BUILDINGOUTRIGGERSAILING
caNoes

INTERNATIONAL MARINE / McGRAW-HILL

Camden, Maine ✦ New York ✦ Chicago ✦ San Francisco ✦ Lisbon ✦ London ✦ Madrid
Mexico City ✦ Milan ✦ New Delhi ✦ San Juan ✦ Seoul ✦ Singapore ✦ Sydney ✦ Toronto

BUILDING OUTRIGGER SAILING
caNoes

Modern Construction Methods for Three Fast, Beautiful Boats

Gary Dierking

The McGraw·Hill Companies

2 3 4 5 6 7 8 9 10   CCW CCW   0 9 8

Library of Congress Cataloging-in-Publication Data
Dierking, Gary.
    Building outrigger sailing canoes : modern
construction methods for three fast, beautiful boats /
Gary Dierking.
        p.   cm.
    Includes bibliographical references and index.
    ISBN-13: 978-0-07-148791-7 (pbk. : alk. paper)
  1. Outrigger canoes—Design and construction.
2. Multihull sailboats—Design and construction.
I. Title.
    VM353.D53 2007
    623.822'3—dc22   2007023801

Questions regarding the content of this book should be
addressed to
International Marine
P.O. Box 220
Camden, ME 04843
www.internationalmarine.com

Questions regarding the ordering of this book should be
addressed to
The McGraw-Hill Companies
Customer Service Department
P.O. Box 547
Blacklick, OH 43004
Retail customers: 1-800-262-4729
Bookstores: 1-800-722-4726

Unless otherwise noted, photos and illustrations by
Gary Dierking.

Contents

Preface

Far in the distant past, when I was maybe thirteen years old, I started sailing small model boats on the pond near our Wisconsin farm. I had some information from library books to guide me, but there was really no one to help or influence me. Steering, of course, was the problem. In the days before radio-control, a quadrant on the rudder was attached to the mainsheet. The harder the sheet pulled, the more the rudder was turned to counteract the weather helm. This was a primitive system and it worked some of the time.

One day after watching my model constantly rounding up into the wind and not holding a course, I spotted an interesting piece of driftwood on the edge of the pond. The driftwood was a piece of pine that had warped into an elegant, curved shape. I took it home and attached a single cross beam, with a pair of waterski-shaped wooden floats at each end. I removed the sailing rig from my balsa monohull and mounted it onto my new double outrigger.

I was elated the first time that it sailed. The little double outrigger not only went very fast, but it also steered a straight course, without any rudder.

I don't know where I got the idea to attach outriggers, but it could have had something to do with the enormous pile of old *National Geographic* magazines that my grandfather had collected. No doubt I had seen outrigger canoes in the photographs that they had published. It took another ten years before I really learned my lesson.

I joined the U.S. Coast Guard after high school to start some real adventure. I had visions of steering boats involved in daring sea rescues, but the reality turned out to be much different. My talent for electronics kept me on shore stations instead of sea duty.

At that time the Coast Guard had LORAN transmitting stations all over the North Pacific, and I spent a full year on Wake Island, a very small ring of coral with a beautiful lagoon. During my stay there, I restored a sunken fiberglass sailing dinghy. The many hours of fast sailing in crystal-clear water while watching the coral heads passing below had a far-reaching effect on my future. An additional three months in Saipan and nine months in Palau ensured that my life would be intimately associated with the Pacific.

After more than four years in the Coast Guard, I decided that I'd better go back to school. I purchased a 28'(8.5m), Swedish-built monohull and lived aboard it in a houseboat marina while working at night and taking classes in the day. The San Francisco Bay area in the 1960s was a hotbed of backyard multihull building. The designs of Arthur Piver and Jim Brown were allowing people who had a big stack of plywood and few years of spare time to build their own boat and cruise long distances.

My friend Rich Clark, also living at the marina, had just completed building a 24'(7.2m) Piver Nugget trimaran, and I went along on its first sail in San Francisco Bay. My experience on the farm pond was duplicated out in the bay on a day when untried boats should have stayed in their berths. We flew along at amazing speeds with fingertip control. Steering was effortless until the under-strength plywood rudder snapped off at the waterline. We were now a good ten miles from home and wondering what to do next. It turned out to be a non-event. By simply sheeting in or out with the two sails, we were able to sail all the way home with very good control. I had no idea at the time that

Pacific sailors had been doing just that for many centuries.

I bought that Nugget trimaran and sailed it for several years throughout San Francisco Bay and down the coast. I could see that this was the type of boat I wanted for my return to the tropical Pacific. The Jim Brown Searunner trimaran designs seemed to be just the right solution, and I started construction of a 37-footer (11.2m) in 1968.

Now you're asking yourself, how's he going to college, earning a living, and building a big boat? I became a college dropout, although I was doing well and enjoying it. The pull of the Pacific islands was too strong to resist, and I was focused on returning there. Four years later, I was ready to go.

Since I had only $1,500 and a boat when I left California, I had to work as much as possible in the various ports I visited. Building the Searunner had given me the skills to apply for a professional boat-building job when I arrived in Honolulu. I spent most of a year at a boatyard there and earned enough for the big jump into the South Pacific. I worked as a surveyor in Pago Pago for a year and designed a monohull cruiser for a crew member of another boat. The hull looked suspiciously similar to my trimaran's center hull.

In French Polynesia, I learned that a lot of local water transportation was done in long, narrow, sharpie-like hulls with a traditional-style outrigger. These were powered with outboard motors and went very fast with low power. I filed this information away for future reference, and with my present designs, I always recommend that the builder try a two-horsepower outboard and prepare to be amazed at the result.

During my time in Hawaii, I built a 16', two-piece plywood outrigger canoe, not unlike some of the sharpie-style hulls I had seen in French Polynesia. I built it in two bolt-together sections so that I could carry it on the deck of my trimaran. It served very well as an extra dinghy while I lived aboard in Honolulu's Keehi Lagoon and inspired the design of the Wa'apa offered in this book.

I built my first strip-planked outrigger canoe when I returned to live in Saipan. I bought a copy of David Hazen's *The Strippers Guide to Canoe-Building* and realized that it was the ideal construction method for rounded hull shapes. While I had already built many plywood hulls, they almost always *looked* like plywood hulls. The 17' (5m) hull that I drew couldn't be identified with any particular island

group but was a combination of features that I liked. It came out drop-dead gorgeous, but it took a while to sell because potential customers were afraid they'd scratch it. It turned out that strippers were a lot tougher than they looked, and the little scratches disappeared with the next coat of varnish.

I built and repaired a lot of different boats during my time in Saipan, including the island's first 45-foot (13.7m) OC6 paddling canoe to be used in competition. The clients wanted a solid fiberglass hull, so I used a one-off fiberglass rod material called C-Flex. It held up very well until a large tree fell across it in one of the regular typhoons.

By this time, I no longer intended to sail long passages. I therefore sold my Searunner, *Bird of Dawning*, to a charter business, built a small house and workshop in the jungle, and built still more small boats for the local population. By 1986, my wife and I were ready for a change.

We moved back to Honolulu, where I landed a job at Aikane Catamarans. It turned out that Aikane Catamarans was owned by Rudy Choy, one of the early pioneers in modern catamaran design. I worked on Rudy's trans-Pacific racer, the 60' (18.3m) Aikane X-5. It had cross-beam problems, and I built a whole new pair from spruce timber and birch plywood.

My most vivid memory of that project was the first sailing test out in the channel between Oahu and Molokai. We were concerned with the massive compression load from the 80' (24.4m) wing mast, especially when the whole boat went airborne off a wave. I rode inside the beam just under the mast, with my flashlight, looking for stress cracks. There were none. A few months later, Rudy accomplished his long-held dream of breaking the speed record between Los Angeles and Honolulu.

During the four years I spent at Aikane, I built three of Rudy's 44' (13.4m) designs in either fiberglass or foam-cored fiberglass, using vacuum bags, epoxy resin, and all of the latest hi-tech fabrics.

After living in Hawaii for a while, you realize that you're unlikely to ever be able to afford a house on the beach. My wife Rose is from New Zealand, and she said it was time to go home, where you could afford to live on the beach (or at least on the harbor front). New Zealand is a fine place for small-boat cruising, with its innumerable bays and beaches. I started thinking more and more about small portable boats with their roots in the traditions of the Pacific. It was time to put together everything I had learned while working and traveling among the islands. I collected all of the books I could find on the subject. Almost all of the available literature was written by archeologists or ethnologists and tended to focus on the size and shape of the object, and very little on how to use it. I decided to start building a series of outrigger sailing canoes, and to learn more about how they worked through direct experience.

My first project was the 31' (9.4m) proa *Te Wa*. The ¼" (6mm) plywood main hull was asymmetric, with the leeward side flatter than the windward side. The single outrigger float, or *ama*, was always kept on the windward side. The ends of the hulls were identical so that it could sail in either direction. When changing tacks, you also had to swap the current bow and stern. The sail and the steering oar had to be moved to the other end of the hull. This procedure was called "shunting," to differentiate it from the more common "tacking." (Shunting and tacking are discussed in detail in Chapter 12.) Once the rig was well set up and your crew member had practiced, the whole procedure could be done in as little as ten seconds.

I'm not the kind of person to just build a boat and sail it without wondering if I can improve it. Changing spars and sails on a 31-footer (9.4m) looked like it might get expensive and time-consuming, so I decided to build a smaller, 16' (4.8m) version to test some new ideas. I drew up the lines for the *Tarawa* to be built in strip composite.

I first rigged the *Tarawa* with the classic Oceanic lateen rig, similar to what I was using on *Te Wa*. It was easy to handle, and I adapted some bungee cords to tend the backstays during the shunt. The *Tarawa* was the prototype for the T2 design offered in this book. The T2 is longer at 18' (5.4 m) but otherwise is similar.

During my years of cruising on the *Bird of Dawning*, I always carried a copy of Euell Gibbons's *Beachcomber's Handbook*. While much of the book is devoted to gathering wild foods in Hawaii, he also built a shunting sailing canoe for offshore fishing. His rig was different than any I'd ever seen or heard of and seemed to be worthy of an experiment. My recent experience with windsurfing gave me some ideas for modifying it, and they were successful. The sail was very powerful and didn't seem to have any vices.

With the increasing popularity of Hawaiian canoe paddling, I thought it was time for me to adapt a smaller, Hawaiian-style canoe to sailing. Hawaiian canoes are optimized for surf handling and have very rounded hull shapes that won't sail well to windward without some other source of lateral resistance. There is anecdotal evidence that traditional canoes used paddles held alongside the hull to allow the canoes to sail somewhat to windward. I decided to break with tradition and use a pivoting leeboard bolted to the side of the hull. At first I used a steering oar, as I had with *Te Wa* and *Tarawa*, but a kick-up rudder was found to be less tiring over long periods of time.

I felt that the Ulua had economic potential, so I made a set of female molds to allow fiberglass copies to be built in a much shorter time. The plans in Chapter 1 show how to build the Ulua in strip composite, and the hull can be built lighter or heavier than the fiberglass production model, depending on your wishes or building skills.

I find building a hull in strip composite to be a very satisfying experience, but not everyone is willing to attempt it. With fond memories of my two-piece canoe dinghy carried on the deck of my cruiser, I decided to redraw it for those builders who really wanted a quick-building plywood hull. The 16' or 24' (4.8m or 7.2m) convertible Wa'apa was the result. It has a simple, flat-bottomed shape sometimes called a "three-board canoe" in Hawaii. Due to the shortage or expense of big logs, many island fisherman now use paddling canoes constructed in much the same way as the Wa'apa.

So there you have it—my convoluted but (or so I think) intriguing story about how I got involved in designing and building outrigger sailing canoes. So far, it's been an amazing, unpredictable life, and I hope that the following chapters will guide you happily toward building your own projects with great success.

Acknowledgments

To the following individuals I wish to express my thanks and gratitude for their help either directly or indirectly during my career as a boatbuilder, sailor, and recently as an author.

In particular, I'd like to thank Wade Tarzia, who knows proas and how to write; Michael Schacht, for convincing me to prepare my designs for the backyard builder; Harmen Heilkema, a close friend and proa designer with long experience; Tim Anderson, for giving my Ulua a good hard test; Kevin O'Neill, who also knows proas and how to write; Bob Holtzman, my editor; the many builders who have purchased plans and given me invaluable feedback; and my wife Rosemary, without whose support this project would have never been completed.

BUILDINGOUTRIGGERSAILING
caNoes

INTRODUCTION

Some Outrigger Basics

From Madagascar, off the east coast of Africa, all the way to Easter Island, the outrigger sailing canoe is one of humankind's most useful tools, and it remains in use today throughout the Indian and Pacific oceans. The outrigger sailing canoe's beauty and elegance, combined with a ruthless functionality and efficiency, make it a very attractive option for anyone wanting to build a small boat.

The evolution of the outrigger sailing canoe has spanned many centuries with little change to the basic configuration. Very few watercraft have undergone such a long development under such exacting conditions. Every island group in the Pacific Ocean has come up with a slightly different solution adapted to either local conditions or traditions. While single and double outriggers have been built in excess of 100 feet (30m) in length, most canoes in daily use today are between 16' (4.8m) and 25' (7.6m). That represents a practical size for the home builder, and the boats you will build in this book are in that size range.

A BRIEF HISTORY OF THE OUTRIGGER CANOE

The people who explored and settled on the islands of the Pacific Ocean did not have a written language, but rather memorized their history and cultural information. This fact makes it difficult to trace the early development of the sailing canoes that explored one third of the earth's surface, beginning as early as 6000 years ago. Most of the valuable information available was collected by early western explorers in the form of notes and drawings (oh, if they'd only had cameras).

At the time of first contact with western explorers, both double-hulled catamarans and single outrigger canoes were in use. The catamarans were favored for hauling heavy freight or a lot of people. The single outrigger canoe was faster and better adapted for chasing schools of fish or for courier use. In some cases, the same hull could be used with a partner as a catamaran or equipped with a single outrigger, depending on its intended use. The double outrigger canoe (trimaran) is not generally seen in Polynesia or Micronesia, but rather in Indonesia and the Philippine Islands.

Both catamarans and single outriggers were seen with shunting and tacking rigs, although the shunting rig was spreading and increasing its influence at the time of western contact.

WHY USE AN OUTRIGGER?

Outriggers are often seen attached to all kinds of watercraft that were not originally designed to be used in this way. Sailing canoes and kayaks are undergoing a revival, and the poor stability of many designs has led some owners to add one or two amas (the floating part of an outrigger) to their craft. Results can be mixed. The extra stability comes at the cost of increased weight and complication in setup and rigging. Two or three hulls are more drag than one, and unless the sail plan is enlarged, you may end up going slower. Hulls originally designed to sail without an outrigger are beamier, and this, combined with the additional ama drag, may cause the performance to be disappointing.

The key to getting an edge in performance is to have a very narrow main hull as has been used throughout the Pacific and Indian oceans. The waterline-length-to-waterline-beam ratio can be as great as 30:1 on large, oceangoing outriggers and double canoes. On the smaller craft with which we are dealing, a 20:1 ratio is about the slimmest practical hull that can still carry the necessary weight. The first time I sailed aboard a 20:1 proa with plenty of wind and a good rig, I was elated to feel an almost total lack of resistance when confronted with a wave face or steep chop. That sail was quite unlike anything I had ever experienced.

The term "proa" originally came from Indonesia. When European explorers first saw the outrigger canoes of the Pacific islands, they called them proas because of their previous experience in Indonesia where the double outrigger canoe is common. Today the term is usually applied to canoes that shunt and always keep their amas to windward. There are even "Atlantic proas" that always keep their amas to leeward. Unfortunately, there is no firm definition for "proa," but I will use it in reference to canoes that shunt, and I will use the term "tacking outrigger" for canoes that tack. Throughout this book, you will encounter various mentions and discussions of tacking and shunting. The most complete description of these procedures is found in Chapter 12, and I recommend that you read this material if you'd like a detailed explanation.

With the designs in this book I have tried to remain as faithful as possible to the design principles that have made the Pacific and Indian Ocean outriggers the enduring successes that they are today. The difference between ancient and modern outriggers is in the materials that we now have available. Some firm traditionalists insist on duplicating the materials available in ancient times in which you built an oceangoing vessel with logs, coconut fiber, and an adze. This is fine, and the results can be a stunning lesson about all of the things you don't really need to build a boat.

I've been a boatbuilder for more than forty years, and in that time I never turned down an opportunity to try some newer, better, or cheaper way to build a boat. I feel that the ancient builders would have been no different, and if a roll of carbon fiber and a drum of epoxy fell out of the sky over Tahiti in 892 A.D., they'd have been happy to use it. As it was, they still laughingly sailed circles around every European ship.

The designs in this book use both ancient and modern engineering solutions. The most obvious structural feature is my prejudice for lashed connections. Using lashings to connect the cross beams to the hull and the ama provides exceptional strength but still allows a small degree of flexibility that reduces the effects of high transient loads experienced by all multihulled craft at sea. While the technique of lashing has been around since the beginning, we now have a full selection of synthetic line to use, from the stretchiest nylon to new fibers that stretch no more than steel cable. For most purposes, I find ordinary polyester/Dacron rope to be just right. Canoes that are used only for paddling often use strips of rubber inner tube for lashing. Rubber is a bit too stretchy for the main connections of a sailing canoe, however, where the rig imposes much greater loads.

LENGTH OF AN OUTRIGGER CANOE

One of the most obvious characteristics of an outrigger sailing canoe is its extreme length-to-beam ratio. Measurements can reveal a waterline length of twenty or more times the waterline beam of the hull. An extremely narrow hull creates a very efficient shape which produces such small waves that it has few of the speed limitations found in beamier displacement hulls. A hull this narrow would, of course, fall over without an ama or another hull to stabilize it.

Oceanic canoes are extravagant with length, as they are seldom confined to modern marinas where you pay by length. Nothing contributes to comfort at sea more than pure length. Having said that, the canoes in this book are all of a length to enable them to be built in your garage and transported on the roof of a car.

WEIGHT OF AN OUTRIGGER CANOE

Modern multihulls are generally quite light in weight compared to traditional working canoes. A light weight does cause some differences in operation compared to traditional practice. Hollow lightweight amas, for instance, cannot provide the necessary ballast to windward that a solid log provides. A lightweight ama necessitates the greater use of movable ballast (human, water, or cargo). Generally I recommend building the structure as light as possible, because once it's built, it is always easier to add weight than to remove it.

SPEED OF AN OUTRIGGER CANOE

Early European explorers of the Pacific Ocean were amazed at the speed and weatherliness of some of the outrigger sailing canoes they encountered. This performance was accomplished without metal fasteners or fittings of any kind, while sails were woven of plant leaf material and were very porous to the wind. Their speed was the result of the low, wave-making shape of the hulls, the huge righting moment derived from an outrigger or second hull, and the lack of heavy ballast. An outrigger sailing canoe's windward sailing ability varied, depending on the local design, but it was superior to that of European vessels of the time. Modern sailing craft are better performers to windward but at a huge cost in expensive, high-modulus (low-stretch) materials in both the sails and rigging.

The canoe designs contained in this book are all capable of reaching speeds up to about 12 knots (14 miles per hour) when you are sailing with the wind on your side (beam reach) or just aft of your side (broad reach). When you are sailing into the wind, the average speed is between 5 and 6 knots. Greater speeds are possible with bigger sails and greater overall beam, and you are certainly welcome to experiment. Over the years, I've become less concerned with ultimate top speed and more concerned with a light canoe's ability to keep going in almost no wind. I'm a sailor and I'll only paddle if I must.

OUTBOARD MOTORS

Clamping a two-horsepower outboard motor to your canoe can greatly increase its versatility. You can easily cruise along at 6 knots at half-throttle. The slim shape of the canoe's hull requires very little power to drive it, so don't be tempted to increase the size of the motor, because the extra thrust is not necessary and the extra weight is not in a good location.

Electric power is also a possibility with the use of an outboard trolling motor and a sealed battery box located near the center of the hull.

If you value your motor, however, leave it at home if you'll be sailing in strong winds, or rig a safety ama (Figure 12-16) to prevent the motor from getting dunked.

SAILING RIGS

Traditional sailing outriggers can be divided into two groups—those that tack and those that shunt. (See Chapter 12 for a complete discussion of shunting and tacking.) Shunting rigs predominate in Micronesia and are also seen in Melanesia, Polynesia, and the Indian Ocean. Shunting canoes are unique in that both ends of the hull are identical and can act as the bow or stern. The ama is always kept on the windward side, where it acts as floating ballast.

To change direction, the sail has to be moved or pivoted to the other end of the hull, while the canoe drifts broadside with its ama (outrigger float) toward the wind. The steering device must also change ends. This is not as complex as it sounds and can be accomplished in less than ten seconds in a well-set-up canoe. Because the canoe is never purposely aimed directly into the wind, there is no possibility of stalling the sail and getting caught "in irons" as you might in a tacking vessel.

The tacking rig is the same as you see in any other part of the world. It is used predominantly in Polynesia and Indonesia. The ones I've shown on the plans are as simple as can be devised with unstayed masts and a single sail. A tacking rig used on a single outrigger canoe means that on one tack the ama will be to windward, and on the other tack it will be to leeward. Modern lightweight amas have sufficient buoyancy to stay afloat when pressed down to leeward. In traditionally built tacking canoes, crew members have to move their weight out onto a balance board extending from the opposite side of the canoe to keep a solid-log ama from submerging.

PADDLING YOUR OUTRIGGER

One or more paddles is an essential part of your equipment when leaving shore. Paddling is often necessary to get away from or into the shore and is very useful if your sailing rig has blown away. All of the designs in this book can be comfortably paddled for short distances. The Wa'apa is the easiest to handle under paddle power. Its hard chines aid in helping the canoe to track in a straight line. The Ulua's hull is optimized to turn quickly while tacking, and a foot pedal–controlled rudder (Figure 10-6) is recommended for long-distance paddling. The T2 can be paddled from either end but is best served by sculling with the steering oar, as shown in Figure 2-14.

One of the paddles onboard should have a larger than normal blade area and be able to double as a steering paddle, to replace a damaged rudder or leeboard.

STRUCTURE OF THE OUTRIGGER CANOE

Traditional sailing outrigger design is finely tuned to take advantage of the low-tech materials available throughout Oceania. The structure and rigging are designed so as to reduce stress concentrations and distribute the loads evenly throughout the structure. Fiber lashings at the important joints between the hull, the beams, and the ama reduce high transient loads that would damage a canoe assembled with metal bolts. Even today, very large multihulls can be successfully assembled with synthetic rope. Modern rope can be chosen from a full range of choices in strength and stiffness to provide the desired degree of elasticity in critical joints, such as where cross beams connect to the hull.

The strip-composite construction method used with the Ulua and T2 designs has been in use for more than thirty years and is well proven to provide a light, strong hull. The plywood structure of the Wa'apa is also a well-proven method.

ACCOMMODATION

Traditionally, shelter onboard a Pacific canoe consisted of no more than a light, thatched tent structure. The narrow hulls made it difficult to sleep inside the hull, but the warm climate allowed sleeping on deck while being sheltered from spray by the thatched structure. Most modern builders do not live in a tropical climate (although they certainly dream of it), and I often get requests for a design with a cabin or tent structure to make cruising more comfortable. This has been done successfully by others, but I prefer to specialize in lightweight canoes that can still be dragged up a beach by one person. It's very hard to make a cabin look like it belongs on an outrigger unless it has only sitting headroom.

MIX AND MATCH

Each of the three basic designs described in this book has several options for the builder. The two-person, 18' (5.4m) Ulua is similar to Hawaiian designs, and because it is strip planked over mold stations, it can be stretched by 50 percent of its design length by simply increasing the spacing between the molds. The beam and depth of the hull remain the same. Steering can be accomplished with a paddle, steering oar, or a kick-up rudder. A pivoting leeboard provides lateral resistance. Any tacking rig can be used, including a surplus windsurfing rig. Ulua can be rigged as a single or double outrigger (trimaran), but you should consider the extra weight of the second ama and the additional length of the cross beams before selecting the latter option.

The T2 has two choices of sailing rig: the classic Oceanic lateen still in use after many centuries, or a modern rig of my design which incorporates windsurfing technology and an easier method of shunting. Steering is accomplished with a paddle, a steering oar, or dual dagger boards. Lateral resistance is provided by the deep "V" hull shape.

The four-person, 24' (7.2m) Wa'apa has the most scope for building options. The Wa'apa is the only plywood design included in this book, and it can be built in three 8' (2.4m) sections, or in one piece. This allows for construction, storage, and transportation in a very small space. The two pointed sections can be joined to form a 16' (4.8m) hull, and with the third midsection inserted between them, a 24' (7.2m) hull is formed. The Wa'apa can be sailed as either a shunting proa or a tacking outrigger. The hull can be stabilized with one or two amas. A leeboard provides lateral resistance, and steering is accomplished with a paddle, a steering oar, a kick-up rudder, or dual dagger boards.

UNITS OF MEASUREMENT

After spending the first half of my life drawing boats in feet and inches, I was forced by circumstances to use metric units. I'm glad I did, because *everything* got simpler. All of my designs are shown in two versions with dimensions in either millimeters or inches. If you are lofting molds from a table of offsets, I recommend that you try doing it in millimeters. A single number of millimeters is less prone to error than using fractions of an inch.

TERMINOLOGY

Some parts of the outrigger sailing canoe simply do not have very descriptive names in the English language. Every Pacific island group has its own language and, hence, different names for the parts of their canoes. The table below gives you at least an idea of some of these names. Also, for any other terms with which you are not familiar, refer to the glossary at the end of the book.

ENGLISH	HAWAII	TAHITI	NEW ZEALAND	MARSHALL ISLANDS
Main Hull	*wa'a*	*va'a*	*waka*	*Wa*
Outrigger Float	*ama*	*ama*	*ama*	*Kubaak*
Outrigger Boom	*iako*	*iato*	*kiato*	*apet, kie*

CHOOSING MATERIALS FOR AN OUTRIGGER CANOE

Choosing suitable timber for your boatbuilding project is important and can be difficult depending upon your location. Cedar-strip planks can be ordered already prepared with cove-and-bead edges, but most builders will choose to save money and cut their own. Western red cedar is the first choice for strip-planking because of its light weight, color, and rot resistance, but many other species are also appropriate. Spruce, pine, other types of cedar, redwood, paulownia, or cypress are a few others that have been used successfully. Planking timber is ideally very lightweight, dry, straight-grained, and available in long, clear lengths. If you cannot find suitable timber in your local area, check through boating or boatbuilding magazines for companies that will supply it.

Timber for gunwales, stems, and chines is ideally harder and heavier than cedar because it has to hold fasteners well and be exposed to more abuse during use. Laminated cross beams can use cedar in the inner layers, with a harder wood like fir or mahogany on the top and bottom.

Plywood can present you with just as difficult a choice unless you have a healthy budget and purchase the most expensive marine grades. BS1088 is a Lloyds standard for marine plywood that ensures mainly the quality of the veneers in all layers. Marine and exterior grades of plywood use the same waterproof adhesive. With marine grade, you are mostly paying for the quality of the inner layers.

If you wish to use a plywood of unknown quality, take a sample and expose it to repeated cycles of boiling and baking in an oven. If you are using ply with one good side and one lesser-grade side, put the knotty side out and glass over it, leaving the better side on the interior of the hull. One-fourth-inch (6mm) plywood is available with three or five plies; the five-ply is far superior. Check the dimensions of plywood sheets, as some are metric sizes and some are imperial (i.e., inch) sizes.

Screws, nails and bolts are ideally made of a non-corrosive metal like silicon bronze or stainless steel. You can use galvanized steel fasteners if they will be fiberglassed over.

HOW TO NAVIGATE THIS BOOK

In the first three chapters of this book, I'll introduce you to each of the three designs being offered, along with the construction drawings and a materials list. Because two of the designs have very different sailing rig options, the next chapter describes in detail how each of these rigs work.

Chapter 5 is a brief course on basic boatbuilding skills and how the materials are used. Chapters 6 and 7 specifically describe each step in the hull construction. Chapters 8 through 11 will guide you through the construction of amas, cross beams, steering devices, and sailing rigs. Chapter 12 teaches you how to make it all work and how to survive the experience. Refer to the glossary for any terms that you do not understand. For further reading on outrigger sailing canoes, Internet links, or to order full-size patterns, refer to the resources chapter.

CHAPTER 1

The Ulua

Length overall	17'9" (5400mm)
Hull width	18" (470mm)
Overall width	6'7" (2000mm)
Draft	8" (200mm) @ 400 lb (182 kg) displacement
Hull weight	64 lb (29 kg)
Weight fully rigged	122 lb (55 kg)
Sailing rig type	Tacking only
Sail area	65 sq ft (6.0 sq m)
Construction method	Strip-planked composite

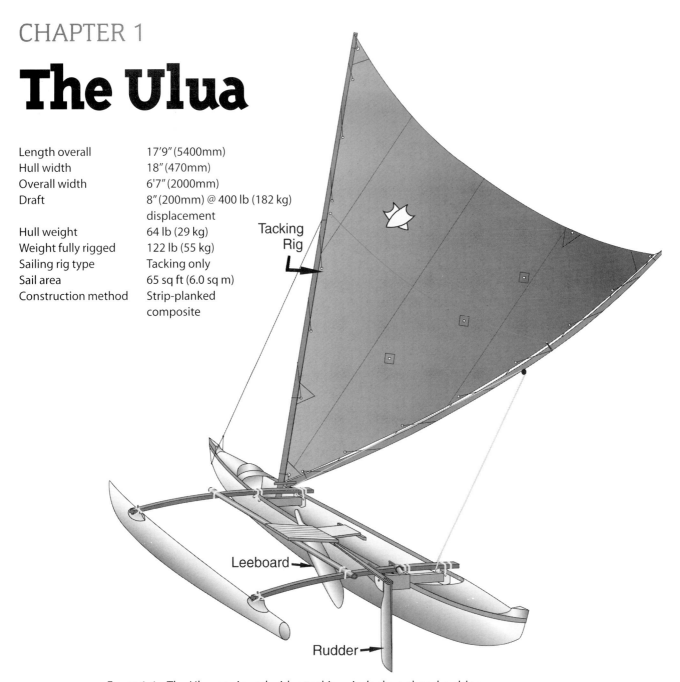

Figure 1-1. The Ulua equipped with a tacking rig, leeboard, and rudder.

◆ "Ulua" is the Hawaiian term for the Giant Trevally fish found in deep, rocky water and off some beaches of the Pacific islands.

The Ulua canoe is based on Hawaiian outrigger canoe design. The channels between the Hawaiian islands are extremely rough and more often than not have strong trade winds blowing. This fact, along with the very small number of natural harbors, provided the breeding ground for a very special canoe. The ability to maintain control during high-surf landings was the most important factor in their design.

The Ulua design broadly resembles the classic Hawaiian canoe, with some differences. The round bottom, which is important in the surf, performs poorly when sailed to windward. I've added a pivoting leeboard for lateral resistance that can be retracted when paddling or when landing in surf. A steering oar or rudder can be used instead of the traditional paddle

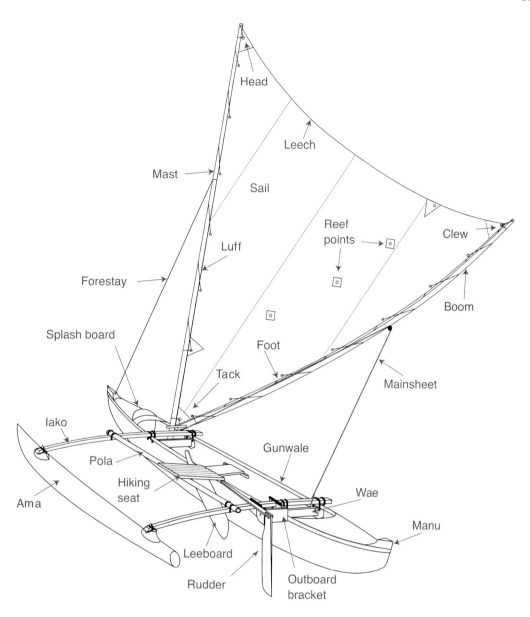

Head

Leech

Mast

Sail

Luff

Reef
points

Clew

Forestay

Boom

Splash board

Foot

Tack

Mainsheet

Iako

Gunwale

Pola

Hiking
seat

Ama

Wae

Manu

Leeboard

Rudder

Outboard
bracket

for steering. The Ulua hull has a little more "V" in the hull than a traditional Hawaiian model, and this improves its speed and windward sailing ability.

Watertight bulkheads in each end of the hull provide reserve buoyancy in the event of damage or capsize. Additional reserve buoyancy can be built in under the two seats in the form of foam blocks or hollow storage compartments. The ama can be either solid foam covered with fiberglass, or hollow and strip planked, with foam or plastic bottles inside for emergency flotation. The large ama is of sufficient size to support cargo stored on the iakos (outrigger booms) along with a crew member on the hiking seat.

A hiking seat enables the crew or helmsperson to shift their weight outboard of the narrow hull's

gunwale to balance the force of the sail. It can consist of a slatted wooden seat or fabric stretched on a frame. The outboard edge is supported by a fore and aft pole resting on the iakos, while the inboard edge rests on the gunwale. At least one hiking seat must be fitted on the ama side of the hull, but an additional seat can be installed on the opposite side, supported by extended iakos.

The sailing rig shown is of a modern Hawaiian type. The availability of fiberglass windsurfing masts allows for a very simple lightweight plug-in rig that can be lowered entirely while at sea and stowed on the iakos. A brailing line folds the boom and sail up against the mast for quick furling and thus avoids dumping the sail onto the crew.

The Ulua can be paddled, sailed, surfed, or powered by a two-horsepower outboard motor. This canoe is capable of extended coastal expeditions and can be car-topped to your favorite launching spot or carried on its side on a trailer with the ama up in the air.

The hull can be stretched to a greater length by increasing the spacing between the molds before the planking begins. You can safely increase the hull length by 150 percent without any changes to the structure.

While the Ulua is an excellent sailing canoe, the shape of the hull is optimized for its ability to turn quickly while tacking. For long-distance paddling, foot pedals, like those used in sea kayaks, can be connected with small lines to the sailing rudder. Steering with your feet allows for stronger paddling without using energy to keep the canoe on a straight course.

MATERIALS FOR BUILDING THE ULUA

Hull

- 60 planks of ¼" × ¾" × 18.5' (6mm × 19mm × 5700mm)
- Enough planks for the hull and end decks can be ripped from 5 pieces of timber, 5½" × ¾" × 18.5' (140mm × 19mm × 5.7m), assuming the use of a thin kerf circular saw blade.

Molds

- 2 sheets of ½" (12mm) or thicker plywood or particle board

Stems

- 2 pieces of 1" × 4" × 30" (25mm × 100mm × 750mm). These can be of cedar or any other softwood.

Gunwales

- 4 pieces of ⅜" × 1" × 18.5' (10mm × 40mm × 5700mm). Harder woods like mahogany or ash are more durable.

Bulkheads and Ring Frame

- 3 pieces of 16" × 18" × ³⁄₁₆" or ¼" (400mm × 450mm × 4 or 6mm) plywood. Bulkheads can be strip composite.

Seats

- 2 pieces of ¾" × 10" × 18" (19mm × 250mm × 450mm). The seats can be of plywood or solid timber.

Iakos

- 10 pieces of ⁵⁄₁₆" × 2⅜" × 6'8" (8mm × 60mm × 2000mm)

Fore and Aft Decks

- 2 pieces of 18" × 3'8", ³⁄₁₆" or ¼" (450mm × 1100mm, 4 or 6mm plywood
- OR: 30 strips of ³⁄₁₆" × ¾" × 44" (4 to 6mm × 19mm × 1100mm) plywood for strip decks

Epoxy Resin

- 3 1-gallon (4-liter) kits of resin and hardener
- Bag of glue powder
- Bag of fairing powder

Fiberglass

- 4 pieces of 6-ounce (200-gram) 18.5' × 26" (6000mm × 650mm) for hull
- 4 pieces of glass for top and bottom of strip deck, 18" × 44" (450mm × 1100mm)
- Miscellaneous strips for glassing in bulkheads
- 2 pieces of 10-ounce (330-gram), 16' × 16" (5000mm × 400mm) for ama, or:
- 4 pieces of 6-ounce (200-gram) fiberglass cloth

Ama

- 2 pieces of 4" × 8" × 12'8" (100mm × 200mm × 4000mm) blue Styrofoam (can use 2" [50mm] foam and glue layers together) ½ sheet; ⅛" or ³⁄₁₆" (3mm or 4mm) plywood for shear web

APPROXIMATE TIME AND COST FOR BUILDING THE ULUA

The amount of time that it takes to complete a sailing Ulua is widely variable and reflects the personal standards and skill of the individual builder. Getting started can seem slow, with little to look at that resembles a canoe, but once planking commences, the hull

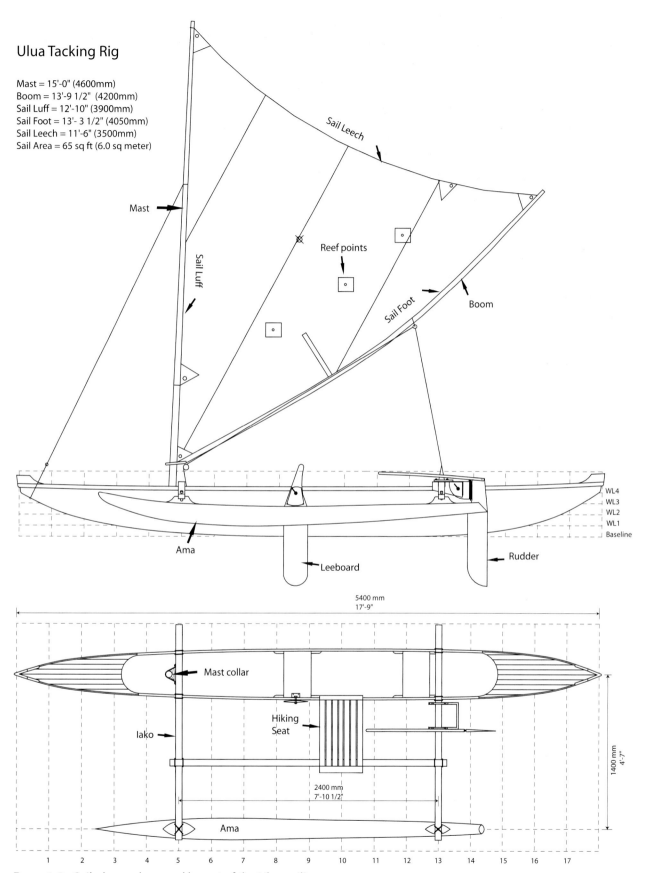

Ulua Tacking Rig

Mast = 15'-0" (4600mm)
Boom = 13'-9 1/2" (4200mm)
Sail Luff = 12'-10" (3900mm)
Sail Foot = 13'- 3 1/2" (4050mm)
Sail Leech = 11'-6" (3500mm)
Sail Area = 65 sq ft (6.0 sq meter)

Sail Leech

Mast

Sail Luff

Reef points

Sail Foot

Boom

WL4
WL3
WL2
WL1
Baseline

Ama

Leeboard

Rudder

5400 mm
17'-9"

Mast collar

Hiking Seat

Iako

1400 mm
4'-7"

2400 mm
7'-10 1/2"

Ama

1 2 3 4 5 6 7 8 9 10 11 12 13 14 15 16 17

FIGURE 1-2. Sail plan and general layout of the Ulua sailing canoe.

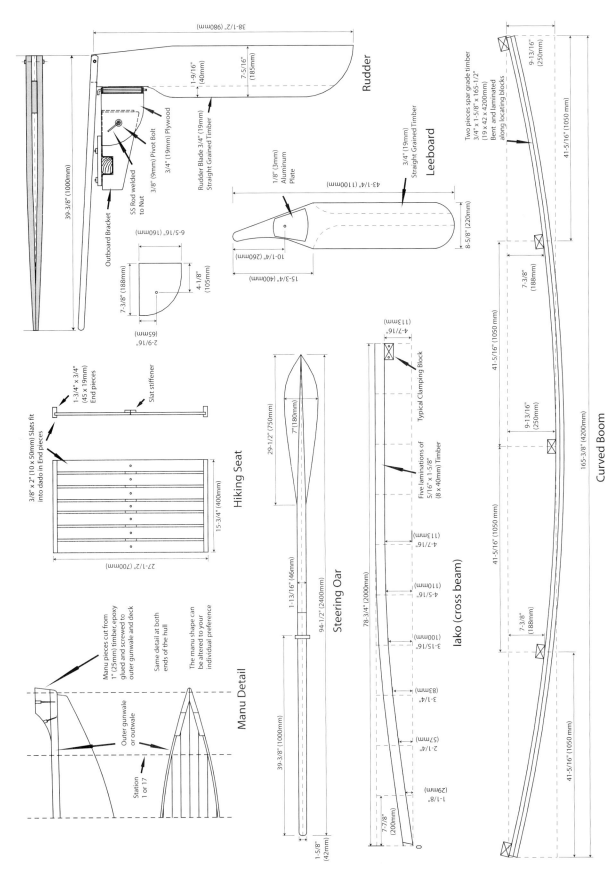

Rudder

38-1/2" (980mm)

1-9/16" (40mm)

7-5/16" (185mm)

39-3/8" (1000mm)

Outboard Bracket

SS Rod welded to Nut

3/8" (9mm) Pivot Bolt

3/4" (19mm) Plywood

Rudder Blade 3/4" (19mm) Straight Grained Timber

6-5/16" (160mm)

7-3/8" (188mm)

4-1/8" (105mm)

2-9/16" (65mm)

Leeboard

1/8" (3mm) Aluminum Plate

3/4" (19mm) Straight Grained Timber

43-1/4" (1100mm)

8-5/8" (220mm)

10-1/4" (260mm)

15-3/4" (400mm)

Curved Boom

Two pieces spar grade timber 3/4" x 1-5/8" x 165-1/2" (19 x 42 x 4200mm) Bent and laminated along locating blocks

9-13/16" (250mm)

41-5/16" (1050 mm)

7-3/8" (188mm)

41-5/16" (1050 mm)

9-13/16" (250mm)

41-5/16" (1050 mm)

7-3/8" (188mm)

165-3/8" (4200mm)

41-5/16" (1050 mm)

Hiking Seat

1-3/4" x 3/4" (45 x 19mm) End pieces

Slat stiffener

3/8" x 2" (10 x 50mm) Slats fit into dado in End pieces

15-3/4" (400mm)

27-1/2" (700mm)

Manu Detail

Manu pieces cut from 1" (25mm) timber, epoxy glued and screwed to outer gunwale and deck

Same detail at both ends of the hull

The manu shape can be altered to your individual preference

Outer gunwale or outwale

Station 1 or 17

Steering Oar

29-1/2" (750mm)

7" (180mm)

94-1/2" (2400mm)

1-13/16" (46mm)

39-3/8" (1000mm)

1-5/8" (42mm)

Iako (cross beam)

4-7/16" (113mm)

Typical Clamping Block

Five laminations of 5/16" x 1-5/8" (8 x 40mm) Timber

4-7/16" (113mm)

4-5/16" (110mm)

3-15/16" (100mm)

78-3/4" (2000mm)

3-1/4" (83mm)

2-1/4" (57mm)

1-1/8" (29mm)

7-7/8" (200mm)

0

FIGURE 1-3. Construction details for the manu, hiking seat, steering oar, iakos, boom, leeboard, and rudder.

10

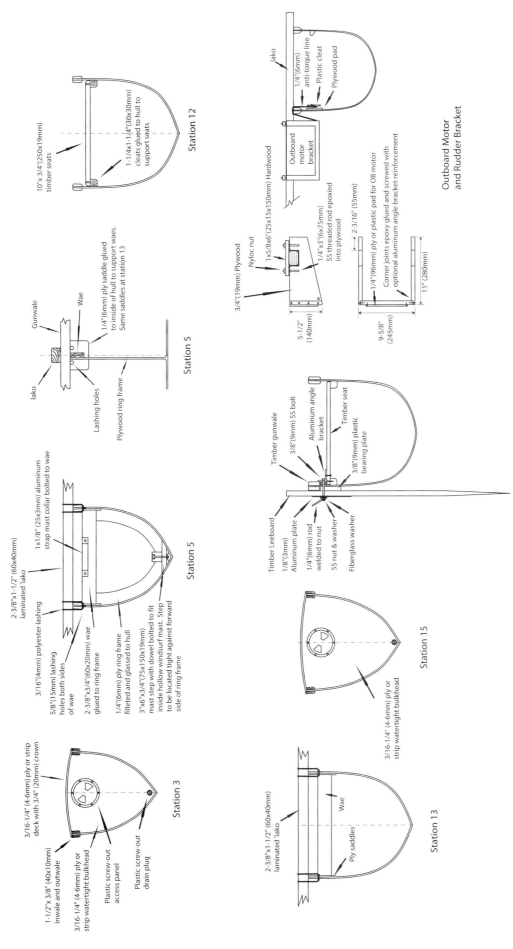

Station 12

10'x 3/4''(250x19mm) timber seats

1-1/4x1-1/4''(30x30mm) cleats glued to hull to support seats

Station 5

Gunwale

Wae

ʻIako

Lashing holes

1/4''(6mm) ply saddle glued to inside of hull to support waes. Same saddles at station 13

Plywood ring frame

Station 5

2-3/8''x1-1/2'' (60x40mm) laminated ʻiako

1x1/8'' (25x3mm) aluminum strap mast collar bolted to wae

3/16''(4mm) polyester lashing

5/8''(15mm) lashing holes both sides of wae

2-3/8''x3/4''(60x20mm) wae glued to ring frame

1/4''(6mm) ply ring frame filleted and glassed to hull

3''x6''x3/4''(75x150x19mm) mast step with dowel bolted to fit inside hollow windsurf mast. Step to be located tight against forward side of ring frame

Station 3

3/16-1/4'' (4-6mm) ply or strip deck with 3/4'' (20mm) crown

1-1/2''x 3/8'' (40x10mm) inwale and outwale

3/16-1/4'' (4-6mm) ply or strip watertight bulkhead

Plastic screw-out access panel

Plastic screw-out drain plug

Outboard Motor and Rudder Bracket

ʻIako

1/4''(6mm) anti-torque line

Plastic cleat

Plywood pad

3/4''(19mm) Plywood

Nyloc nut

1x5/8x6''(25x15x150mm) Hardwood

Outboard motor bracket

1/4''x3''(6x75mm) SS threaded rod epoxied into plywood

2-3/16'' (55mm)

1/4''(96mm) ply or plastic pad for OB motor

Corner joints epoxy glued and screwed with optional aluminum angle bracket reinforcement

5-1/2'' (140mm)

9-5/8'' (245mm)

11'' (280mm)

Timber Leeboard

1/8''(3mm) Aluminum plate

1/4''(6mm) rod welded to nut

SS nut & washer

Fiberglass washer

Timber gunwale

3/8''(9mm) SS bolt

Aluminum angle bracket

Timber seat

3/8''(9mm) plastic bearing plate

Station 15

3/16-1/4'' (4-6mm) ply or strip watertight bulkhead

Station 13

2-3/8''x1-1/2'' (60x40mm) laminated ʻiako

Wae

Ply saddles

FIGURE 1-4. Structural cross sections and outboard motor bracket construction.

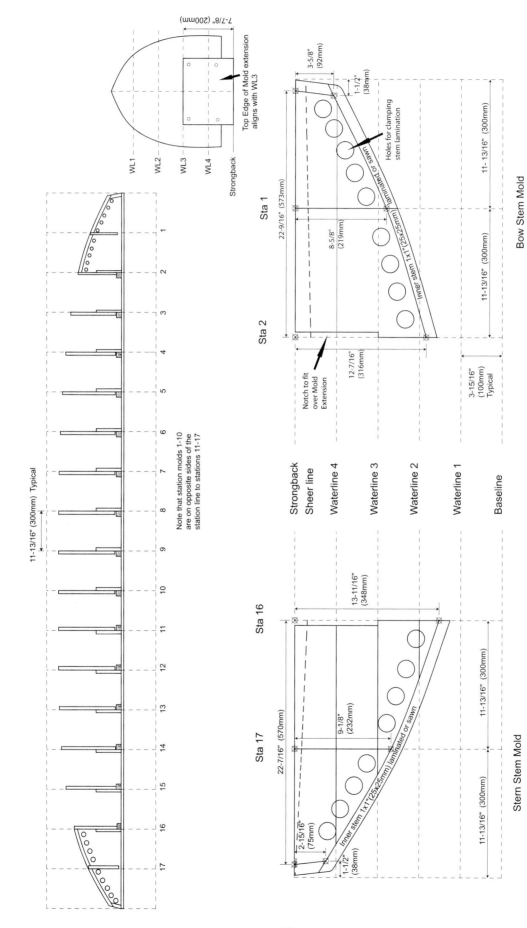

FIGURE 1-5. Stem and mold section setup.

12

Ulua Table of Offsets

Station Number	1	2	3	4	5	6	7	8	9	10	11	12	13	14	15	16	17
Sheer To Baseline	470 / 1-6-4	463 / 1-6-2	458 / 1-6-0+	455 / 1-5-7+	453 / 1-5-6+	451 / 1-5-6	451 / 1-5-6	451 / 1-5-6	451 / 1-5-6	451 / 1-5-6	451 / 1-5-6	452 / 1-5-6+	454 / 1-5-7	457 / 1-6-0	462 / 1-6-1+	470 / 1-6-4	483 / 1-7-0
Sheer Half Breadth	86 / 0-3-3	140 / 0-5-4	168 / 0-6-5	185 / 0-7-2+	198 / 0-7-6+	208 / 0-8-1+	215 / 0-8-3+	218 / 0-8-4+	220 / 0-8-5+	220 / 0-8-5+	220 / 0-8-5+	219 / 0-8-5	215 / 0-8-3+	209 / 0-8-2	196 / 0-7-5+	167 / 0-6-4+	104 / 0-4-1
WL 4 Half-Breadth	71 / 0-2-6+	130 / 0-5-1	164 / 0-6-3+	185 / 0-7-2+	200 / 0-7-7	210 / 0-8-2	217 / 0-8-4+	219 / 0-8-5	221 / 0-8-5	221 / 0-8-5	221 / 0-8-5	220 / 0-8-5	215 / 0-8-3+	208 / 0-8-1+	191 / 0-7-4	155 / 0-6-0+	87 / 0-3-3+
WL3 Half-Breadth	32 / 0-1-2	104 / 0-4-1	150 / 0-5-7	179 / 0-7-0+	197 / 0-7-6	208 / 0-8-1+	215 / 0-8-3+	218 / 0-8-4+	220 / 0-8-5+	220 / 0-8-5+	220 / 0-8-5+	219 / 0-8-5	212 / 0-8-3	200 / 0-7-7	176 / 0-6-7+	128 / 0-5-0+	45 / 0-1-6
WL2 Half-Breadth		43 / 0-1-5+	105 / 0-4-1	146 / 0-5-6	172 / 0-6-6	189 / 0-7-3+	199 / 0-7-6+	206 / 0-8-1	210 / 0-8-2	212 / 0-8-2+	211 / 0-8-2+	208 / 0-8-1+	198 / 0-7-6+	177 / 0-6-7+	138 / 0-5-3+	72 / 0-2-6+	
WL1 Half-Breadth				65 / 0-2-4+	108 / 0-4-2	137 / 0-5-3	155 / 0-6-1	167 / 0-6-4+	175 / 0-6-7	178 / 0-7-0	176 / 0-6-7+	170 / 0-6-5+	152 / 0-6-0	118 / 0-4-5	58 / 0-2-3		
WL .5 Half Breadth						75 / 0-3-0	104 / 0-4-1	118 / 0-4-5	126 / 0-4-7+	128 / 0-5-0	124 / 0-4-7+	113 / 0-4-4	93 / 0-3-5+	54 / 0-2-1			
Keel to Baseline	254 / 0-10-0	158 / 0-6-2	97 / 0-3-6+	56 / 0-2-1+	30 / 0-1-1+	14 / 0-0-4+	4 / 0-0-1+	1 / 0-0-0+	0 / 0-0-0	0 / 0-0-0	0 / 0-0-0	0 / 0-0-0	6 / 0-0-2	24 / 0-0-7+	60 / 0-2-3	126 / 0-4-7+	240 / 0-9-3+
30 Degree Diagonal	104 / 0-4-1	104 / 0-4-1	157 / 0-6-1+	196 / 0-7-6	226 / 0-8-7	247 / 0-9-6	263 / 0-10-3	272 / 0-10-5+	277 / 0-10-7	279 / 0-11-0	277 / 0-10-7	271 / 0-10-5+	258 / 0-10-2+	233 / 0-9-1+	192 / 0-7-4+	128 / 0-5-0+	41 / 0-1-5

The table of offsets enables you to reproduce the curved shape of the hull molds. The top number in each box is in millimeters, and the bottom number is feet, inches, and eighths of an inch. A plus sign adds a sixteenth of an inch. For example: 1-6-1+ equals one foot, 6 inches, and three-sixteenths of an inch.

Draw a centerline, baseline, waterlines, strongback line, and the 30-degree diagonal, ensuring that the waterlines are parallel and spaced correctly. Measure and mark the offsets or half breadths, tack a small nail at each point, and bend a timber batten along the nails. Draw along the batten with a pencil.

Note that stations 1 and 17 have a strip removed from their centerlines to enable them to straddle the stem molds. The strip to be removed must be exactly as wide as the thickness of your stem molds.

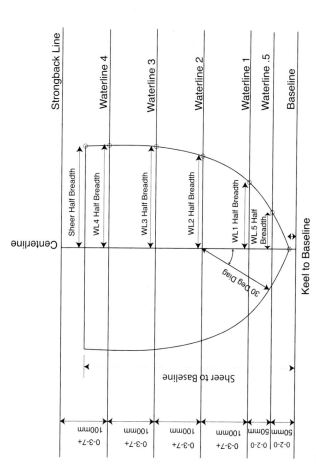

FIGURE 1-6. Table of offsets and mold section lofting.

FIGURE 1-7. (ABOVE LEFT) Ulua sailing on a starboard tack, with the ama to leeward and the sailor seated in the hull. (Photo courtesy Rose Turner)

FIGURE 1-8. (ABOVE) Ulua sailing on a port tack, with the ama to windward and the sailor on the hiking seat. (Photo courtesy Rose Turner)

FIGURE 1-9. (LEFT) Dan St. Gean's stretched Ulua equipped with double outriggers. (Photo courtesy Dan St. Gean)

FIGURE 1-10. (BELOW) Kent Robertson's stretched Ulua equipped with double outriggers and raised iakos. (Photo courtesy Kent Robertson)

FIGURE 1-11. An Ulua resting on the beach during a Hauraki Gulf cruise. (Photo courtesy Tim Anderson)

FIGURE 1-12. Michael Wise's Ulua equipped with a fabric trampoline. (Photo courtesy Michael Wise)

will take shape rapidly. The average time to set up, plank, and fiberglass a bare hull is about 100 hours. The total time to complete a ready-to-sail Ulua is a minimum of 300 hours.

The minimum cost of materials is about U.S. $1,200. Half of this amount is for the epoxy resin and fiberglass. The sailing rig can be home made with a plastic tarp sail and a used Windsurfer mast for a very low cost, or you can have a sail maker provide a sail for a few hundred dollars more. Outrigger sailing canoes will perform exceptionally well without expensive materials or hardware.

CHAPTER 2

The T2

Length overall	17'9" (5400mm)
Hull width	16" (406mm)
Overall width	9' (2740mm)
Draft	12" (305mm) @ 350 lb (160 kg) displacement
Hull weight	65 lb (29.5 kg)
Weight fully rigged	135 lb (61 kg)
Sailing rig type	Shunting only
Sail area	87 sq ft (8.1 sq m)
Construction method	Strip-planked composite

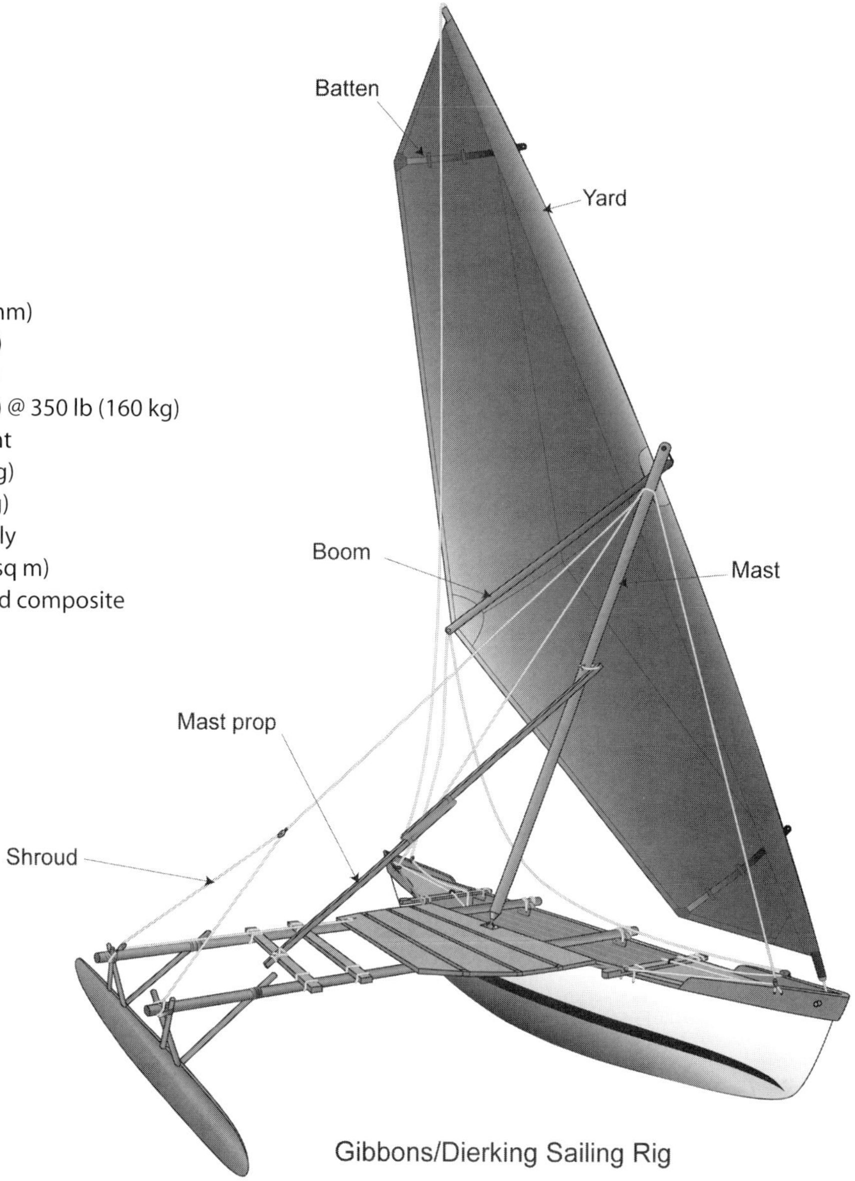

Gibbons/Dierking Sailing Rig

FIGURE 2-1. The T2 sailing canoe can be fitted with either an Oceanic lateen rig (see next page) or a Gibbons/Dierking rig as shown here.

The T2 is based on the designs of Micronesian sailing canoes. The T2 hull mostly resembles canoes found in the Marshall Islands and nearby Kiribati and, at 18' (5.4m), would be used primarily for fishing and transportation within an atoll lagoon. The hull is a deep, rounded "V" with an asymmetric shape and is constructed with the strip-composite method. Each end of the hull is identical and the T2 is sailed with either end as the bow. The ama is always kept on the windward side and can be flown above the water to reduce drag.

The T2 can be sailed with either the classic Oceanic lateen rig or a modification of a rig developed by Euell Gibbons (widely known for his books on gathering wild foods) in the 1950s. The Oceanic lateen rig is very old but still very powerful. If you are an experienced sailor, you will have to develop some new instincts when handling it. It is very forgiving of incorrect sheeting angles and will maintain its power at a point where a more conventional rig would have stalled. The Gibbons rig shown in Figures 2-1, 2-4, and 2-11 is completely untraditional with its roots in windsurfing and will appeal to the sailor who is interested in high speed. My version of the Gibbons rig is still experimental, and you won't see many of them around, but it is worth the time and effort to build one if you enjoy developing new technology.

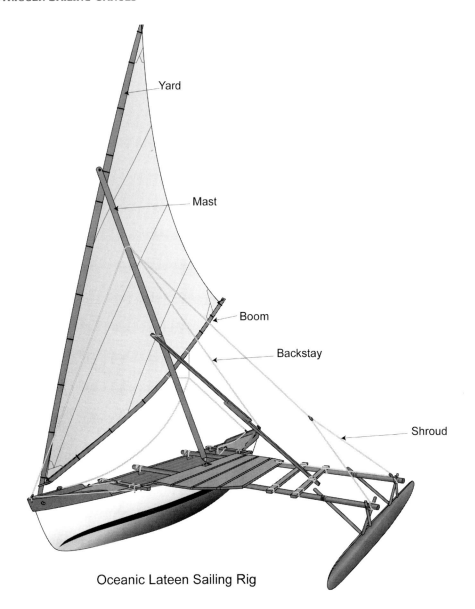

Oceanic Lateen Sailing Rig

The T2 is a sport canoe for one or two people and is not designed to carry heavy loads. The cockpit has a floor above the waterline, which allows it to be self-draining. Watertight bulkheads in each end, combined with the sealed area below the cockpit, allow the T2 to be sailed in extreme conditions without any concern for how much water enters. Seating is provided on a platform over the windward side, supported by the iakos. Because you will always be sitting on the windward side, there is no need to change sides when changing direction during a shunt.

A steering oar is the recommended way to steer and can be used to scull the canoe when becalmed. The fore-and-aft position of crew weight has a great effect on the steering and can be used to avoid use of the steering oar on all points of sail except for a broad reach or run.

The asymmetric, deep "V" hull shape requires no foils or leeboard for lateral resistance. The lack of underwater foils reduces the windward performance only marginally and can give you great confidence when you are sailing fast in shallow water. The asymmetric hull helps to counteract the forces of the long-boomed lateen sail and the ama drag that try to turn the canoe into the wind.

I've made a couple of modifications from traditional Micronesian design. Most shunting rigs require that the mast rake forward in the direction of travel in order to balance the sail force with the underwater shape. This rig requires running backstays to control

18

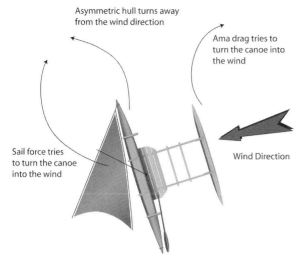

Asymmetric hull turns away from the wind direction

Ama drag tries to turn the canoe into the wind

Wind Direction

Sail force tries to turn the canoe into the wind

FIGURE 2-2. The asymmetric main hull of the T2 compensates for the forces resulting from the long boom and the drag from the ama.

the amount of mast rake. The T2 uses strong bungee cords to take up the slack in the backstays as the mast changes rake during the shunting. The bungee cords try to hold the mast at its vertical center point. Pulling the sail toward the bow stretches the bungee cord until a stopper ball on the backstay runs into the block attached to the stern. All of this means that the backstays are essentially self-tending, and that to shunt, all you have to do is pull the sail to the opposite end of the hull.

MATERIALS FOR BUILDING THE T2

Hull

- 70 planks of ¼" × ¾" × 18.5' (6mm × 19mm × 5700mm)
- Enough planks for the hull; end decks can be ripped from 6 pieces of timber, 5½" × ¾" × 18.5' (140mm × 19mm × 5700mm), assuming the use of a thin kerf circular saw blade.
- 2 sheets of ½" (12mm) or thicker plywood or particle board

Stems

- 2 pieces of 1" × 4" × 38" (25mm × 100mm × 950mm) clear, soft timber ripped into thin slices

Gunwales

- Inwale: 2 pieces of ½" × 1" × 18.5' (12mm × 25mm × 5700mm)
- Outwale: 2 pieces of ¾" × 1" × 12.8' (19mm × 25mm × 3900mm)
- Gunwales are best made of timber that is heavier and more durable than cedar.

Bulkheads, End Decks, and Cockpit Floor

- All of these parts can be made from one sheet of ¼" (6mm) plywood.

Hiking Seat

- 4 pieces of ¾" × 5½" × 6' (19mm × 140mm × 1800mm). A soft, lightweight wood like cedar or redwood can be left bare for nonslip seating.

Iakos

- 10 pieces of ⁵⁄₁₆" × 2⅜" × 9' (8mm × 60mm × 2700mm) fir, spruce, or pine
- *OR:* 2 pieces of 2" to 2¼" (50 to 55mm) aluminum tubing with minimum ³⁄₃₂" (2mm) wall thickness. Some alloys are stiffer than others; T6 is best.

Epoxy Resin

- 3 each, 1-gallon (4-liter) kits
- Bag of glue powder
- Bag of fairing powder

Fiberglass

- 4 pieces of 6-ounce (200-gram), 18.5' × 32" (6000mm × 800mm) for hull
- 4 pieces of glass for top and bottom of strip deck, 16" × 56" (400mm × 1400mm)
- Miscellaneous strips for glassing in bulkheads
- 2 pieces of 10-ounce (330 gram), 13' × 16" (3900mm × 400mm) for ama
- *OR:* 4 pieces of 6-ounce (200-gram) fiberglass cloth

Ama

- 2 pieces of 4" × 8" × 12'8" (100mm × 200mm × 4000mm) blue Styrofoam (can use 2" [50mm] foam and glue layers together) sheet; ⅛" or ³⁄₁₆" (3 or 4mm) plywood for shear web

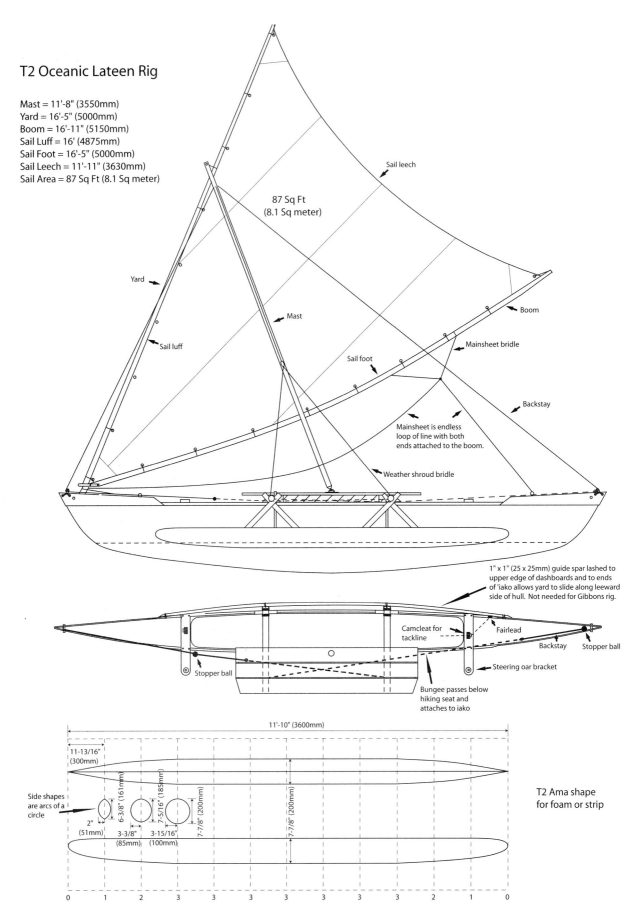

T2 Oceanic Lateen Rig

Mast = 11'-8" (3550mm)
Yard = 16'-5" (5000mm)
Boom = 16'-11" (5150mm)
Sail Luff = 16' (4875mm)
Sail Foot = 16'-5" (5000mm)
Sail Leech = 11'-11" (3630mm)
Sail Area = 87 Sq Ft (8.1 Sq meter)

87 Sq Ft
(8.1 Sq meter)

Sail leech

Yard

Mast

Boom

Sail luff

Sail foot

Mainsheet bridle

Backstay

Mainsheet is endless
loop of line with both
ends attached to the boom.

Weather shroud bridle

1" x 1" (25 x 25mm) guide spar lashed to
upper edge of dashboards and to ends
of 'iako allows yard to slide along leeward
side of hull. Not needed for Gibbons rig.

Camcleat for
tackline

Fairlead

Backstay

Stopper ball

Stopper ball

Steering oar bracket

Bungee passes below
hiking seat and
attaches to iako

11'-10" (3600mm)

11-13/16"
(300mm)

Side shapes
are arcs of a
circle

6-3/8" (161mm)

7-5/16" (185mm)

7-7/8" (200mm)

7-7/8" (200mm)

2"
(51mm)

3-3/8"
(85mm)

3-15/16"
(100mm)

T2 Ama shape
for foam or strip

0   1   2   3   3   3   3   3   3   2   1   0

Figure 2-3. Oceanic lateen sail plan, running backstay layout, and ama plan.

T2 Gibbons / Dierking Rig

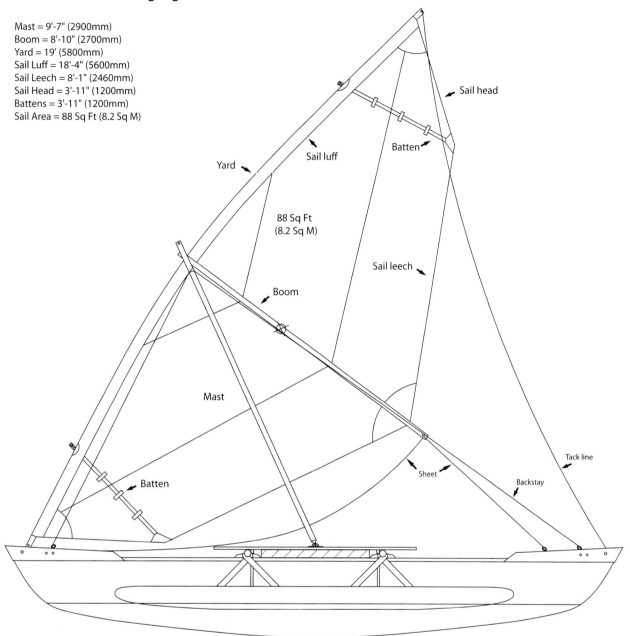

Mast = 9'-7" (2900mm)
Boom = 8'-10" (2700mm)
Yard = 19' (5800mm)
Sail Luff = 18'-4" (5600mm)
Sail Leech = 8'-1" (2460mm)
Sail Head = 3'-11" (1200mm)
Battens = 3'-11" (1200mm)
Sail Area = 88 Sq Ft (8.2 Sq M)

Sail head

Sail luff

Batten

Yard

88 Sq Ft
(8.2 Sq M)

Sail leech

Boom

Mast

Sheet

Tack line

Backstay

Batten

FIGURE 2-4. A Gibbons/Dierking sail plan.

APPROXIMATE TIME AND COST FOR BUILDING THE T2

The amount of time that it takes to complete a T2 is widely variable and reflects the personal standards and skill of the individual builder. The average time to set up, plank, and fiberglass a bare hull is about 100 hours. The total time to complete a ready-to-sail T2 is a minimum of 300 hours.

The minimum cost of materials is about U.S. $1,200. Half of this amount is for the epoxy resin and fiberglass. The ability to "scrounge" used or discarded building materials, hardware, or sails can greatly reduce the cost of the finished canoe.

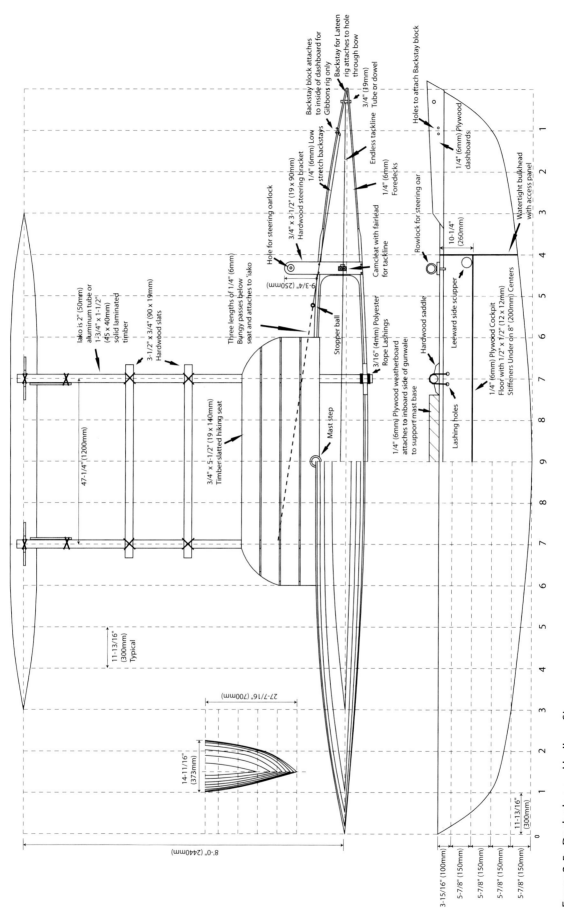

Iako is 2" (50mm) aluminum tube or 1-3/4" x 1-1/2" (45 x 40mm) solid laminated timber

3-1/2" x 3/4" (90 x 19mm) Hardwood slats

11-13/16" (300mm) Typical

47-1/4" (1200mm)

3/4" x 5-1/2" (19 x 140mm) Timber slatted hiking seat

Three lengths of 1/4" (6mm) Bungy passes below seat and attaches to 'iako

27-7/16" (700mm)

14-11/16" (373mm)

Hole for steering oarlock

3/4" x 3-1/2" (19 x 90mm) Hardwood steering bracket

1/4" (6mm) Low stretch backstays

Backstay block attaches to inside of dashboard for Gibbons rig only

Backstay for Lateen rig attaches to hole through bow

3/4" (19mm) Tube or dowel

Endless tackline

1/4" (6mm) Foredecks

9-3/4" (250mm)

Camcleat with fairlead for tackline

Stopper ball

3/16" (4mm) Polyester Rope Lashings

1/4" (6mm) Plywood weatherboard attaches to inboard side of gunwale

Mast step

Hardwood saddle

Leeward side scupper

1/4" (6mm) Plywood Cockpit Floor with 1/2" x 1/2" (12 x 12mm) Stiffeners Under on 8" (200mm) Centers

Lashing holes

Rowlock for steering oar

10-1/4" (260mm)

Watertight bulkhead with access panel

1/4" (6mm) Plywood dashboards

Holes to attach Backstay block

8'-0" (2440mm)

11-13/16" (300mm)

3-15/16" (100mm)
5-7/8" (150mm)
5-7/8" (150mm)
5-7/8" (150mm)
5-7/8" (150mm)

FIGURE 2-5. Deck plan and hull profile.

22

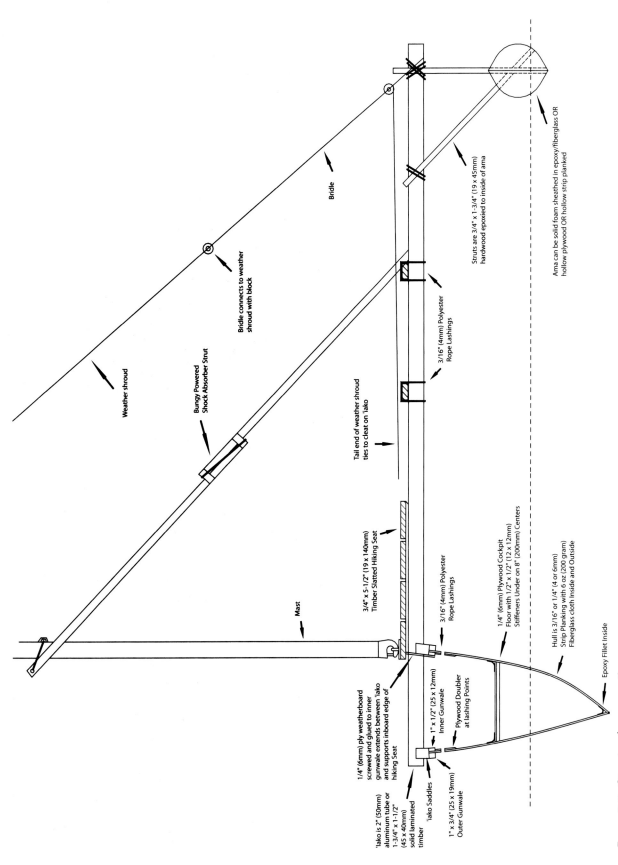

Weather shroud

Bridle

Bridle connects to weather
shroud with block

Bungy Powered
Shock Absorber Strut

Struts are 3/4" x 1-3/4" (19 x 45mm)
hardwood epoxied to inside of ama

3/16" (4mm) Polyester
Rope Lashings

Ama can be solid foam sheathed in epoxy/fiberglass OR
hollow plywood OR hollow strip planked

Tail end of weather shroud
ties to cleat on 'iako

Mast

3/4" x 5-1/2" (19 x 140mm)
Timber Slatted Hiking Seat

3/16" (4mm) Polyester
Rope Lashings

1/4" (6mm) Plywood Cockpit
Floor with 1/2" x 1/2" (12 x 12mm)
Stiffeners Under on 8" (200mm) Centers

Hull is 3/16" or 1/4" (4 or 6mm)
Strip Planking with 6 oz (200 gram)
Fiberglass cloth Inside and Outside

Epoxy Fillet Inside

1/4" (6mm) ply weatherboard
screwed and glued to inner
gunwale extends between 'iako
and supports inboard edge of
hiking Seat

'iako is 2" (50mm)
aluminum tube or
1-3/4" x 1-1/2"
(45 x 40mm)
solid laminated
timber

1" x 1/2" (25 x 12mm)
Inner Gunwale

Plywood Doubler
at lashing Points

'iako Saddles

1" x 3/4" (25 x 19mm)
Outer Gunwale

FIGURE 2-6. Structural cross section.

23

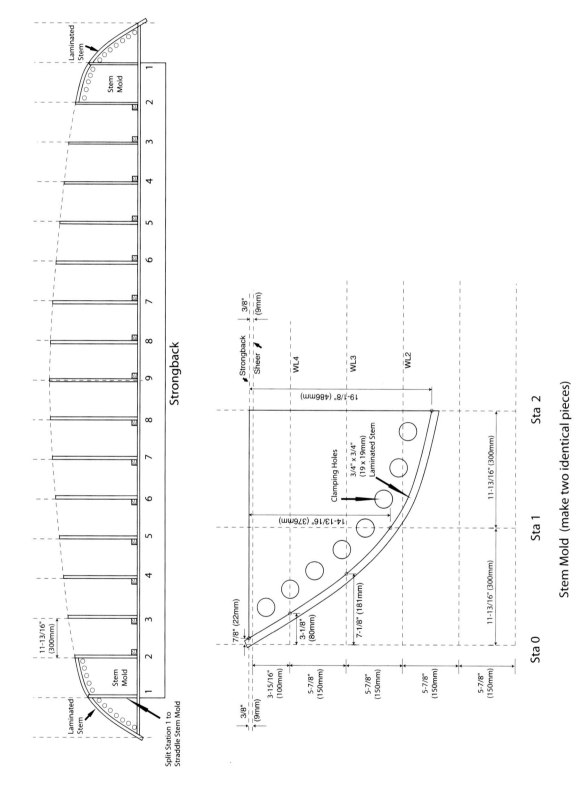

Strongback

Laminated Stem

Stem Mold

11-13/16" (300mm)

Split Station 1 to Straddle Stem Mold

Laminated Stem

Stem Mold

3/8" (9mm)

Strongback

Sheer

WL4

WL3

WL2

19-1/8" (486mm)

Clamping Holes

3/4" x 3/4" (19 x 19mm) Laminated Stem

14-13/16" (376mm)

7/8" (22mm)

3-1/8" (80mm)

7-1/8" (181mm)

11-13/16" (300mm)

11-13/16" (300mm)

Sta 0

Sta 1

Sta 2

3/8" (9mm)

3-15/16" (100mm)

5-7/8" (150mm)

5-7/8" (150mm)

5-7/8" (150mm)

5-7/8" (150mm)

Stem Mold (make two identical pieces)

FIGURE 2-7. Mold section setup and stem mold layout.

T2 Table of Offsets

Hull Offsets Leeward Side

Station Number	1	2	3	4	5	6	7	8	9
Sheer Half Breadth	26 / 0-1-0	52 / 0-2-0+	76 / 0-3-0	96 / 0-3-6	113 / 0-4-3+	129 / 0-5-0+	141 / 0-5-4+	146 / 0-5-6	146 / 0-5-6
WL4 Half Breadth	24 / 0-0-7+	48 / 0-1-7	71 / 0-2-6+	90 / 0-3-4+	107 / 0-4-1+	121 / 0-4-6	129 / 0-5-0+	136 / 0-5-3	136 / 0-5-3
WL3 Half Breadth	12 / 0-0-4	35 / 0-1-3	55 / 0-2-1+	72 / 0-2-6+	86 / 0-3-3	98 / 0-3-7	107 / 0-4-1+	112 / 0-4-3+	113 / 0-4-3+
WL2 Half Breadth		16 / 0-0-5	31 / 0-1-2	44 / 0-1-6	57 / 0-2-2	68 / 0-2-5+	75 / 0-2-7+	79 / 0-3-1	81 / 0-3-1+
WL1 Half Breadth			0 / 0-0-0	10 / 0-0-3	20 / 0-0-6+	30 / 0-1-1+	35 / 0-1-3	39 / 0-1-4+	41 / 0-1-5
Keel to Baseline	310 / 1-0-1+	204 / 0-8-0+	150 / 0-5-7	114 / 0-4-4	81 / 0-3-1+	51 / 0-2-0	25 / 0-1-0	8 / 0-0-2+	0 / 0-0-0

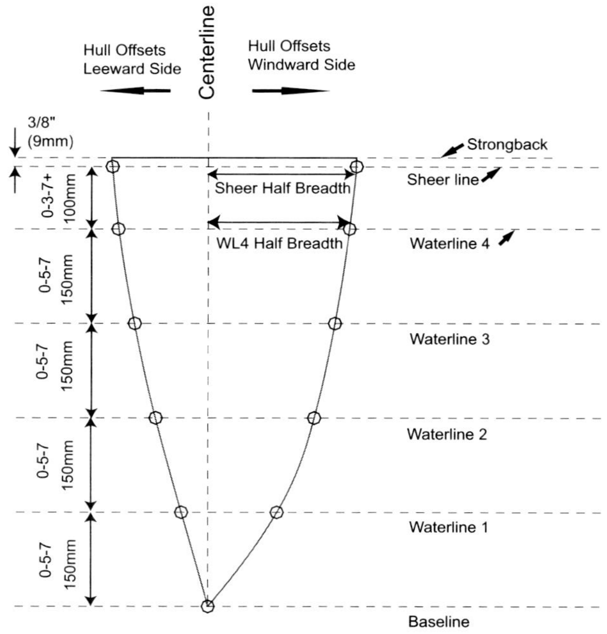

Hull Offsets Windward (ama) Side

Station Number	1	2	3	4	5	6	7	8	9
Sheer Half Breadth	63 / 0-2-4	118 / 0-4-5	159 / 0-6-2	190 / 0-7-4	210 / 0-8-2	221 / 0-8-5+	225 / 0-8-7	226 / 0-8-7	227 / 0-8-7+
WL4 Half Breadth	55 / 0-2-1+	111 / 0-4-3	151 / 0-5-7+	182 / 0-7-1+	202 / 0-7-7+	211 / 0-8-2+	213 / 0-8-3	215 / 0-8-3+	216 / 0-8-4
WL3 Half Breadth	32 / 0-1-2	90 / 0-3-4+	132 / 0-5-1+	161 / 0-6-3	179 / 0-7-0+	189 / 0-7-3+	191 / 0-7-4	192 / 0-7-4+	194 / 0-7-5
WL2 Half Breadth		48 / 0-1-7	91 / 0-3-4+	122 / 0-4-6+	142 / 0-5-4+	154 / 0-6-0+	159 / 0-6-2	161 / 0-6-2+	162 / 0-6-3
WL1 Half Breadth			0 / 0-0-0	37 / 0-1-4+	67 / 0-2-5	88 / 0-3-3+	99 / 0-3-7	103 / 0-4-0+	105 / 0-4-1
Keel to Baseline	310 / 1-0-1+	204 / 0-8-0+	150 / 0-5-7	114 / 0-4-4	81 / 0-3-1+	51 / 0-2-0	25 / 0-1-0	8 / 0-0-2+	0 / 0-0-0

The table of offsets enables you to reproduce the curved shape of the hull molds. The top number in each box is in millimeters, and the bottom number is feet, inches, and eighths of an inch. A plus sign adds a sixteenth of an inch. For example: 1-6-1+ equals one foot, 6 inches, and three-sixteenths of an inch.

Because the hull is asymmetric, the offsets or half breadths are different on each side of the hull. The two sides are designated as a windward and a leeward side.

Both ends of the hull are identical so that most of the molds are used twice. Make two molds of stations 1-8, and one of station 9 amidships.

Draw a centerline, baseline, waterlines, and strongback line, ensuring that the waterlines are parallel and spaced correctly. Measure and mark the offsets or half breadths, tack a small nail at each point, and bend a timber batten along the nails. Draw the curved line along the batten with a pencil.

FIGURE 2-8. Table of offsets and mold section lofting.

25

FIGURE 2-9. (ABOVE LEFT) The author's *Tarawa*, ready to set sail.

FIGURE 2-10. (ABOVE) *Tarawa* with a Dierking/Gibbons rig. (Photo courtesy Rose Turner)

FIGURE 2-11. (LEFT) Guy Rinfret's *Bororo*, fitted with an Oceanic lateen rig. (Photo courtesy Guy Rinfret)

FIGURE 2-12. (BELOW) *Bororo* under sail. (Photo courtesy Guy Rinfret)

Figure 2-13. *Bororo's* hull graphics. (Photo courtesy Guy Rinfret)

FIGURE 2-14. *Bororo* being sculled with the steering oar. (Photo courtesy Guy Rinfret)

CHAPTER 3

The Wa'apa

Length overall	23'8" (7200mm)
Hull width	21¼" (540mm)
Overall width	11' (3370mm)
Draft	6" (150mm) @ 675 lb (306 kg) displacement
Hull weight	174 lb (79 kg), 58 lb (26 kg) per section
Weight fully rigged	275 lb (125 kg)
Sailing rig type	Tacking or Shunting
Sail area	84 sq ft (7.8 sq m) Tacking, 126 sq ft (11.7 sq m) Shunting
Construction method	Plywood

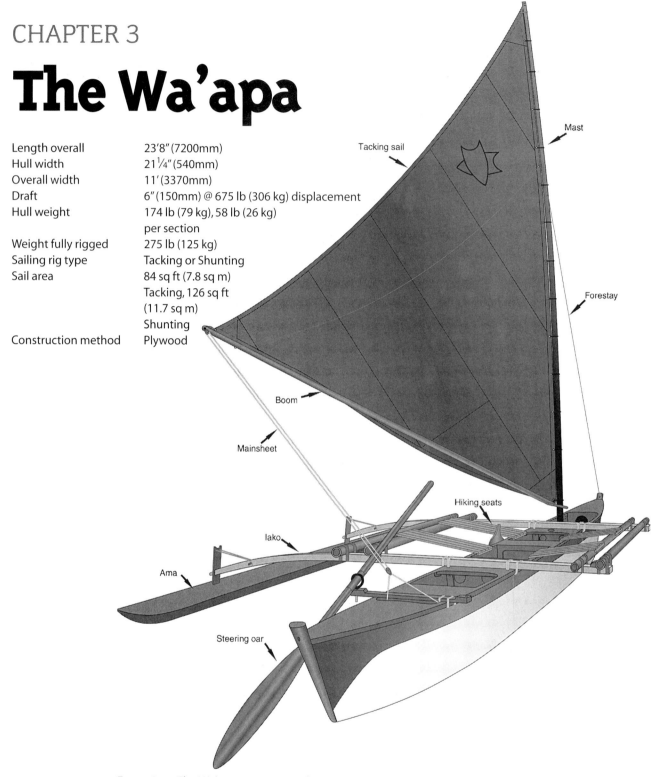

FIGURE 3-1. The Wa'apa outrigger sailing canoe equipped with a tacking rig.

In the late 1800s, when sawn lumber began to appear in Hawaii and other Pacific islands, the local canoe builders immediately saw its use as an easier way to build canoes. While perhaps slightly less efficient than round-bottomed shapes, a flat-bottomed, dory-shaped hull has now become the standard working canoe seen in many places throughout the Pacific. The first models were simply built of three wide planks and came to be known as "three-board canoes," or "wa'apa" in Hawaiian.

I built a 16-footer in the 1970s that unbolted in the center for easier stowage onboard my cruising trimaran. It proved to be a useful dinghy and a fun sailer for exploring. This design is similar in shape to that one, but it allows for a center section to be added, which stretches the boat to 24'. The 24-footer seats four crew members and can be sailed as a tacking outrigger or a shunting proa. The tacking configuration uses hiking seats on both sides of the hull, whereas the shunting version carries them only on the ama (windward) side of the hull.

The Wa'apa can be built as a one-piece hull if you choose, but one of its prime advantages is that no hull or ama section is longer than 8' (2.4m). It can be built, stored, and transported in a small space. The three-section main hull and a two-piece plywood ama require only six sheets of ¼" (6mm) plywood. The hull sides and ama can be built with ³⁄₁₆" (4mm) plywood to save weight.

Waterline length is a wonderful thing, and it is cheap to build when hull beam and depth remain the same. This design is extremely versatile in that many different options can be included with the basic design. It can be sailed as a tacking outrigger, where the ama runs either on the windward or leeward side, or as a shunting proa, where the ama is always kept on the windward side.

RIG CHOICE

Choosing between the two rigs is difficult and really is a matter of personal choice. The shunting proa has the potential for greater performance but requires a more complicated rig. The mast is stayed, requiring two backstays and a weather shroud. Steering is accomplished from either end with a long oar, a pair of dagger boards in the ends, or a pair of kick-up rudders. An endless tack line controls the butt of the yard and, when shunting, you simply pull the yard from one bow to the other without leaving your seat. The butt of the yard can slide along below the gunwale of the hull's leeward side.

One of the characteristics of the lateen or crab-claw rig is that the butt of the yard wants to swing to windward during a shunt. Keeping the butt below the gunwale prevents this annoying trait and avoids the necessity of installing a guiding track, or guiding the butt along by hand. The backstays that control the fore-and-aft rake of the mast can be controlled by a bungee cord that tries to hold the mast vertical. Pulling the butt of the yard to either bow will stretch

the bungee cord. A pair of spiller lines or lazy jacks are rigged to depower the sail in squalls and to hold the boom, yard, and sail off of the deck when the sail is lowered with the halyard.

The tacking rig is very simple, with an unstayed windsurfing mast, no halyard, and a spiller/brailing line for brailing the sail up against the mast. This is especially convenient, as the sail is quickly stowed out of the way of paddlers. The whole rig is easily pulled out and stowed on the iakos. The rig shown in Figure 3-4 uses a straight boom with a loose-footed sail. While not as visually attractive as a curved boom, this system allows you to reef the sail by simply rotating the mast and winding the sail up on it. The boom outhaul controlling the clew of the sail is led forward along the boom to an easily reached cleat.

Long, narrow-beamed canoes are very sensitive to weight distribution. The location of crew members or cargo weight has an effect on the fore-and-aft sailing balance of the canoe. Concentrating weight aft increases the lateral resistance of the hull in that area and will cause lee helm, or the tendency to turn away from the wind. Weight concentrated forward will have the opposite effect. Using a fixed rudder aft, or on the iako, instead of an oar, will also change the balance. For this reason, in Figure 3-4 I have shown two mast-step locations for the tacking rig. This will allow you to adjust for different loading conditions or steering setups.

THE HULL

The hull is a flat-bottomed dory shape, although a dory would have more flare in the sides. I'm opposed to extreme flare in the sides, as I feel it slows the hull considerably when sailing into waves.

Because each hull section is slightly shorter than a sheet of plywood, no scarf joints or butt blocks are necessary.

Each hull section is connected to the next with four ⁵⁄₁₆" (8mm) stainless-steel bolts. Washers cut from inner tubes or wetsuit material are placed between the hull sections to keep water out of the bolt holes.

The hull sides and decks can be made from either ¼"(6mm) or ³⁄₁₆" (4mm) plywood. Plywood with five plies is much better than three plies. The bottom panels should be ¼" (6mm) to avoid damage when the hull is resting on rocks. It is not necessary to fiberglass the entire hull if it is built from

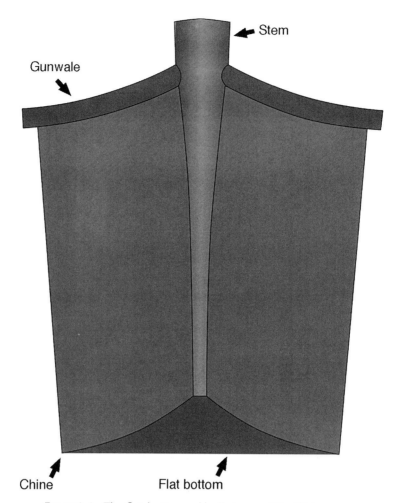

FIGURE 3-2. The flat-bottomed hull shape of the Wa'apa.

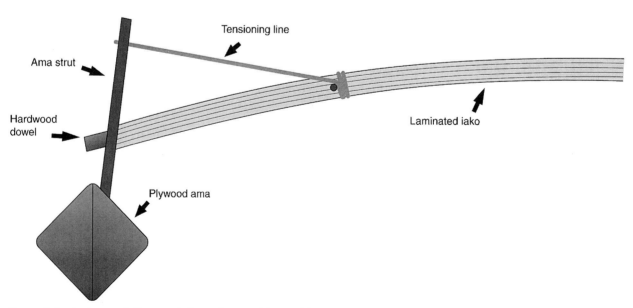

FIGURE 3-3. A plywood, diamond-shaped ama with a quick-connecting strut.

¼" (6mm) plywood. The prototype was glassed only on the bottom, lapping 2" (50mm) up over the chine. The rest of the hull was painted with water-based acrylic house paint. Be sure to apply several primer coats and avoid paints that say they require no primer.

There are several possible options for the deck layout. The drawings in Figures 3-4, 3-5, 3-6, 3-7, and 3-8 show all open hulls, with a watertight bulkhead at each end for emergency flotation. It is possible to completely deck over either of the two end sections, or even all three, with hatches strategically placed so that you can put your feet into the hatch when paddling. This is a good option if you are planning to use the canoe in very rough offshore conditions.

THE AMA

The ama shown in Figure 3-3 is a square, four-sided box mounted with the "V" at the deck and bottom. It can also be broken down into two sections, with bulkheads and ¼" (6mm) bolts at its midpoint. A 16' (4.8m) ama can be made from one sheet of plywood. Although it has nicely curved ends, all of the joints are square with no beveling required.

The single hardwood strut is a strong, simple system to attach the ama to the iakos. It is quick to rig and unrig and allows good flexibility in the pitching axis.

While a 16' (4.8m) ama is fine for the three-section canoe, it is a bit oversized for the two-section configuration. You may want to build a second, shorter ama if you intend to paddle the two-section canoe frequently.

THE DOUBLE OUTRIGGER OPTION

While most of my designs feature only one ama, the double-outrigger option can be very attractive. If you're single-handing a lot on fairly long trips, the ability to fall asleep at the helm and not worry about capsizing can be very comforting. The double outrigger, or trimaran, has a long history and is still common in the Indian Ocean, where there are hundreds of thousands of them. Of course, you're going to have to build an extra ama and always carry that

weight with you. For that reason, I recommend building foam/fiberglass amas, as they are the lightest that you can build easily.

The iakos for the double outrigger can be either the laminated, swooping, gull-wing shape often seen, or a simple, straight, hollow box beam, which is stiffer and easier to build. The top and bottom of the hollow beams are ¾" × 2¾" (19mm × 70mm) timber, and the sides are ¼" (6mm) plywood. A key point to remember is that the amas should be above the water when the canoe is loaded and held level.

In order to raise the iakos as high above the water as possible, you can build the center hull section with a higher freeboard than for the end sections. There is enough room on the sheet of plywood to increase the width of the side panel by 4" (100mm). Two of the station 2 bulkheads and the station 3 frame would also have to be extended upward. The iakos are slightly closer together with this option, as they rest entirely on the center section. The standard arrangement has the iakos cover the joint between the hull sections.

MATERIALS FOR BUILDING THE WA'APA

This list of materials will build the three-piece, 24' (7.2m) hull.

Three-Piece Hull

STANDARD
- 5 sheets of ¼" (6mm) plywood

LIGHTWEIGHT
- 4 sheets of ³⁄₁₆" (4mm) plywood and 1 sheet of ¼" (6mm) plywood
- Use ¼" (6mm) for bottom panels

Gunwales
- 49' (15 lineal m) of ¾" × 1¼" (18mm × 30mm) clear timber

Chines
- 49' (15 lineal m) of 15mm × 25mm (⅝" × 1") clear timber

Bulkhead Perimeters

- 12.6' (3.2 lineal m) of ¾" × 1" (18mm × 25mm) clear timber
- 8' (2.4 lineal m) of ¾" × 1⅜" (18mm × 35mm) clear timber
- 18.4' (5.6 lineal m) of ¾" × 2" (18mm × 50mm) clear timber

Stems

- ¾" × 3" × 4' (18mm × 75mm × 1200mm) of plywood or solid softwood

Seat Supports

- 11.8' (3.6 lineal m) of ¾" × 1¼" (18mm × 30mm) clear timber

Plywood Ama

- 1 sheet of ³⁄₁₆" or ¼" (4mm or 6mm) plywood
- 64' (19.2 lineal m) of ⅝" × ⅝" (16mm × 16mm) clear timber
- 6' (1.8 lineal m) of ¾" × 3½" (18mm × 90mm) hardwood

Iako (Cross Beams)

SOLID LAMINATED

- 14 pieces of 2¾" × ⁵⁄₁₆" × 10.8' (70mm × 8mm × 3.3m)
- 1' (300mm) of 1¼" (30mm) hardwood dowel

HOLLOW BOX BEAM (DOUBLE OUTRIGGER)

- 4 pieces of 2¾" × ¾" × 13.2' (70mm × 18mm × 4m) fir, spruce, mahogany, or pine
- ½ sheet of ¼" (6mm) plywood
- 2' (600mm) of 1¼" (30mm) hardwood dowel

Epoxy Resin

- 1 each of 1-gallon (4-liter) kit if used for glue and sheathing of bottom only
- 3 each of 1-gallon (4-liter) kit if used for glue and to sheath entire hull and ama

APPROXIMATE TIME AND COST FOR BUILDING THE WA'APA

Being built of plywood, the Wa'apa requires less construction time than a strip-planked composite hull. The basic components (hull, ama, and iakos) will require about 160 hours, depending on the level of finish that you desire. Sheathing the entire hull in fiberglass (rather than just the bottom) will add another ten hours to the total time. The structure can be built in less time, but appearance and longevity may suffer.

The cost of building the basic structure will be a minimum of U.S. $1,000, with an additional U.S. $500 if you wish to completely sheath the hull and ama with fiberglass. The cost of a sailing rig can range from U.S. $20 to U.S. $2,000, depending on what you want and where you get it.

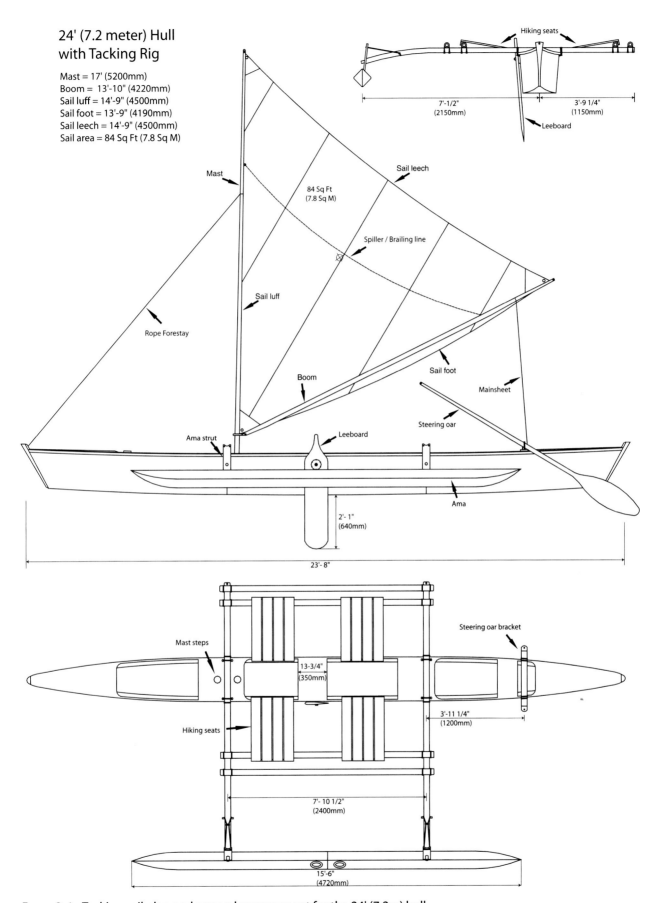

24' (7.2 meter) Hull with Tacking Rig

Mast = 17' (5200mm)
Boom = 13'-10" (4220mm)
Sail luff = 14'-9" (4500mm)
Sail foot = 13'-9" (4190mm)
Sail leech = 14'-9" (4500mm)
Sail area = 84 Sq Ft (7.8 Sq M)

Hiking seats

7'-1/2"
(2150mm)

3'-9 1/4"
(1150mm)

Leeboard

Mast

Sail leech

84 Sq Ft
(7.8 Sq M)

Spiller / Brailing line

Sail luff

Rope Forestay

Boom

Sail foot

Mainsheet

Ama strut

Leeboard

Steering oar

2'- 1"
(640mm)

Ama

23'- 8"

Mast steps

Steering oar bracket

13-3/4"
(350mm)

3'-11 1/4"
(1200mm)

Hiking seats

7'- 10 1/2"
(2400mm)

15'-6"
(4720mm)

FIGURE 3-4. Tacking sail plan and general arrangement for the 24' (7.2m) hull.

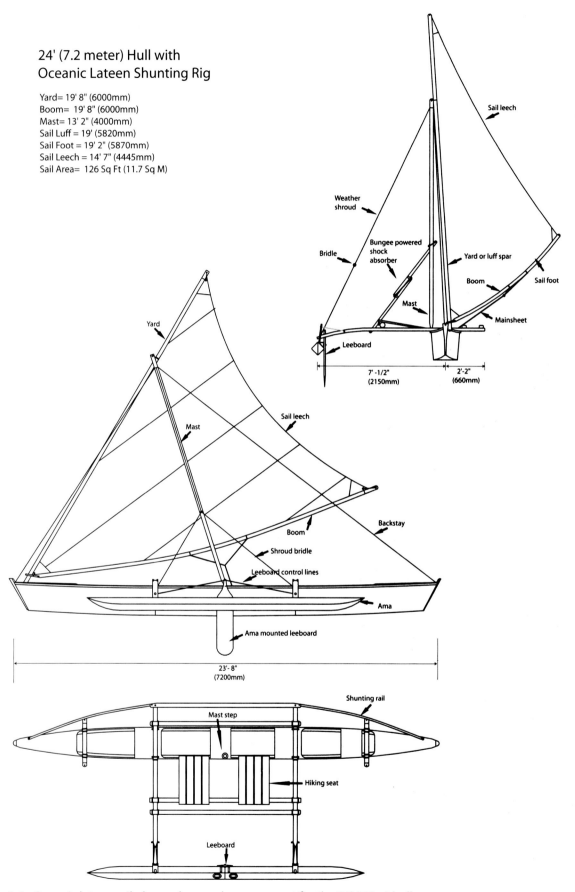

24' (7.2 meter) Hull with Oceanic Lateen Shunting Rig

Yard= 19' 8" (6000mm)
Boom= 19' 8" (6000mm)
Mast= 13' 2" (4000mm)
Sail Luff = 19' (5820mm)
Sail Foot = 19' 2" (5870mm)
Sail Leech = 14' 7" (4445mm)
Sail Area= 126 Sq Ft (11.7 Sq M)

Sail leech

Weather shroud

Bridle

Bungee powered shock absorber

Yard or luff spar

Boom

Sail foot

Mast

Mainsheet

Leeboard

7'-1/2"
(2150mm)

2'-2"
(660mm)

Yard

Sail leech

Mast

Backstay

Boom

Shroud bridle

Leeboard control lines

Ama

Ama mounted leeboard

23'- 8"
(7200mm)

Shunting rail

Mast step

Hiking seat

Leeboard

FIGURE 3-5. Oceanic lateen sail plan and general arrangement for the 24' (7.2m) hull.

34

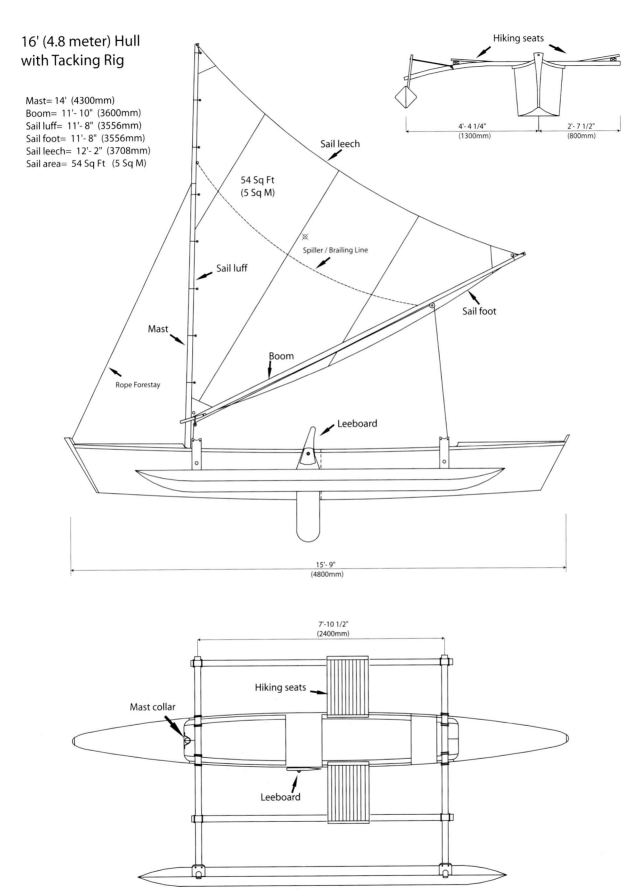

16' (4.8 meter) Hull
with Tacking Rig

Mast= 14' (4300mm)
Boom= 11'- 10" (3600mm)
Sail luff= 11'- 8" (3556mm)
Sail foot= 11'- 8" (3556mm)
Sail leech= 12'- 2" (3708mm)
Sail area= 54 Sq Ft (5 Sq M)

Hiking seats

4'- 4 1/4"
(1300mm)

2'- 7 1/2"
(800mm)

Sail leech

54 Sq Ft
(5 Sq M)

Spiller / Brailing Line

Sail luff

Sail foot

Mast

Boom

Rope Forestay

Leeboard

15'- 9"
(4800mm)

7'-10 1/2"
(2400mm)

Mast collar

Hiking seats

Leeboard

FIGURE 3-6. Tacking sail plan and general arrangement for the 16' (4.8m) hull.

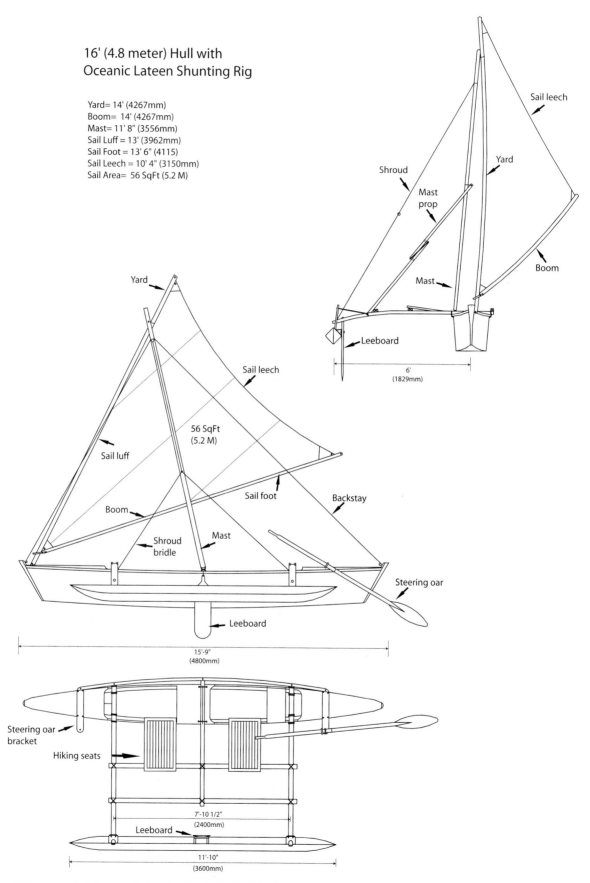

16' (4.8 meter) Hull with
Oceanic Lateen Shunting Rig

Yard= 14' (4267mm)
Boom= 14' (4267mm)
Mast= 11' 8" (3556mm)
Sail Luff = 13' (3962mm)
Sail Foot = 13' 6" (4115)
Sail Leech = 10' 4" (3150mm)
Sail Area= 56 SqFt (5.2 M)

Sail leech

Shroud

Mast
prop

Yard

Mast

Boom

Leeboard

6'
(1829mm)

Yard

Sail leech

56 SqFt
(5.2 M)

Sail luff

Sail foot

Backstay

Boom

Shroud
bridle

Mast

Steering oar

Leeboard

15'-9"
(4800mm)

Steering oar
bracket

Hiking seats

Leeboard

7'-10 1/2"
(2400mm)

11'-10"
(3600mm)

FIGURE 3-7. Oceanic lateen sail plan for the 16' (4.8m) hull.

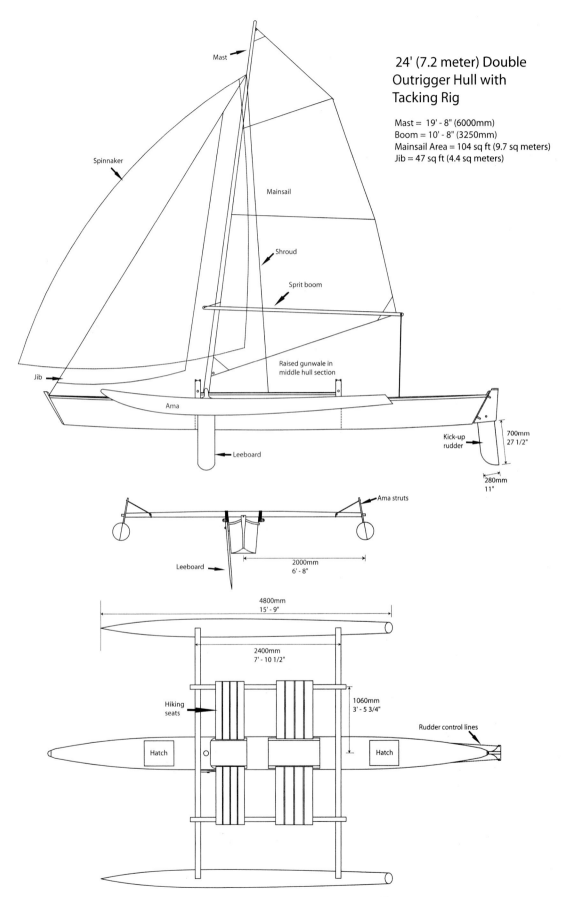

FIGURE 3-8. Tacking sail plan for the 24' (7.2m) double outrigger–equipped hull.

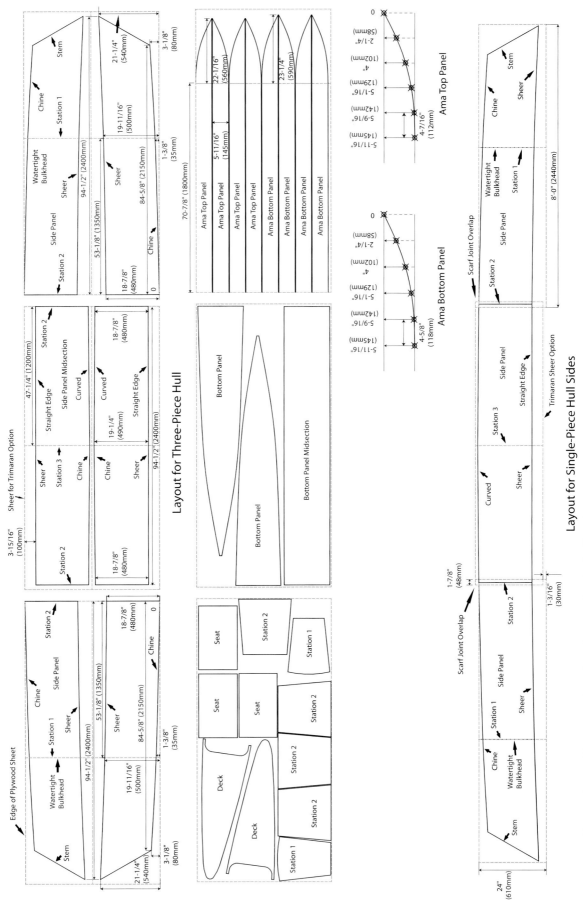

Layout for Three-Piece Hull

Layout for Single-Piece Hull Sides

Ama Top Panel

Ama Bottom Panel

FIGURE 3-9. Plywood panel layout and cutting diagram for the hull and ama.

38

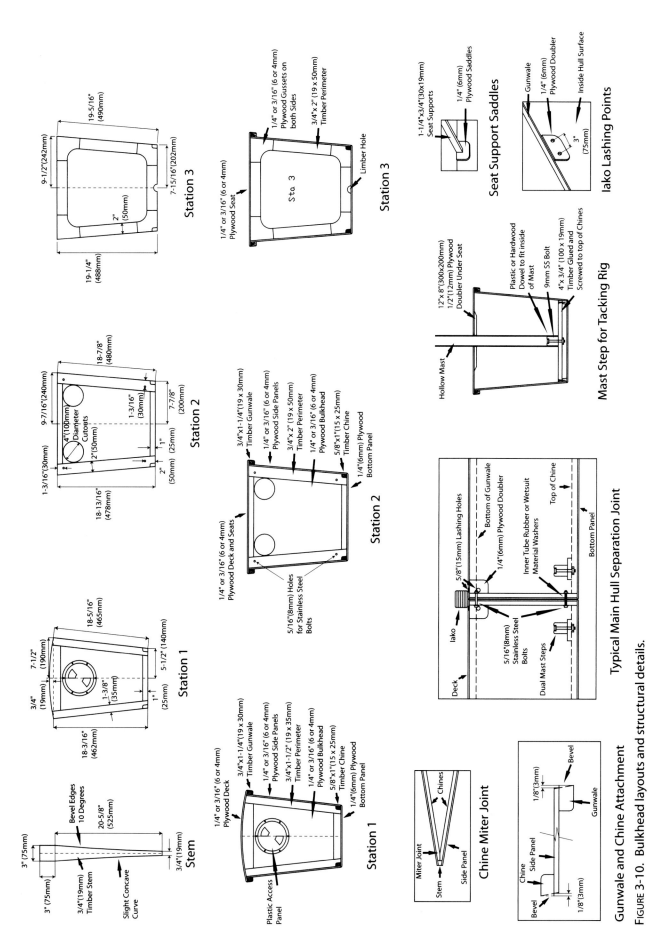

Station 3

19-5/16"(490mm)
9-1/2"(242mm)
2"(50mm)
7-15/16"(202mm)
19-1/4" (488mm)

1/4" or 3/16" (6 or 4mm) Plywood Gussets on both Sides
3/4"x 2" (19 x 50mm) Timber Perimeter
Limber Hole
1/4" or 3/16" (6 or 4mm) Plywood Seat
Sta. 3

Station 3

1-1/4"x3/4"(30x19mm) Seat Supports
1/4" (6mm) Plywood Saddles

Seat Support Saddles

Gunwale
1/4" (6mm) Plywood Doubler
Inside Hull Surface
3" (75mm)

Iako Lashing Points

Station 2

18-7/8" (480mm)
9-7/16"(240mm)
4"(100mm) Diameter Cutouts
2"(50mm)
1-3/16" (30mm)
7-7/8" (200mm)
1-3/16"(30mm)
18-13/16" (478mm)
2" (50mm)
1" (25mm)

3/4"x1-1/4"(19 x 30mm) Timber Gunwale
1/4" or 3/16" (6 or 4mm) Plywood Side Panels
3/4"x 2" (19 x 50mm) Timber Perimeter
1/4" or 3/16" (6 or 4mm) Plywood Bulkhead
5/8"x1"(15 x 25mm) Timber Chine
1/4"(6mm) Plywood Bottom Panel

Station 2

1/4" or 3/16" (6 or 4mm) Plywood Deck and Seats
5/16"(8mm) Holes for Stainless Steel Bolts

12"x 8"(300x200mm) 1/2"(12mm) Plywood Doubler Under Seat
Plastic or Hardwood Dowel to fit inside of Mast
9mm SS Bolt
4"x 3/4" (100 x 19mm) Timber Glued and Screwed to top of Chines
Hollow Mast

Mast Step for Tacking Rig

Station 1

18-5/16" (465mm)
7-1/2" (190mm)
3/4" (19mm)
5-1/2" (140mm)
1-3/8" (35mm)
1" (25mm)
18-3/16" (462mm)

Stem

3" (75mm)
Bevel Edges 10 Degrees
20-5/8" (525mm)
3/4"(19mm) Timber Stem
Slight Concave Curve
3" (75mm)
3/4"(19mm)

1/4" or 3/16" (6 or 4mm) Plywood Deck
3/4"x1-1/4"(19 x 30mm) Timber Gunwale
1/4" or 3/16" (6 or 4mm) Plywood Side Panels
3/4"x1-1/2" (19 x 35mm) Timber Perimeter
1/4" or 3/16" (6 or 4mm) Plywood Bulkhead
5/8"x1"(15 x 25mm) Timber Chine
1/4"(6mm) Plywood Bottom Panel
Plastic Access Panel

Station 1

5/8"(15mm) Lashing Holes
Bottom of Gunwale
1/4"(6mm) Plywood Doubler
Inner Tube Rubber or Wetsuit Material Washers
Top of Chine
Bottom Panel
Iako
5/16"(8mm) Stainless Steel Bolts
Dual Mast Steps
Deck

Typical Main Hull Separation Joint

Miter Joint
Chines
Stem
Side Panel

Chine Miter Joint

Bevel
1/8"(3mm)
Gunwale
Chine
Side Panel
Bevel
1/8"(3mm)

Gunwale and Chine Attachment

Figure 3-10. Bulkhead layouts and structural details.

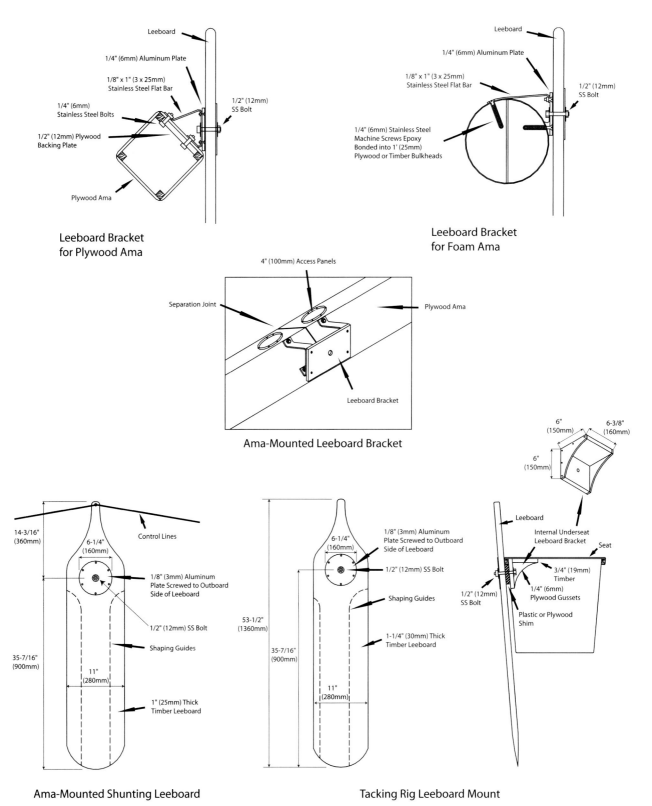

Leeboard

1/4" (6mm) Aluminum Plate

1/8" x 1" (3 x 25mm)
Stainless Steel Flat Bar

1/4" (6mm)
Stainless Steel Bolts

1/2" (12mm) Plywood
Backing Plate

Plywood Ama

1/2" (12mm)
SS Bolt

**Leeboard Bracket
for Plywood Ama**

Leeboard

1/4" (6mm) Aluminum Plate

1/8" x 1" (3 x 25mm)
Stainless Steel Flat Bar

1/2" (12mm)
SS Bolt

1/4" (6mm) Stainless Steel
Machine Screws Epoxy
Bonded into 1' (25mm)
Plywood or Timber Bulkheads

**Leeboard Bracket
for Foam Ama**

4" (100mm) Access Panels

Separation Joint

Plywood Ama

Leeboard Bracket

Ama-Mounted Leeboard Bracket

14-3/16"
(360mm)

6-1/4"
(160mm)

Control Lines

1/8" (3mm) Aluminum
Plate Screwed to Outboard
Side of Leeboard

1/2" (12mm) SS Bolt

Shaping Guides

35-7/16"
(900mm)

11"
(280mm)

1" (25mm) Thick
Timber Leeboard

Ama-Mounted Shunting Leeboard

6-1/4"
(160mm)

1/8" (3mm) Aluminum
Plate Screwed to Outboard
Side of Leeboard

1/2" (12mm) SS Bolt

Shaping Guides

53-1/2"
(1360mm)

35-7/16"
(900mm)

11"
(280mm)

1-1/4" (30mm) Thick
Timber Leeboard

Tacking Rig Leeboard Mount

6"
(150mm)

6-3/8"
(160mm)

6"
(150mm)

Leeboard

Internal Underseat
Leeboard Bracket

Seat

3/4" (19mm)
Timber

1/4" (6mm)
Plywood Gussets

Plastic or Plywood
Shim

1/2" (12mm)
SS Bolt

FIGURE 3-11. Leeboard construction details and mounting options.

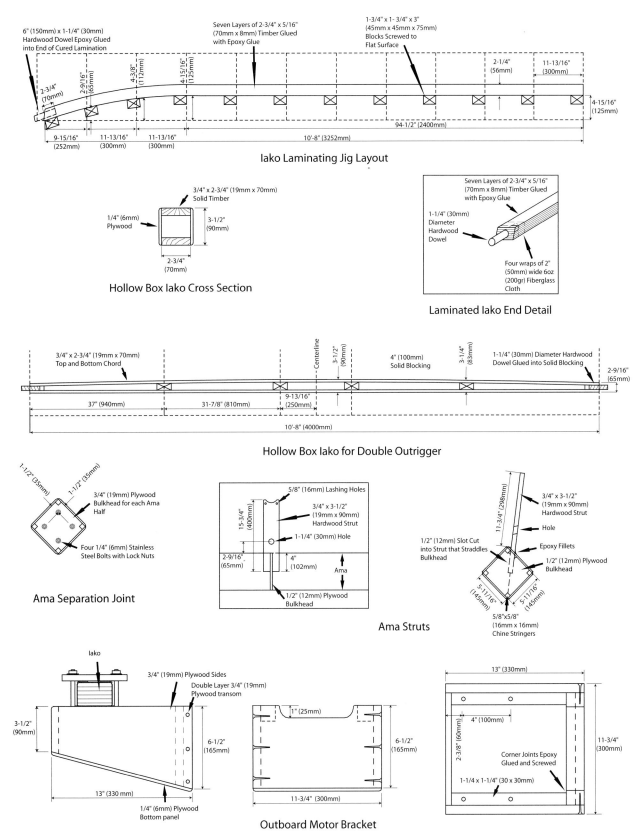

Iako Laminating Jig Layout

Hollow Box Iako Cross Section

Laminated Iako End Detail

Hollow Box Iako for Double Outrigger

Ama Separation Joint

Ama Struts

Outboard Motor Bracket

FIGURE 3-12. Construction details for iakos, ama struts, and outboard motor bracket.

41

FIGURE 3-13. (ABOVE LEFT) 24' (7.2m) Wa'apa with tacking rig. (Photo courtesy Rose Turner)

FIGURE 3-14. (ABOVE) Wa'apa sailing on port tack with the ama to windward. (Photo courtesy Rose Turner)

FIGURE 3-15. (LEFT) Wa'apa viewed from the stern. (Photo courtesy Rose Turner)

FIGURE 3-16. (BELOW LEFT) Wa'apa disassembled and stacked for storage.

FIGURE 3-17. (BELOW) Four $\frac{5}{16}$" (8mm) stainless-steel bolts are used to connect the hull sections together.

CHAPTER 4
Sailing Rigs

The sailing rigs shown for the designs in this book are divided between those that *tack* and those that *shunt*. Tacking rigs are familiar to almost everyone who has sailed anything from a dinghy on up to a square-rigged ship. The tacking rig is used on a hull that has a true bow and a true stern and that changes direction by passing its bow through the eye of the wind. Shunting rigs are completely reversible, where the leading edge of the sail is shifted to the opposite end of the hull and the former bow becomes the stern after the shunt is completed. A shunting rig therefore requires a double-ended hull that can sail with either end forward. During a shunt, the eye of the wind passes over the ama instead of the bow, as with a tacking rig.

Both types of rig have advantages and disadvantages, and deciding between them is mostly a matter of personal choice. The tacking rig can be simpler, with fewer stays and control lines, but it requires stronger and heavier cross beams to resist the upward forces and lateral transient forces when sailing with the ama to leeward. A tacking rig also requires an ama with sufficient buoyancy to keep it from submerging when it is to leeward. A shunting rig always has the ama on the windward side and can use lighter cross beams because they never experience the bending loads that a tacking rig imposes.

You can now see that the hull and rig are a closely integrated system, and not every choice of rig and hull can be made to work together. For instance, an asymmetric hull should only be used with a shunting rig, but a shunting rig can be used on a symmetric or asymmetric hull.

THE OCEANIC LATEEN RIG

The Oceanic lateen rig differs from the lateen seen in the Middle East by the addition of a boom, which gives it greater efficiency when sailing off the wind. The Oceanic lateen is used on canoes that shunt rather than tack.

In most cases, the mast will tilt toward the current bow to keep the center of effort of the sail forward of amidships. Running backstays are used on all but the smallest canoes. One or more weather shrouds leading to a bridle near the ama are always used. Traditionally, the backstays had to be released and retensioned during each shunt because the mast was tilted in the opposite direction. In my design, the lower ends of the backstays are led to powerful bungee cords that try to pull the mast vertical. Pulling the tack of the sail to either end will stretch the backstay bungee at the opposite end while the slack in the forward backstay is taken up by the other bungee. A stopper knot or plastic ball in the backstay ensures that the amount of mast rake stays constant. The bungees are terminated at the cross beams under the hiking seat.

The shunting procedure is unfamiliar to most sailors but is easily mastered. Generally, a well-set-up canoe can complete a shunt in ten seconds. (Note: For a more detailed description of shunting, see Chapter 12.)

Assuming that you are sailing to windward, the first step is to bear away until the wind is blowing directly over the ama, at ninety degrees to the centerline of the hull. This can be accomplished by sheeting in hard, shifting your weight aft, or using the steering oar.

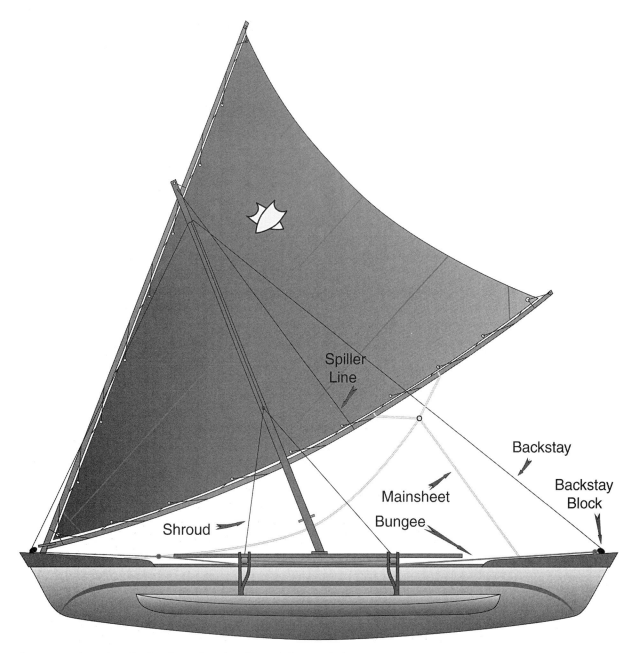

FIGURE 4-1. Running rigging for a shunting Oceanic lateen rig.

Next, release the sheet so that the sail is luffing and the boom is straight out to leeward. Then, release the tack of the sail from the bow, causing the mast to go vertical. Pull the yard by hand, or with an endless running tack line, to the other bow, pulling the mast with it. If you have one steering oar, change it to the other end, or if you have two, retract the one and extend the other. Sheet in the sail and go. Because you'll be starting on a beam reach, an eased boom will make the canoe head into the wind. Sheet in harder as you reach the desired course.

With some rig designs, the butt of the yard will pass along the hull above the deck, allowing you to have only one sheet line. On others where the yard butt passes below the gunwale, a separate sheet for each tack is needed, with the unused sheet looped around the front of the yard. The most convenient way to rig separate sheets is to use an endless loop of line with both ends terminating on the boom.

While sailing with a shunting rig, you must always be aware of the possibility of back-winding. If you sail too close to the wind or catch a gusting header, the sail and boom will go back against the mast and may render the canoe uncontrollable. With some rigging setups, the whole rig may fall over into the water. There is a way to keep your rig from falling over. You can use a mast prop, which is a pole lashed to the mast about a third of the way up and extending out to the outrigger platform. Some traditional props are curved to act as a spring.

The mast prop shown for the T2 (Figure 2-6) consists of two straight, overlapping struts with a bungee cord loop to make the prop act as a shock absorber. If the sail is back-winded, the struts slide past each other but are constrained by the bungee, allowing the rig to lay over about thirty degrees from vertical. This relieves the force that is trying to sink the ama and capsize the canoe. In some cases, you can recover from a back-winding with a strong sweep of the steering oar or paddle. The spiller/brailing line

shown in Figure 4-1 is useful in many ways. It can be used to brail up the boom and sail in the event of a back-winding and allow you to get back on course more easily. Or, you can lower the sail, get the canoe turned around, and rehoist the sail.

If you don't wish to use a mast prop, you can fit a lee shroud from the mast to the leeward side of the canoe, but this can get in the way of the shunting maneuver.

I prefer my sailing amas to be buoyant enough to withstand a back-winding in at least moderate winds. Traditional solid amas would submerge immediately when back-winded.

The brailing/spiller line is useful in sudden squalls to reduce the power in the sail. You can have two separate spiller lines rigged with one on each side of the boom. Pulling the leeward spiller raises the boom and introduces a ridge across the sail, effectively reducing

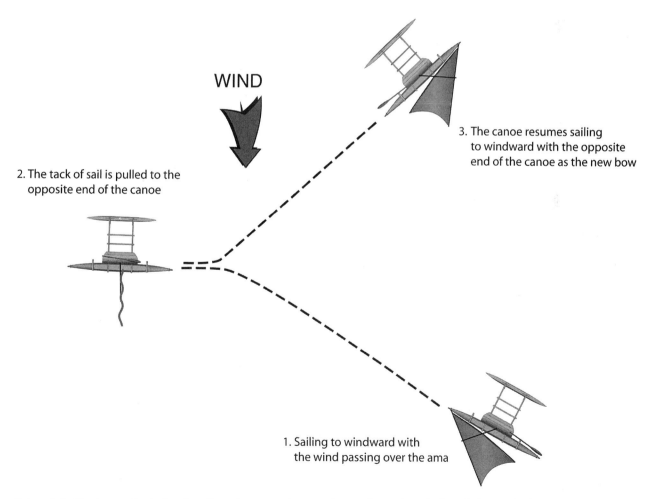

WIND

3. The canoe resumes sailing to windward with the opposite end of the canoe as the new bow

2. The tack of sail is pulled to the opposite end of the canoe

1. Sailing to windward with the wind passing over the ama

FIGURE 4-2. To change tacks by shunting, the canoe is turned away from the wind until the ama is broadside to the wind direction. The sail is shifted to the opposite bow while the canoe is stopped and drifting slowly to leeward. The sail is sheeted in and the canoe resumes its course to windward.

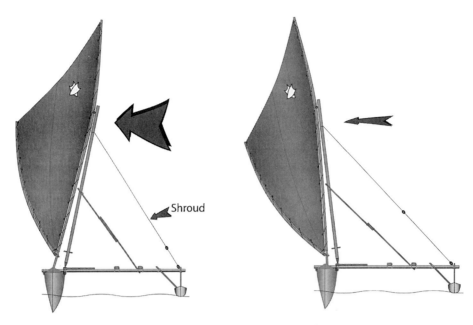

The mast is tilted to windward in strong winds by tightening the shroud.

In light winds the mast is eased to vertical or to leeward.

FIGURE 4-3. In strong winds, the mast and sail can be tilted to windward to reduce the projected area and heeling force. In light winds, the mast should be laterally vertical or tilting slightly to leeward to help the long boom swing out to leeward during a shunt.

its area. Pulling the windward spiller lifts the boom and creates a deeper camber in the sail that can be more efficient in light winds. Spillers are also useful for holding the sail and boom off of the deck or water when the sail is lowered with the halyard.

The weather shroud is normally a running shroud that can be used to tilt the mast and sail to windward or leeward. With a bridle rigged to the outboard ends of the iakos, the shroud can be adjusted while sailing with a block and tackle. In strong winds, the mast can be tilted to windward to reduce heeling by moving some of the weight of the rig to windward and introducing a small lift component. In very light winds, shunting is easier if the mast is allowed to tilt to leeward, because it prevents the boom from trying to swing inboard.

Shunting outriggers do have one elegant structural advantage over tacking outriggers. Keeping the ama to windward at all times removes the bending loads that would occur if a buoyant ama were to leeward, as in modern trimarans. The iakos are loaded primarily in compression and thus can be constructed more lightly than those of a tacking outrigger.

FIGURE 4-4. Force triangle of a shunting proa structure.

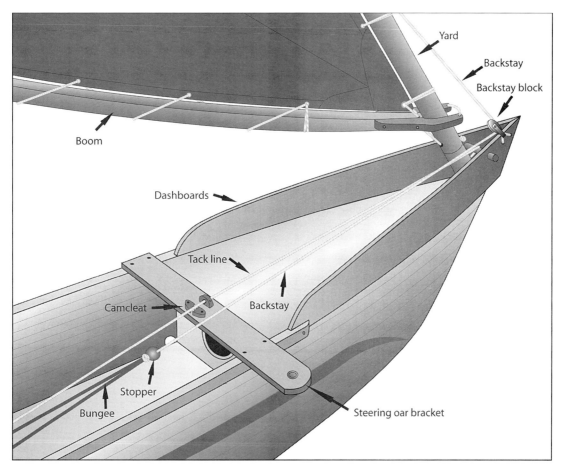

FIGURE 4-5. T2 foredeck rigged with an Oceanic Lateen sail. This shows the traditional arrangement where the end of the yard rests on the foredeck.

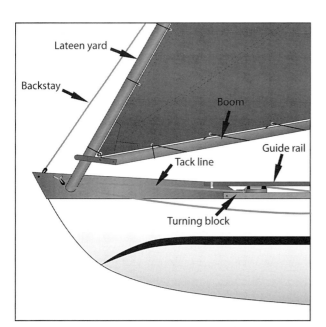

FIGURE 4-6. T2 foredeck rigged with lateen yard hanging along leeward side of hull. This arrangement can make shunting easier on small canoes.

The shunting rig geometry is important to understand to avoid surprises the first time you try to shunt. By the way, it's easy to test your whole shunting procedure on your lawn or the beach by simply orienting the canoe with the wind coming directly over the ama.

Refer to Figure 4-8 to see how a small variation in the ratio of the mast length to the distance, from the butt end of the yard to its attachment point on the mast, can affect the path of the yard's butt as it passes from bow to bow. The butt of the yard with the longer mast tilted well forward (as is used in the Caroline Islands) will follow a path high above the deck. This is necessary in canoes with a lee platform. Traditionally, small huts were constructed on the lee platform, and a forward-tilted rig would allow the yard to pass over the lee platform. Rigs where the yard butt passes above the deck are more difficult for the single-handed sailor to handle because of the tendency of the yard butt to swing to windward, caused by the weight of the long boom off to leeward.

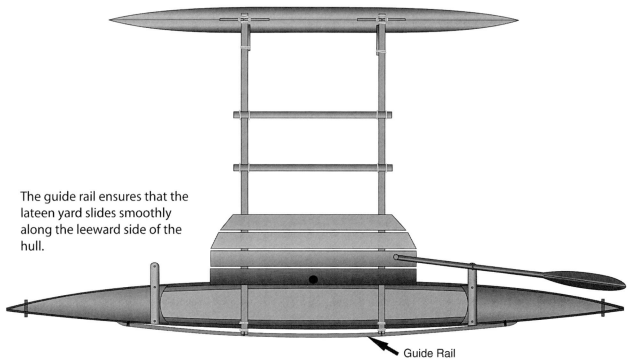

The guide rail ensures that the lateen yard slides smoothly along the leeward side of the hull.

Guide Rail

FIGURE 4-7. A guide rail is fitted to ensure a smooth passage when pulling a lateen yard along the leeward side of the hull.

On rigs with a shorter mast that is angled more upright, the yard butt will pass along the hull below the gunwale. This can work to your advantage if you are single-handing, because you can simply pull the yard along with an endless line attached to its butt. A guide rail (see Figure 4-7) prevents it from catching on projecting cross beams or steering brackets. The T2 lateen sail plan will allow the yard to slide along below the gunwale. The yard does not have to rest on the foredeck while sailing. It can be hung by its tack line along the leeward side of the bow, with the tack line leading through a fairlead or block.

THE GIBBONS RIG

In the early 1950s, Euell Gibbons built a 24' (7.2m) plywood outrigger sailing canoe in Hawaii for offshore fishing. He had been a professional boatbuilder and had also done quite a bit of research on Micronesian sailing craft. He came up with a modification of the Oceanic lateen rig that enabled him to single-handedly sail and shunt his canoe with less effort. He used a fixed vertical mast stepped amidships. The halyard attached to the center of the yard and allowed the boomless sail to be tilted toward either bow. Because the mast did not tilt, the center

of effort ended up aft of the hull's center and generated a strong weather helm. To compensate for the weather helm, he mounted an oversized rudder on the aft iako, which steered the canoe and also provided the needed lateral resistance to the aft end of the canoe. To shunt, he released the yard that was tacked down to the bow and pulled down the other end of the yard to the other bow. He would then lift the rudder from its mount, reinsert it on the other iako, sheet in, and take off.

Even with the oversized rudder, the aft center of effort made the canoe difficult to steer on broad reaches. To help in this regard, Gibbons would sometimes put up a spinnaker.

I'd read the story in his *Beachcomber's Handbook* back in the seventies, but it took more than twenty years and the advent of good windsurfing sails before I put it all together. I knew, first of all, that a sprit boom would improve the performance of the sail because Gibbons had no boom at all. I also added a pair of sail battens to widen and flatten the head of the sail and make it more efficient. People are always trying to adapt windsurfing rigs to canoes, but they never seem to look or perform to their full potential. The combination of Euell Gibbons's original idea and modern windsurfing technology has given us a viable rig option for modern shunting proas.

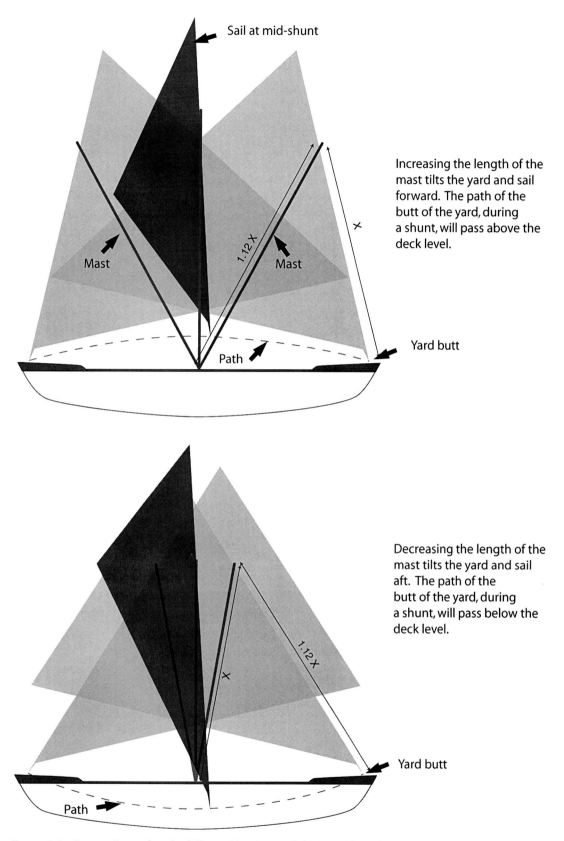

Sail at mid-shunt

Increasing the length of the mast tilts the yard and sail forward. The path of the butt of the yard, during a shunt, will pass above the deck level.

1.12 X

X

Mast

Mast

Yard butt

Path

Decreasing the length of the mast tilts the yard and sail aft. The path of the butt of the yard, during a shunt, will pass below the deck level.

1.12 X

X

Yard butt

Path

FIGURE 4-8. Comparison of paths followed by the yard during a shunt between differently raked leading edges and mast lengths. The top arrangement is used when the yard must pass over a leeward platform built on extended cross beams. The bottom arrangement is used with a guide rail.

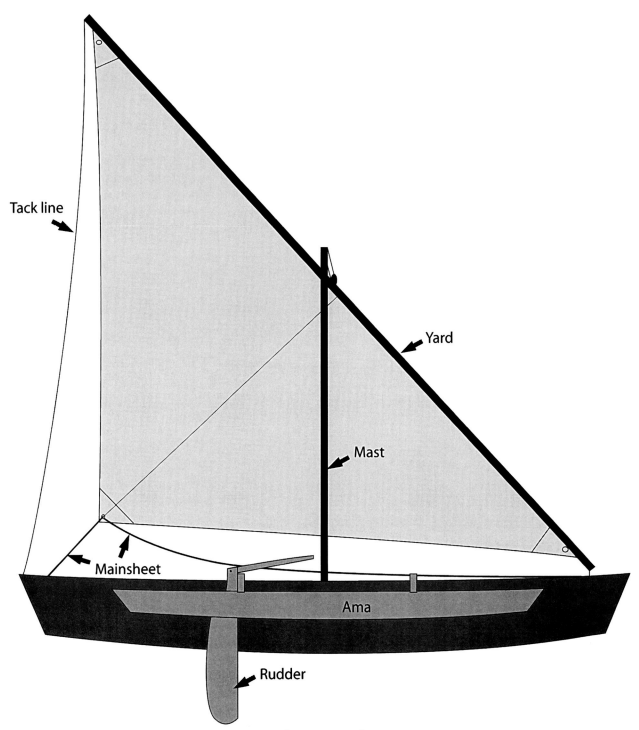

Tack line

Yard

Mast

Mainsheet

Ama

Rudder

FIGURE 4-9. Euell Gibbons's original shunting rig used in Hawaii in the 1950s.

The downside to almost every Oceanic rig, however, is its inability to reef in the manner of more familiar rigs. The Gibbons/Dierking rig is no better in that respect, and the best solution is to simply have smaller duplicate sails with yards either carried on deck (in the case of larger canoes) or changed on the beach (like with a Windsurfer). This is not the hassle

that you would suspect, and the resulting smaller rig is cleaner than any reefed sail.

The most unusual aspect of my version is the attachment of the sprit boom. The boom actually hangs permanently from the masthead, and to raise the sail, the yard is hauled up the boom on a sliding collar or on a loop of parrel beads. The battens also are installed in an unusual manner, with the pocket openings at the leading edge to allow the sail to be furled completely when lowered.

The addition of a tilting mast in my design does make the rig more complex than Gibbons's original configuration but puts the center of effort where it belongs and greatly relieves the steering load.

This sailing rig also allows the use of a smaller, overlapping rig inside of the main rig, sort of like a staysail inside of a jib. Both sails are shunted simultaneously. The added complication, however, would be more easily dealt with in a larger canoe.

The backstays are bungee-powered, as in my lateen rigs, so that when you release the endless line holding the tack to the bow, the mast immediately springs to the vertical position. The line leading to the former head of the sail is now pulled, and the sail tilts over to the new position.

Note that all shunting maneuvers must be done with the wind coming square over the ama. The canoe will be drifting slowly to leeward, but since the shunt only takes ten seconds or less, you won't drift very far.

Although the mast is quite short, it does need to be stiff. Aluminum tubing, hollow wood, or

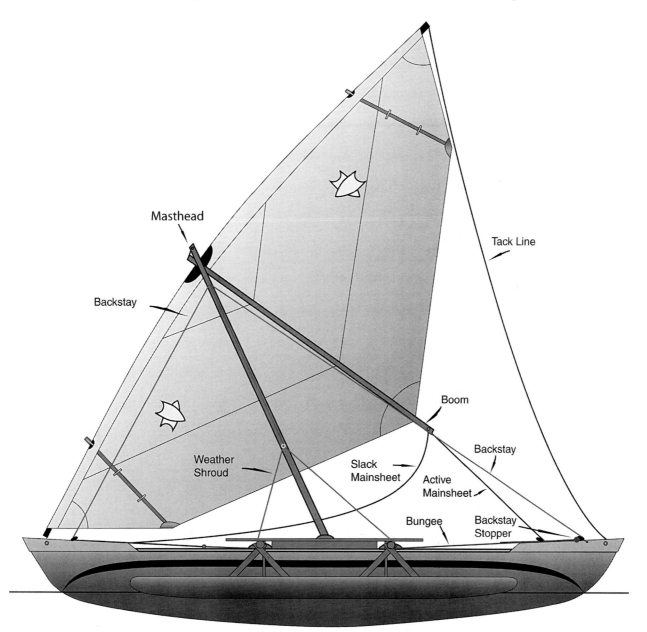

FIGURE 4-10. Major components of the Gibbons/Dierking rig. Note that the boom is permanently hung from the masthead.

51

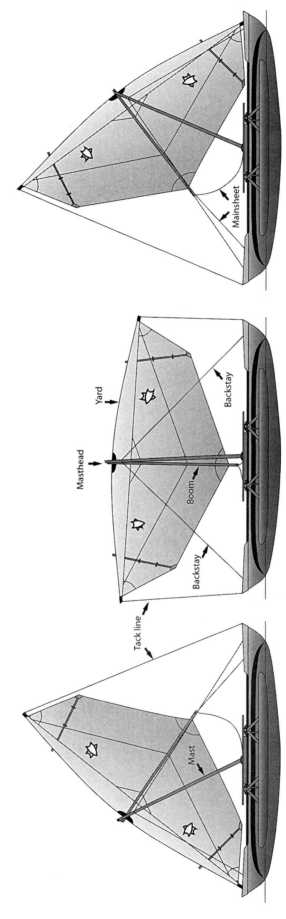

FIGURE 4-11. The method of shunting the Gibbons/Dierking rig is similar to that used for the lateen rig. The canoe is oriented with the ama to windward, the tack line holding the yard end to the bow is released, and the tack line to the opposite bow is taken in. The sail tilts over to the new bow and is sheeted in. The canoe now resumes its course to windward.

fiberglass tubing are all candidates for masts. Not only does the mast on both the Gibbons/Dierking and the Oceanic lateen rig need to tilt fore and aft, it also needs to be able to tilt to windward and leeward. The rig can be canted to windward in strong winds to reduce heeling force and convert some of it into lift.

As the mast tilts back and forth with each shunt, and to windward or leeward with varying wind strengths, the mast base must allow for this range of motion. The simplest approach is a shallow socket carved from wood into which the rounded butt of the mast can rest. It is very important to have the mast lashed into a socket like this to prevent it from jumping out, as it is prone to do in a back-winded situation. The very best mast base is a standard spinnaker pole end fitting. At the base, the fitting clips into either a fixed eye or a sliding track, and this is a convenient way to shift the center of effort on both the Gibbons/Dierking rig and the Oceanic lateen. Moving the mast base forward also moves the sail's center of effort forward, which, in turn, can relieve the load on the steering oar. Some traditional proas in Oceania had multiple mast-step sockets for this purpose. Spinnaker pole ends can be obtained secondhand and are available for both

wood and aluminum spars. Windsurfer mast bases with their universal joints and sliding tracks will also work.

The halyard needs to be made of a low-stretch line like polyester braid, as it is highly loaded and controls the amount of draft in the sail. A stretchy halyard will cause a baggy sail shape. The diameter should be at least $\frac{5}{16}$" (8mm) to make it easy on the hands. A 2:1-ratio halyard would not be a bad idea.

The yard or luff spar can be made of timber (hollow or solid), aluminum tubing, bamboo, or windsurfing masts. In the case of tapered materials like bamboo or windsurfing masts, use two sections sleeved and joined with their large ends in the middle of the spar.

Because the boom is hung from the masthead, a row of adjustment holes or a sliding track can be mounted at the masthead to fine tune the rig. Moving the boom attachment point higher will shift the center of effort of the sail forward.

The structure of the sail is somewhat similar to a windsurfing sail, with a sleeve along the luff and the necessity of aligning the warp of the fabric parallel with the leech to withstand the high tension there. Because there are actually two differently aligned leeches, you'll get the best results

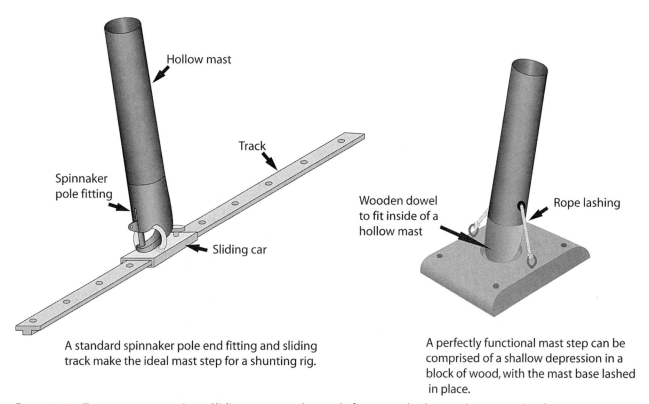

Hollow mast

Track

Spinnaker pole fitting

Sliding car

A standard spinnaker pole end fitting and sliding track make the ideal mast step for a shunting rig.

Wooden dowel to fit inside of a hollow mast

Rope lashing

A perfectly functional mast step can be comprised of a shallow depression in a block of wood, with the mast base lashed in place.

FIGURE 4-12. Two mast-step options. Sliding steps can be made from standard spinnaker or windsurfing hardware.

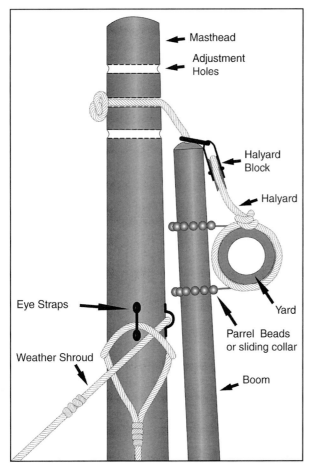

FIGURE 4-13. Gibbons/Dierking rig masthead. A sliding track can be used instead of the adjustment holes. A short length of tube lashed to the yard and sliding on the boom can replace the parrel beads. Note that the boom hangs from the masthead.

with a miter cut or a seam running parallel to the boom.

The single full-length batten at each end of the sail is mounted on the windward side, with a short, sewn pocket only at the leech. Two or three intermediate fabric straps are sewn on the sail to hold the batten in place. The batten extends out past the luff spar and is tensioned with a small line looped around the luff spar. This arrangement, which is the opposite of conventional practice, makes furling a lowered sail much easier. After the yard has been lowered almost to the deck, the battened ends of the sail will still be sticking up in the air. Releasing the batten-tensioning lines on the yard allows that part of the sail to be pushed down along the battens.

The Gibbons/Dierking is a true one-sided sail. In other words, one side of the fabric will always be

the windward side. In the study of flow over wing sections, research has shown that a smooth, low-drag surface is more important on the upper, low-pressure side of a wing. This corresponds to the leeward side of a sail. To take advantage of this fact, obstructions such as battens are located on the windward or high-pressure side.

Staying on the subject of more advanced aerodynamics, a straight, asymmetric wing spar, with its flatter side to windward, could replace the standard round yard. The greater thickness of a wing spar would add great stiffness if this rig were to be scaled up for a larger canoe. Taking this one step further, a rigid, asymmetric wing sail could be used, or if you have one, a composite wing from a sailplane.

THE HAWAIIAN RIG

I call the simple tacking rig used on the Ulua a Hawaiian-style rig. It is the least complicated of all the rigs shown here and only has two strings to pull—the mainsheet and a spiller or brailing line.

This rig is based on a windsurfing mast that is light, stiff, and available everywhere. A hollow wooden spar of slightly larger diameter would also work. Although I sailed mine for several years with no stays at all, I've found that a simple, ¼" (6mm), low-stretch rope forestay, attached about two thirds of the way up the mast, improved the sail shape when close-hauled in stronger winds.

The curved boom is not strictly necessary but does look the part and is easy to make. Although the curved boom shown on the Ulua looks quite elegant, it does not allow reefing of the sail unless the rig is taken down. The Wa'apa sail plan shows a loose-footed sail with a straight boom. A loose foot allows the sail to be reefed by turning the mast and winding up some of the sail after the outhaul has been loosened.

Either the curved-boom laced foot or the straight-boom loose foot can be used on both the Ulua and the Wa'apa.

A tacking outrigger is probably not quite as efficient as a shunting rig, because on one of the tacks the ama will be depressed into the water, causing more drag than when it's on the windward side. In practice, the speed difference is not really noticeable, but some other peculiarities are. When the ama is to leeward, its drag tends to turn the canoe to leeward.

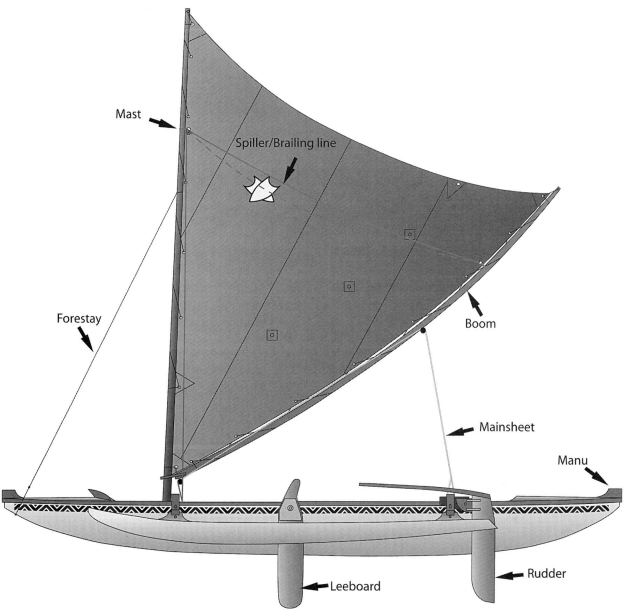

Mast

Spiller/Brailing line

Forestay

Boom

Mainsheet

Manu

Rudder

Leeboard

FIGURE 4-14. Hawaiian tacking rig. A rope forestay can improve the sail shape while sailing to windward in strong breezes.

This affects the basic sailing balance between the lee-board's lateral resistance and the sail's center of effort. However, by pivoting the leeboard fore or aft, the balance can be regained.

STUB-MAST RIGS

Another type of tacking rig used on some modern Hawaiian sailing canoes has a short stub mast set into the hull, with a longer luff spar hoisted parallel to it with a halyard. This can be an advantage in

that it allows the use of shorter spars for the luff of the sail, and the rig can be lowered more easily with the short halyard. The luff spar needs either a wind-surfing universal joint at its base (see Figure 4-18) or a socket with a lashing.

The stub mast also enables you to use any old windsurfing rigs you may have stored away. The fully rigged sail can still be lowered on to the iakos by releasing the short halyard attached to the end of the wishbone boom. The bracket shown in Figure 4-18 clamps to the iako.

A tacking canoe is shown sailing to windward on a port tack, with the wind passing over the left (ama) side. Crew weight on the hiking seat is necessary to prevent the ama from lifting. The canoe turns through the eye of the wind (with the sail luffing) and settles on a starboard tack with the wind passing over the right (starboard) side of the hull. The ama is now to leeward and is being depressed by the force of the sail.

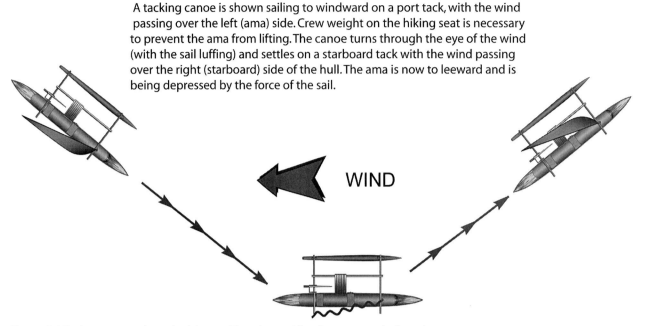

WIND

FIGURE 4-15. A canoe equipped with a tacking rig working its way to windward.

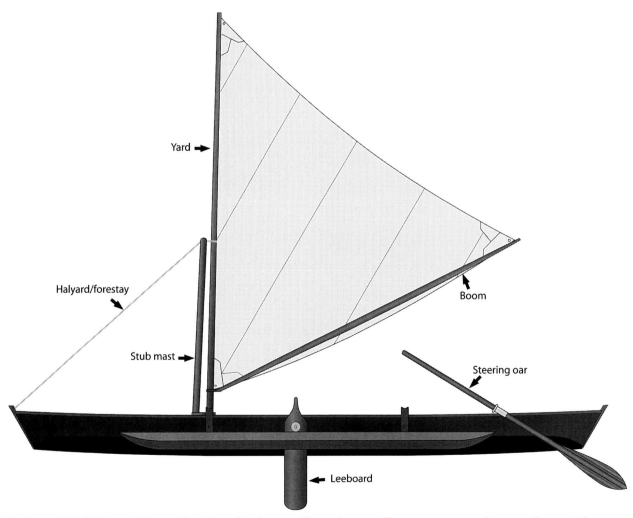

Yard

Halyard/forestay

Stub mast

Boom

Steering oar

Leeboard

FIGURE 4-16. A Wa'apa with a tacking rig and stub mast. The stub mast allows you to spread more sail area with a standard windsurfing mast because it is stepped at deck level.

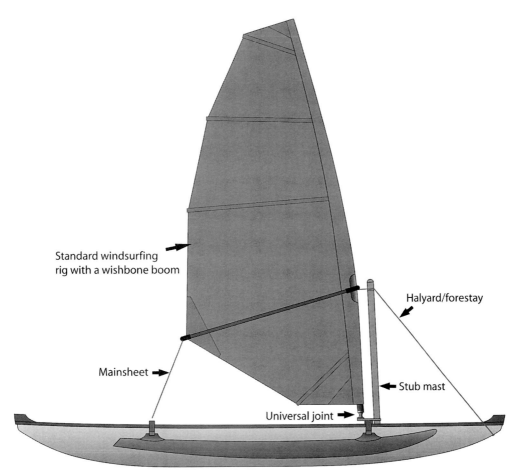

FIGURE 4-17. Ulua with a stub mast and windsurfing sail.

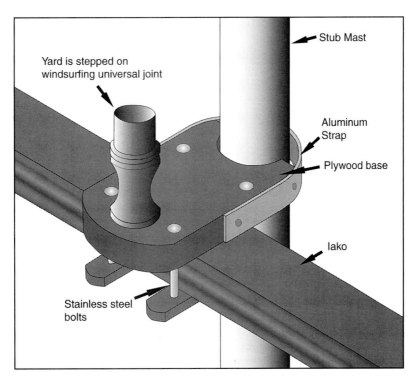

FIGURE 4-18. A stub-mast adapter is shown clamped to an Ulua iako with four bolts. The yard or luff spar of the sail connects to the universal joint and allows you to lower the entire rig.

CHAPTER 5
Boatbuilding Basics

◆ The designs in this book use two very different construction methods. The Ulua and the T2 are strip planked, and the Wa'apa is built from plywood panels.

STRIP-PLANKING VERSUS PLYWOOD

There are many strip-planked canoes and kayaks around that look like finely built furniture with many intricate-looking joints, and because of this, many beginning boatbuilders are reluctant to try this method. It's true that the materials may cost a little more than a plywood hull and more hours of labor are involved, but the result can be highly professional, even for someone who's never built anything before. It doesn't actually require any *traditional* boatbuilding skills. Assembling the hull one plank at a time ensures that there will be no big mistakes. The fairness (smooth curvature) of the hull can be checked at every step. Even the worst-case scenarios can be fixed with putty and a coat of paint instead of a clear varnish finish.

A strip-plank project first requires a *strongback,* which is a straight, level, flat surface on which to mount the *molds.* The molds are temporary plywood or particle-board shapes that define the cross-sectional shape of the hull. The hull is built upside down with its keel at the top. The molds are screwed to the strongback at specified intervals. Two special *stem molds* define the ends of the hull. Permanent *stems* are laminated over the stem molds and beveled by hand to allow the planks to lay against them. The mold edges are covered with plastic tape to prevent the planks from sticking to the molds. Beginning at the gunwale,

thin strips of wood are stapled to the molds and glued to the stems. Each additional plank is edge-glued to the previous one, until planking ends at the keel. No plank-edge beveling is required until the last few planks.

Strip-planked hulls derive most of their strength from the fiberglass sheathing that is applied both inside and outside the hull. The wooden strips act as a core material between the fiberglass skins to create a very strong but light, sandwich-composite panel. The lengthwise grain of the wood also contributes longitudinal strength. Most damage to a strip-composite hull is only cosmetic, with most "write-offs" the result of the canoe flying off of a car roof, rather than anything you will experience on the water.

The plywood construction of the Wa'apa is simple and quick. It can be built as a one-piece hull or in two or three bolt-together sections. There is no strongback or temporary structure to hold it together. The plywood side panels are prefabricated on a flat table and bent around two bulkheads and a stem timber. The plywood bottom is nailed and glued into place, and the hull is basically complete after the installation of foredecks and seats.

The hull could be built using the popular "stitch-and-tape" method, but I feel that you'll have better results using conventional chine timbers to join the side and bottom panels. Because the chine is already attached to the side panel during the assembly, its stiffness causes the panel to bend in a very smooth curve, avoiding the wavy chines sometimes seen in stitch-and-tape hulls.

A fiberglass sheathing over the exterior of a plywood hull is not structurally necessary but can help to avoid problems later with some species of plywood. Douglas fir or pine plywood will "check" or develop hairline cracks in a paint finish if the panel hasn't been sheathed. Most tropical marine plywood will hold a paint finish without checking. I recommend at least sheathing the bottom and the chines to provide increased abrasion resistance.

TOOLS

Power Tools

- Jigsaw: A jigsaw is probably the most used power tool in any boatbuilding project. Spend the extra money to get one with variable speed and adjustable orbital cut.
- Table saw or portable circular saw: You'll need one of these to cut your planks for a stripper and to make gunwales, chines, or cross beams. A circular saw can be fitted to a portable table for ripping, or it can be fitted with a commercial or homemade rip-guide attachment.
- Drill: This can be either battery powered or plugged into the wall. You'll need a variety of bits for screw pilot holes or countersinking.
- Random orbital sander: This is probably the best all-around type of sander.
- Router (optional): This is used to make optional bead and cove planks when fitted under a router table. It is also useful for rounding the edges of gunwales and chines.
- Thickness planer (optional): This is useful for smoothing planks to an exact thickness and preparing strips for laminated beams. It can save a lot of sanding. Be sure to have ear protection.
- Vacuum cleaner (optional): A shop vacuum is great for cleaning the hull surface inside and out and can also be connected to some sanders.

Hand Tools

- Staple gun: If you're building a stripper, this tool will get a lot of use. Your stapler must be capable of driving ⁹⁄₁₆" (14mm) staples. Consider that you may have to disassemble it regularly to clean out hardened glue. The Arrow T50 has served me well.
- Japanese pull saw: Next to the jigsaw, I find the Japanese pull saw to be the most valuable tool in the shop. It is the absolute best tool for working with small strips and performing many other tasks. It is extremely sharp when new but is not easily sharpened.
- Block plane: Using a low-angle blade is best. Keep it very sharp for a pleasing experience.
- Staple puller: This can be found in a store, but I've always made mine by bending the tip of an old, flat-tip screwdriver and sharpening the edge.
- Clamps: Use either sliding-bar or "C" clamps. You'll want at least a dozen, preferably many more. No shop has ever had too many. Plastic spring-powered clamps are also useful.
- Scissors
- Wood chisels
- Flat rasp
- Screwdrivers
- Hammer
- Utility knife
- Putty knife
- Ruler
- Square
- Tape measure
- Level
- Sliding bevel gauge

Safety Gear

- Dust masks
- Disposable gloves
- Safety glasses

MATERIALS

Choosing materials for your project can be a real headache, and in many cases it's more about what you can get rather than what you would like to have.

Plywood is perhaps the trickiest material to choose, and you'll often not have much choice from your local supplier. The easiest (and most expensive) way to solve this problem is to buy proper marine-grade plywood. Marine-grade plywood is manufactured with completely waterproof glue and will have no unseen voids in its inner plies. The plies on the outer surface will also be thicker, unlike in some cheaper grades that have paper-thin surface layers.

Marine-grade plywood made from wood species such as okoume (gaboon), meranti, or Douglas fir are all good choices. Note that Douglas fir plywood does not seal well with a paint-only finish and should be completely sheathed in fiberglass.

If you can't resist purchasing some bargain-priced plywood at the local building supply, do the following test to see if it's suitable for the marine environment. Take a sample of the plywood and boil it for an hour or so. Put it into a slow oven, dry it completely, and repeat the process. If it's not delaminating after this test, it's probably okay for your canoe. Plywood that is ¼" (6mm) comes in either three-ply or five-ply. The five-ply is definitely superior. Some cheaper three-ply exterior grades have a thick inner ply and very thin outer plies. An unseen void in the inner ply doesn't leave much between you and the ocean.

The choice of solid timber for your project will depend on its intended use. Chines and bulkhead perimeters are normally made with medium-density softwoods like Douglas fir, spruce, or pine. Western red cedar, while ideal for strip-planking, is too soft to hold fastenings well, or to be used as a gunwale where it would be easily damaged. Outer gunwales are preferably made of a harder timber like ash or mahogany.

Laminated cross beams (iakos) can be made entirely from one species of softwood or optimized by using a harder wood on the top and bottom layers, with a very light, timber-like cedar for the inner layers.

Western red cedar is the premiere planking material for a strip-planked hull. It is very light, easy to work, and rot-resistant. Western red cedar is, however, toxic to some people when it is sanded and can cause asthma-like symptoms. Any lightweight, knot-free timber can be used for strip-planking, from balsa to pine.

There are many brands of epoxy resin that are suitable for your project. Look for brands that have good documentation for their use in marine structures and that have a range of additives available for making your own glue and fairing mixtures. Some epoxies are more toxic to skin than others. Do some research through boating magazines and the Internet to get information on the relative safety of different brands of epoxy resin.

WORK SPACE

I built my first real boat when I was fifteen years old, in an unused upstairs bedroom. When spring arrived and the ice had melted in the lake, it was time to get it outside. In spite of my calculations, it wouldn't fit down the stairway and instead went out an upstairs window to many waiting hands. That was probably one of the least ideal situations, but at least canoes will fit through smaller windows than, say, scows.

Ideally, you'd have a large barn structure with big doors opening out toward the shoreline of a picturesque harbor, but in most cases you'll be building in a garage, basement, or carport.

You'll need a work space that is dry and out of direct sunlight. Damp wood and epoxy don't get along well together, and direct sunlight will cause epoxy to harden before you're finished working with it. While working with epoxy resin, try to stay within a temperature range of 65°F (17°C) to 85°F (29°C). Many modern glues and resins require a minimum temperature to cure to their full strength, so if you're working during a cold winter, your space will need to be heated. *Be aware that you may be producing flammable fumes that could ignite from your heat source.*

You'll need enough space to walk around the ends of the hull, and to have a workbench and a small table or cart to hold the epoxy supplies. Ripping planks on a table saw requires a clear space twice the length of the longest plank. You can deal with this by either moving the saw outdoors or ripping with a portable circular saw indoors. If you're building with plywood, cut as many of the pieces as possible before beginning the assembly to give yourself adequate space for the laying out and cutting.

Sanding can produce a lot of dust, which means that good ventilation is necessary, especially with toxic woods such as western red cedar (see the section in this chapter on materials). Also consider how to keep the dust and fumes out of your living space.

Good lighting is necessary and could save some embarrassment when you finally move the hull out into the sunlight. Shining a strong light down the side of your hull in a dark workshop will reveal the quality of your workmanship in stark terms.

Portable, tent-like structures used for greenhouses are okay as long as you have a way to shade the hull from direct sunlight while sheathing or coating anything with epoxy resin. Retired shipping containers can be purchased near seaports in sizes of 20' (6m) or 40' (12m) and make good, secure workshops. They have the extra advantage of being portable and not requiring building permits.

LOFTING

Lofting is just another term for drawing something at full scale. With the dimensions shown in the plans, you'll be able to re-create mold shapes and other parts full size. You can loft either on paper or onto the panel itself. In most cases, it's quicker to draw the part right onto the panel to be cut out.

You'll need some thin finishing nails or brads, a hammer, a square, an accurate ruler, and a flexible batten or spline to bend into a curve. Battens can be strips of aluminum flat bar or can be cut from wood or acrylic plastic. A fiberglass batten from a windsurfing sail works well. A batten for a given curve should be as stiff as possible but still be able to bend the required amount without breaking or popping out the nails.

For a strip-planking mold, begin by drawing the centerline, the baseline, the strongback line, and the parallel waterlines, accurately and square to each other. The offset dimensions (see Figure 5-1) indicate the distance between the centerline and the edge of the mold, along each of the waterlines. The vertical dimensions indicate the distance from the keel to the baseline, the sheer line to the strongback, and the spacing between waterlines.

Carefully measure the distances, and tap in a thin finishing nail at each point. Choose a slender batten and bend it along the nails. Use the stiffest batten that will follow the curve without breaking or pulling out the nails. Sight along the curve to detect any unfairness. Any error in measurement will usually be quite obvious when the batten is held against the nails.

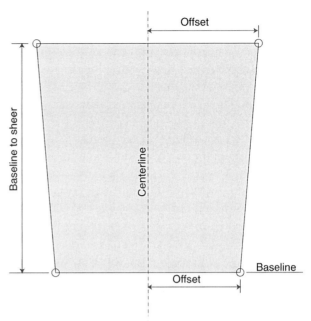

FIGURE 5-2. To loft a bulkhead for the Wa'apa, draw a baseline and a centerline at a right angle to it. The baseline will also be the bottom of the bulkhead. Measure the "baseline-to-sheer" dimension vertically up from the baseline, and the offset dimension horizontally from the centerline. The intersection of these dimensions will determine the position of the upper (sheer) and lower (chine) corners of the bulkhead.

If it looks satisfactory, tap in another set of nails along the other side of the batten to hold it in place. Draw a line along the batten so that it passes through the measured points. Repeat the procedure for the other half of the mold.

Lofting parts for a plywood hull is easier with fewer points to plot and only straight lines to draw. Start by drawing a centerline and a baseline at right angles to it. Measure the offsets shown, and connect the dots with straight lines.

When lofting large plywood panels, such as the sides of the Wa'apa hull, use the edge of the plywood sheet as the baseline. Check to be sure that the plywood sheet has straight edges and square corners.

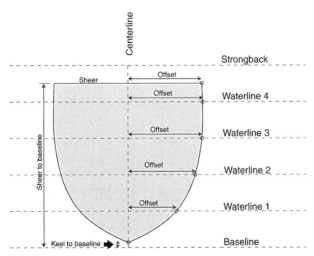

FIGURE 5-1. To create a mold station from a table of offsets, begin by drawing a horizontal baseline, a vertical centerline at a right angle to the baseline, and a series of waterlines parallel to the baseline and spaced at the indicated intervals. Offsets are measured from the centerline out along the waterlines. A series of offsets connected by a fair curve will determine the shape of the mold.

GLUES

Almost all of the structural joints in modern boatbuilding projects depend on glue. It will pay dividends for you to become very well informed about all types of glue, and which glues are suitable for the marine environment.

The most versatile of all modern adhesives is epoxy. In fact, you can buy the basic resin and use it for every gluing and coating job in the project. Epoxy comes as two separate chemicals—a resin and a hardener—both with the consistency of syrup. They are usually combined in a ratio of four or five parts resin to one part hardener, although some brands use different ratios. In all cases, getting the ratio right is critical to achieving good results. You can purchase pumps from your dealer that will measure the epoxy in the right amounts, or you can weigh it on a balance scale.

It is also important to mix the epoxy very completely for a minute or more, as any molecules that haven't found a mate will remain uncured and will weaken the result. Once the epoxy is mixed, it can be used directly to either coat a bare wood surface for waterproofing, or to saturate fiberglass cloth.

To use the epoxy for glue, a modifier in the form of various powders is added to attain the desired consistency. The glue powder is available from the resin supplier. To make an epoxy-based putty for filling holes and fairing a surface, a different powder is added that will cure to a more easily sanded material than the hard-glue mixture.

Epoxy is an excellent all-around choice for assembling plywood hulls and laminated structures, but it is unnecessary for edge-gluing planks when you are strip-planking. A strip-composite hull has the planking sandwiched between two layers of fiberglass that does a good job of holding them together, making the use of a waterproof glue like epoxy between the planks an unnecessary expense. Just use the common white, or yellow aliphatic carpenters' glue, between planks, and you'll have a much easier time sanding later.

A more recent arrival in the waterproof glue choices is polyurethane glue. It is a one-part glue so does not require any mixing. It can be used for edge-gluing planks and even foams up to fill any small gaps. It can also be used for general-purpose laminating but doesn't always bond well to very dry wood. It is usually recommended by the manufacturer that you wipe the surfaces to be glued with a damp sponge first before applying the glue. If you're going to use it for anything besides edge-gluing strips, I'd recommend gluing up some scraps to test its adhesion.

Resorcinol glue is another option for some parts of your canoe. It is rated as the most waterproof of all glues but requires perfectly fitting joints and a high clamping pressure. It can be used for laminated beams or spars where good clamping pressure is available. It comes in the form of a powder and syrup that must be mixed together.

All glues can have adhesion problems with oily woods such as teak. When gluing teak, it is best to wipe the contact surfaces with acetone to degrease them just before applying the glue. Some epoxies can have problems with white oak, too, so glue up a test sample with your materials before using them in your canoe.

All glues *except* epoxy require good contact and clamping pressure for a strong bond. Epoxy is the opposite in that high clamping pressure can "starve" the joint—in other words, squeeze too much of the glue out and it gives you a weaker bond. So if you're a rough joiner and there are a lot of gaps, epoxy is your friend.

Normally, you do not thin epoxy, because it becomes less waterproof if you do. There are special epoxy thinners for cleaning brushes, etc., but lacquer thinner or acetone will also work. Avoid cleaning epoxy from your skin with thinner, as it only helps it to penetrate deeper into your skin. Vinegar can help to remove fresh epoxy with fewer harmful effects.

The downside of epoxy is that some people are allergic to the hardener. This results in an itchy rash where contact has been made. Once you become sensitized to it, you may never be able to use it again. Your best defense is to always wear disposable plastic or rubber gloves. This applies to polyurethane glue, too, but mostly because once it's on your hands it takes days to wear off.

In the days before epoxy was widely available, strip canoes and plywood boats were sheathed with the cheaper polyester resin. While this is fine for an all-fiberglass hull or a foam-sandwich hull, polyester does not bond to wood as well as epoxy. Polyester is also not as waterproof.

SCREWS, NAILS, AND STAPLES

While glue is the primary structural fastener in these small canoe designs, mechanical fasteners are still used in many places. After many years of use, the integrity of the wood fibers bonded with the glue can deteriorate if they are not carefully sealed from moisture. Screws or nails will act as your backup. An important rule to remember is that the length of a nail or screw should be at least three times the thickness of the plywood through which it passes. Fastening ¼" (6mm) plywood to a framework requires at least a ¾" (18mm) nail or screw.

In the case of a plywood hull like the Wa'apa, the plywood sides and bottom are glued and nailed

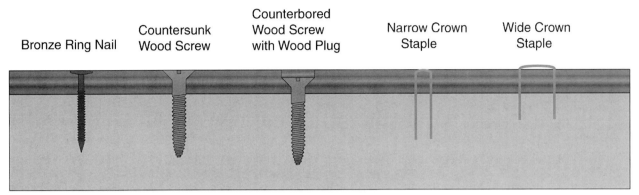

| Bronze Ring Nail | Countersunk Wood Screw | Counterbored Wood Screw with Wood Plug | Narrow Crown Staple | Wide Crown Staple |

FIGURE 5-3. The most commonly used mechanical fasteners in small-boat construction.

along the gunwale and chine. The nails or screws clamp the joint together while the glue hardens. Bronze or stainless-steel annular ring nails are the first choice for nails. The ridges along the shafts of the nails give great holding power, making them very difficult to remove once they are hammered in flush. Use a steel punch to set the heads just below the plywood surface so that they can be covered with putty and sanded flush.

In the case of a strip hull like the Ulua, screws are used to attach the gunwales, seats, and other small parts to the hull. Always drill a pilot hole for screws before driving the screw into place. Special bits are available for each size of screw and will ensure that they have maximum holding power. Screws can be countersunk flush with the surface, or counterbored below the surface, with special drill bits available for that purpose. Counterbored screws can be covered with wooden plugs, which are available from some stores, or you can make your own with a plug-cutting bit available from specialty tool dealers. Wooden plugs are especially attractive along the gunwale and are quick and easy to install. Each plug is glued and tapped into place, and when the glue has hardened, the excess plug is shaved off with a sharp chisel. Sandpaper, wrapped around a block, will finish it flush with the surrounding surface.

Screws come with a variety of slot styles, with the plain, slotted head; the Phillips head; the Pozi drive (similar to the Phillips); and the square drive. Avoid using the plain, slotted heads if possible, because the screwdriver can easily slip out the side and damage the wood. A plywood hull can also be fastened along the sheer and chine with power-driven, narrow-crown staples. Staples are available in stainless steel and sometimes bronze. Practice on scrap material, and adjust your air-powered or electric

stapler to drive the staple just below the surface of the material.

Wide-crown, plain, steel staples are used to hold strip planks in place while the glue hardens. These are usually driven with a hand-powered staple gun and are only available up to $\frac{9}{16}$" (14mm) in length. By allowing the crown of the staple to stay above the surface, you will be able to remove it later without damaging the soft surface of the plank.

A staple remover can be bought or made from an old flat screwdriver. Bend the tip of the screwdriver with a hammer and vise, and file it to a sharp edge.

When removing a staple, hold a putty knife flat on the planking up close to the staple. Hook the tip of the removal tool under the crown, and lever it against the putty knife. If one of the staple legs breaks off, use a needle-nose pliers to pull it out. Sometimes the staples are driven through plastic banding strips to prevent damage to the planking and to allow easier removal.

CUTTING PLYWOOD

In most cases, a handheld jigsaw (also known as a saber saw) can be used to cut out bulkheads, panels, and other small parts from sheet plywood. It is difficult to cut a fair curve or a straight line with a jigsaw; therefore, depending on your skill level, cut outside of the line, and shave down to the line with a block plane or sanding board. For cutting a long, straight section, clamp a straight, stiff board parallel to the line to act as a guide. Use the special blades designed for plywood to avoid splintering the edge.

A circular saw can also be used to cut long, curved pieces or straight lines with a guide. To cut curves, retract the blade to just clear the bottom surface of the panel. A fine-toothed blade will reduce splintering.

CUTTING STRIP PLANKS

Commercially manufactured red cedar planks for strip building are available in some areas and can be expensive, but there are several ways of making your own. When I built my first stripper, I only had a handheld circular saw, a jigsaw, a drill, and electric sanders. I clamped the ¾" × 6" (20mm × 150mm) planking stock to a couple of sawhorses, and by using a rip guide attached to the saw, I walked along the plank, taking off ¾" (6mm) slices. This method has the advantage of needing only half the space required for feeding planks though a stationary machine. You can make a rip guide by bolting a strip of timber parallel to the blade on the bottom side of the circular saw.

The next most inexpensive method of cutting planks is to get one of the portable tables under which you can clamp your circular saw, thus turning it into a table saw.

Using a table saw is the most common method to rip the planks. You'll need good supports for the timber feeding in and out, and a feather board to hold the plank tightly against the rip fence. Use a push stick to keep your fingers away from the blade. Thin kerf blades are available to reduce waste.

A feather board is used to keep smaller pieces of stock pressed firmly against your table saw or router's fence. The design of a feather board allows the stock to pass in one direction and causes resistance if it is moved in the other direction. A feather board is basically a board with an angled end and ⅛" to 14" wide "fingers" cut into the beveled end. As stock is forced between the fence and the feather board, these fingers move slightly to allow the stock to pass. The firm squeeze helps keep the stock tight against the fence and helps ensure a more accurate cut. In addition to keeping your stock up against the fence, the fingers help reduce the chance of kickback. For more advanced work, such as with a router table, a second feather board can be clamped to the fence to hold the stock down on the table.

You can also use a band saw to rip planks, and due to its narrow cut, it has the advantage of wasting the least amount of wood. The surface will be more

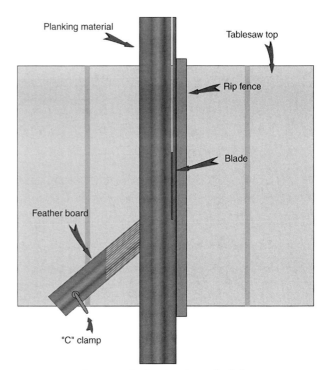

FIGURE 5-4. The use of a feather board while ripping strip planks is highly advisable and will prevent accidents while you are cutting thin planks.

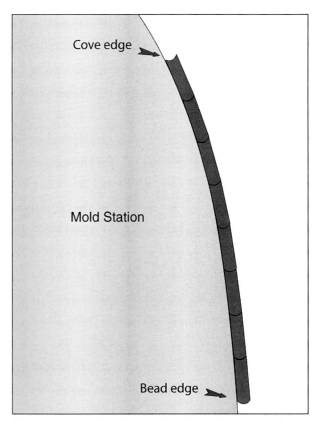

FIGURE 5-5. Bead and cove planking against a mold station.

64

FIGURE 5-6. A slash-grain board ripped into vertical grain planks.

irregular, however, and more may have to be sanded off later or cleaned up with a thickness planer.

Bead and cove edges make the alignment of the planks on the mold easier and fit the edges together better when you are planking over a tight radius. A special pair of router bits must be purchased in order to do this yourself. If you decide to make your own bead and cove planking, you'll need a router, a router table to mount it, and the special router bits. Use feather boards to hold the plank both against the fence and down to the table.

Bead and cove edges are not as essential with the outrigger canoes designs shown here because there are no tight curves to plank. I've only built with square-edged planks, and the joints are not really noticeable. Normally, it is unnecessary to fill any gaps between square-edged planks unless you can see through the gap. Sanding dust mixed with glue makes a good gap filler. Be sure to mask off the adjacent planks to avoid staining the surface.

It is not always possible to get full-length timber for planking. Structurally, there is no need to scarf shorter lengths together before putting them on the mold. A simple butt joint done in place on the mold is fine. If you still want to splice the planks before planking, you can make quick scarf joints by building a jig to fit up against a fixed disc sander made from your table saw. Sanding is better than sawing with such thin, fragile strips.

When the planks are in place on the mold, the outer and inner faces should be *edge grain*, or *vertical grain*. The grain lines should run straight and be spaced closely. If you rip slices from a flat or *slash* grain plank, the slices will exhibit vertical grain when they are turned on their sides on the mold. A sanded hull with all edge grain will come out fairer than one with flat-grain planks. Sanding flat or slash-grain planks causes the softer areas to be removed, with hard ridges remaining.

SCARFING TIMBER

A scarf joint is a way of making short pieces of timber or plywood into longer pieces, without making them thicker or weaker at the joint. Gunwales and spars are most commonly in need of scarf joints. If done carefully, they will look very nice with a varnished finish.

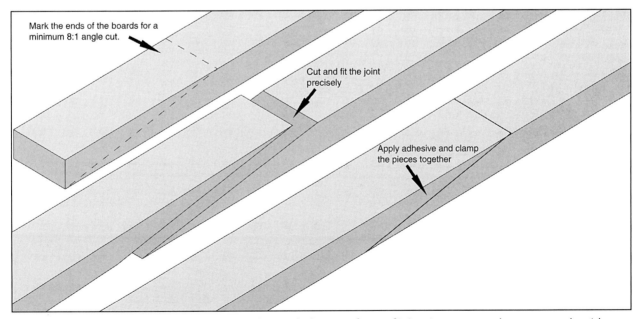

FIGURE 5-7. Timber planks can be spliced together with the use of a scarf joint. Long, tapered cuts are made with a saw to the ends of each piece to be joined. A plane or a sanding block is used to fit the ends exactly together. Adhesive is applied, and the joint is clamped together.

The length of the joint should be a minimum of eight times the thickness of the material. A ¾" (19mm) thick gunwale would require a scarf joint at least 6" (152mm) in length. Plywood that is ¼" (6mm) requires a joint that is 2" (48mm) in length.

Cutting the taper on the ends of the pieces must be precise. The first step is to draw the actual cutting line on three sides of the material. Make sure that the end of the timber strip is square before measuring back from it.

One strategy is to remove most of the material with a power tool and do the final precision work with a plane and sanding block. Clamp the piece securely to a table or workbench. You can remove the bulk of the material in several ways. A power plane, disc grinder, jigsaw, or wide chisel can be used to remove most of the stock. Just don't cut too close to the line. Use a sharp block plane and a hard sanding block or board to get down to the line. Make sure that the surface is flat without any high points in the middle. Once you have the two parts shaped, fit them together on edge on a flat surface, and use the plane or sanding block to get a good fit.

Epoxy glue (discussed earlier in this chapter) is the best adhesive to use if your fit is not perfect. Mix some resin and hardener, but do not add the thickener yet. Paint a thin coat of the unthickened epoxy on the mating surfaces, and allow it to soak into the absorbent end grain. Omitting this step can cause a weaker joint, because the end grain will absorb the resin and leave mostly filler.

Mix the thickening powder into the remaining resin, and coat the two mating surfaces. Lay the joint flat on the table, and use a straightedge across the top and sides of the joint to align the surfaces. Put a temporary staple into each side to prevent them from sliding around. Wrap plastic sheeting or waxed paper around the joint, and clamp the piece against a straight piece of timber with at least two spring clamps or C-clamps.

If you have several joints to make, these can all be clamped together, as long as each one is individually wrapped with plastic. When the glue has cured, clean up the surfaces with sandpaper on a sanding board.

Scarfing Plywood

If you elect to build the Wa'apa plywood hull in one piece, you will have to splice standard-length sheets into longer lengths. Scarfing is the best way to do this.

Scarfing plywood uses a similar procedure to that used with solid timber. You will need a wide enough table or work surface to support the edge of the joint. Be sure that the surface is straight and flat, and that you have a firm, square edge under the end of the plywood sheet. Use a stiff board that is as long as the width of the plywood, and some clamps to hold the sheet firmly to the work surface.

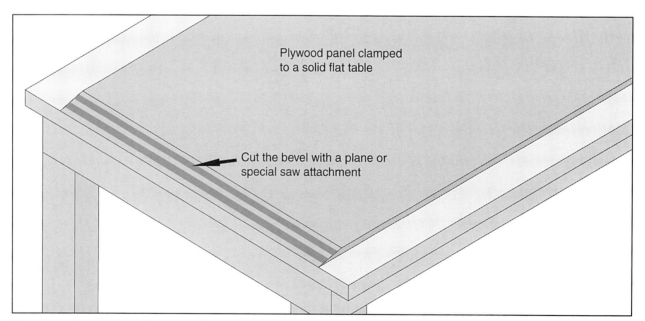

Plywood panel clamped to a solid flat table

Cut the bevel with a plane or special saw attachment

FIGURE 5-8. Plywood scarf joints can be roughly cut with a plane or grinder and fitted more precisely with the use of a sanding block or plane.

Again, you can remove most of the material with planes or grinders, but be careful not to splinter the delicate edges. (A circular-saw attachment designed for cutting scarfs in plywood is available from Gougeon Brothers, Inc., the company that makes West System epoxy [see the resources section at the end of the book].) The glue lines between the laminates of the plywood will help you to produce a flat surface, because they will be straight when the surface is flat.

Plywood scarfs can be cut one at a time, or they can be stacked and staggered so that both sheets can be done at the same time. The first sheet is laid down with its edge even with the table's edge. The second sheet is laid on top of the first sheet with its edge aligned with the end of the first sheet's scarf. So, if you're scarfing ¼" (6mm) plywood, the second sheet's edge would be 2" (48mm) back from the first sheet's edge.

When you are gluing a plywood scarf, prime the surfaces with unthickened epoxy as in the timber joints, apply the thickened glue after the first coat soaks into the wood, and line up the two sheets with the joint over a flat, solid surface covered with plastic sheeting. Press the joint together to squeeze out any excess glue before determining its position, then use a straightedge on the top surface and along the edges to bring the two pieces into perfect alignment. Then hold them together

by driving at least two wide-crown staples through the joint.

Two options are available for applying the necessary clamping pressure, depending on how the plywood will be finished. If you plan on a clear finish with a minimum number of blemishes, you can stack heavy weights on a stiff board that covers the joint. It is also possible to jam struts between the ceiling and the joint for downward pressure.

Another way to pressure the joint is with power-driven staples through thin ply, or by using scrap timber. The timber can be split away when the glue is hard, and the staples can be pulled with vise grips and a putty knife to protect the surface. You can also use small nails hammered through the same timber or plywood scraps.

There are few limits as to how long you can make a sheet of plywood. I have personally made 60' (18m) long sheets from ³⁄₁₆" (4mm) plywood.

JOINING PLYWOOD SHEETS WITH FIBERGLASS

Another way exists to join plywood sheets without any cutting or shaping of the ends. The sheets are butted edge to edge, and fiberglass tape is applied to both sides of the joint. This has proven to be as strong as the traditional scarf joint.

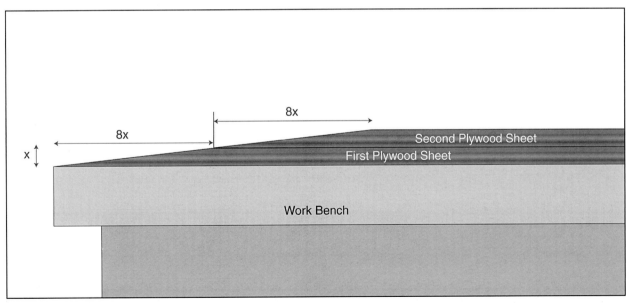

FIGURE 5-9. By stacking both sheets of plywood to be joined with the top sheet set back by the width of the cut, both cuts can be done at the same time and with greater accuracy.

Apply fiberglass tape to both sides of the joint at the same time. You'll need a flat surface to support both sheets butted together, like the floor or a large table. Cover the work surface area with clean, flat, plastic sheeting. Lay down a 4" (100mm) wide strip of 6-ounce (200-gram) fiberglass cloth, and wet it out with epoxy. Coat all of the contact areas on both sides of the two pieces of plywood. Butt them together, centered over the strip of wet fiberglass.

Wet out the second strip of fiberglass on top of the butt joint, and cover it with more plastic sheeting. Lay a flat piece of board or a strip of heavy plywood on top of the joint, and weigh it down with anything heavy—the more the better.

As a last check, be sure that the two pieces of plywood are still butted together solidly. The next day, the fiberglass strips can be lightly sanded and are ready for use.

There are also a couple of enhancements to this method. To obtain a perfectly flush joint, you can sand away some of the surface of the plywood on both sides, before applying epoxy, to recess the fiberglass tape. Only remove about 1/32" (1 mm) of material.

Another enhancement is to use *peelply* between the wet fiberglass and the plastic sheet. Peelply is simply lightweight nylon, or polyester fabric, that can be peeled off of the epoxy after it has cured. Peelply has the advantage of leaving a clean, textured surface that requires little or no sanding. Peelply can be used on many places to which you know you'll have to bond later, because it keeps the surface clean until you are ready to peel off the peelply (and bond to that surface). It is available from epoxy dealers, or you can use white, uncolored nylon from a fabric store.

JOINING PLYWOOD SHEETS WITH BUTT BLOCKS

One of the oldest and most commonly used ways to join plywood sheets is through the use of *butt blocks*, or *butt straps*.

Butt-block splices will locally stiffen the panel considerably and should only be used where the panel does not have to be forced into a tight bend. A layer of fiberglass on the outside is necessary to prevent a crack

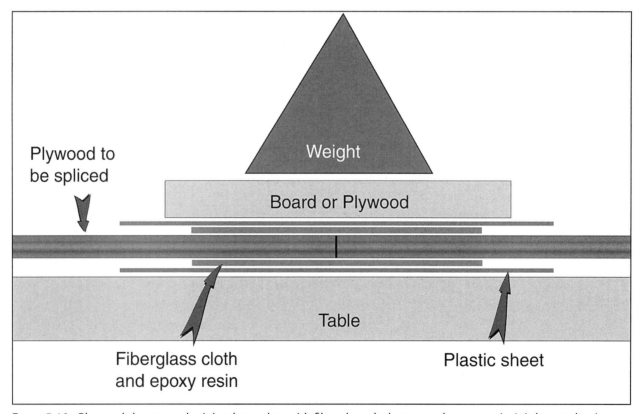

FIGURE 5-10. Plywood sheets can be joined together with fiberglass cloth tape and epoxy resin. It is best to laminate both sides of the plywood joint at the same time, rather than trying to turn a sheet with cured fiberglass tape on only one side.

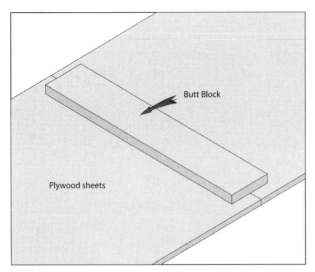

FIGURE 5-11. Joining plywood sheets with a butt block. Screws, nails, or a heavy weight can be used to hold the joint together until the adhesive cures.

appearing at the joint. The stiffening effect can be used to your advantage by locating the joint in such a way as to allow it to replace a frame.

The butt block itself should be plywood to prevent splitting. A thick butt block is the easiest to install, as you can use short nails or screws passing through the plywood panel into the butt block. A thin butt block, which is the same thickness as the panels, should be joined primarily with adhesive, although mechanical fasteners may be added for extra security.

Butt-block splices are not recommended in the one-piece Wa'apa design option, because the joints are located over bulkhead locations and would require that the bulkheads be cut smaller to adjust to the increased thickness of the panel.

FILLETING

With the advent of epoxy resins, filleting has become a popular way to join or seal joints in plywood or composite panels. Fillets are used in my designs primarily to bond and seal watertight bulkheads. Filleting material is a mixture of mixed epoxy and a filler material or thickener to make a stiff putty. The filler material will determine the strength and density of the fillet. Fillers can consist of glue powder, which is a combination of colloidal silica and cotton fiber, lightweight fillers like microspheres or microballoons, or even wood sanding dust. Glue

powder or wood dust will result in a high-density fillet that is excellent for bonding and sealing watertight bulkheads. It can be left without a fiberglass layer applied over it.

Low-density fillets require one or more layers of fiberglass tape. It is easiest to apply the glass tape to a fillet before the fillet hardens. This will result in the best possible bond, and without any preparatory sanding.

The filleting tool, similar to a spatula, is made from scrap timber or plywood with the end rounded to the desired radius.

To make a fillet, thoroughly mix a small batch of epoxy. Too large a batch will produce more heat during the reaction and may cause the epoxy to harden before you have applied all of it. Reserve a portion of the unthickened epoxy to prime any bare wood surfaces. Add the thickener after the resin and hardener are mixed. Keep adding small amounts of filler until the mixture is stiff enough to stand without slumping. It should have the consistency of peanut butter.

Prime the wood surfaces with unfilled epoxy before putting in the fillet. If the surface has previously been coated, hand sand it, and clean the surface with epoxy thinner or acetone.

If you have only a small amount of filleting to do, apply the material with the filleting tool by daubing it along the joint. If you have a long fillet to make, put the mixture into a small zip-lock plastic bag or a cake-decorating bag; cut the corner from the bag and squeeze out the mixture along the joint. Use the filleting tool to smooth and shape the radiused joint, and use a narrow, flat putty knife to clean the excess from the surface.

If you see your fillets starting to sag after you've put them in place, use the putty knife to remove them, and mix in more filler.

FILLING, SANDING, AND FAIRING

Completing a hull with a truly professional finish can require a lot of filling, fairing, and sanding. Filling is the application of any kind of putty to fill low areas or nail and screw heads that are below the surface. If you're planning on a clear, varnished finish, you won't be able to fill low areas of the hull. Instead, you will have to sand or shave down the higher areas to match. A painted finish can require more preparation than a varnished one, because the grain of the

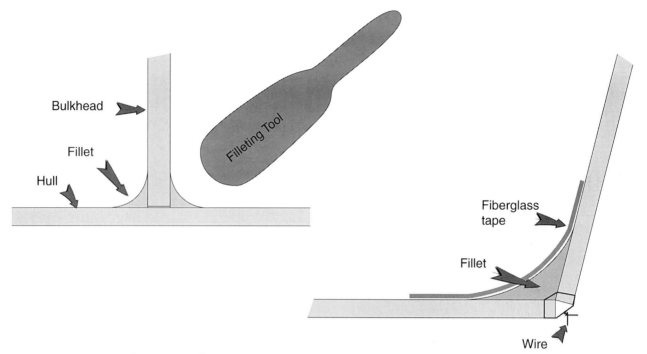

FIGURE 5-12. Two uses for an epoxy fillet—the first to bond a bulkhead in place, and the second to form a chine with the "stitch-and-tape" method.

varnished wood sometimes disguises imperfections that would be obvious if it were coated in paint.

Most strip-composite canoes are finished with varnish. The fiberglass sheathing will be almost completely transparent but will still need the UV protection from an exterior-grade or spar varnish.

Try to minimize any filling of the surface if the hull is to be varnished. Gaps between planks can be filled with commercial wood-putty mixtures, or a mixture of sanding dust (not sawdust) and epoxy or white glue. Use masking tape on both sides of the gap to prevent staining the adjacent surface. Staple holes do not need filling, as the first coat of resin will fill them. A hull that is to be painted will have defects such as nail and screw heads. Punch nail heads below the surface and fill them with the same material. In addition, you can use one of the commonly available polyester-based putties used for automotive bodywork. This material is especially useful if you're in a hurry, since it can be applied, sanded, and painted within an hour. Because this material is usually a pink color when mixed with its polyester hardener, it is not suitable for a surface to be varnished. It is best used only where the surface will be sheathed in fiberglass later and is not as permanent if it is simply painted over. One of the lightweight epoxy fillers is best under a paint-only surface.

Sanding and fairing are two very different processes. Sanding just tries to make the surface smooth and will make the hills and valleys equally smooth and devoid of scratches. Just running a vibrator or random orbital sander over a surface will make it smooth, but not necessarily fair. Fairing is the process of removing the hills and filling the valleys to make the hull surface a fair curve from end to end. The amount of fairing required for a strip hull can be greatly reduced by doing careful work during the stripping process. After each plank is stapled in place, sight down its length to ensure that it lies in a fair curve. A bit of shimming and adjustment to the molds at this stage can save a lot of fairing work later.

The best tools for fairing any hull up to even 100' (30m) consist of a selection of long sanding boards. Sanding boards up to 16" (400mm) in length are available from automotive-supply stores and have a thin foam surface that helps the sandpaper cut. Longer boards up to 4' (1200mm) are easily made in the shop. The thickness of the board can be varied to make it flexible enough to conform to the overall curvature of the hull. Commercial boards are equipped with clamps to hold the sandpaper, but shop-built boards can use either staples at the ends and along the edges, or spray contact adhesive, to hold the sandpaper in place.

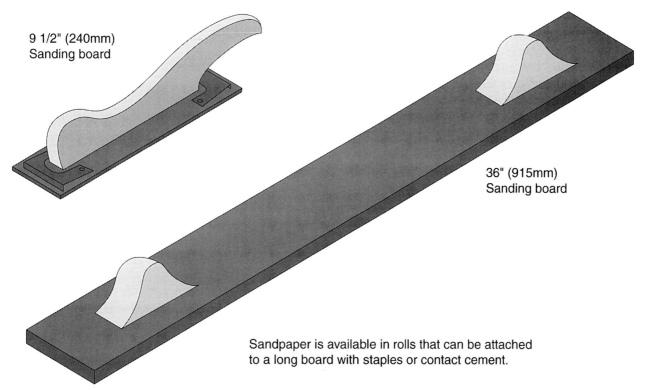

9 1/2" (240mm)
Sanding board

36" (915mm)
Sanding board

Sandpaper is available in rolls that can be attached
to a long board with staples or contact cement.

FIGURE 5-13. Long sanding boards are the only way to achieve a truly fair surface.

Excessively coarse sandpaper like 36 or 40 grit should not be used, because you'll have to sand too much away later to get rid of the scratches. Begin with 60 to 80 grit if you need to remove a lot of wood. Final sanding, before glassing a strip hull, should be done with 120-grit paper. Use a damp sponge to wipe the surface, and look for scratches that haven't been sanded away. Once you've coated the hull with epoxy, the scratches are there forever. Be sure to allow it to dry until the next day before applying any epoxy.

Fine sanding to smooth the surface can be done by hand but is much easier with a vibrating sander or random orbital sander. Belt sanders are too aggressive for soft cedar surfaces unless you are a master with them.

SHEATHING WITH FIBERGLASS AND RESIN

The fiberglass sheathing on both the outside and the inside of the hull is vital for developing the full strength of a strip-composite hull. A plywood hull can gain abrasion resistance and a more durable surface finish with a sheathing of fiberglass cloth impregnated with epoxy resin. The layer of fiberglass will also contribute to panel stiffness.

One layer of 6-ounce (200-gram) woven fiberglass cloth is required on both sides of a strip-planked hull. Increasing the weight of fabric on the outside will increase abrasion resistance, whereas increasing the fabric weight on the inside will increase the impact resistance. Heavier fabrics or multiple layers will, however, reduce the clarity of a varnished finish.

Narrow canoe hulls are best glassed one side at a time, with the fabric overlapped 2" (50mm) along the keel and stem. When you are purchasing the fiberglass cloth, keep it rolled, not folded, because wrinkles can be difficult or impossible to remove.

Unroll the fabric onto the hull with a finished edge that is 2" (50mm) past the keel line. You'll have to cut the finished edge away when you get to the stems. Leave 2" (50mm) of fabric hanging past the edge of the hull at the gunwale, because this will help to catch epoxy drips. Put a strip of masking tape, 1" (25mm), away from the edge of the fabric at the keel to stop resin from running down the side of the hull. Crease the tape as you put it on so that you will have a turned-up edge. Gently stretch out the fabric, pulling from the ends. A big, soft, dry paintbrush or a clean dust brush can help with removing wrinkles.

Epoxy is best applied in a temperature range of 65°F (17°C) to 85°F (29°C). Epoxy will cure faster at warmer temperatures and also when mixed in larger amounts. So the rule is that, in cooler weather, you can mix larger batches, because you'll have plenty of time to work, but in hotter weather, you must use many small batches. The clarity of the fiberglass sheathing will depend upon the temperature of the shop and the resin. If you're working at the cooler end of the range, it will require more time and effort to get the resin to penetrate the fabric. Excessive brushing or rolling will create foam bubbles in the resin, which can result in a milky finish.

Ideally, the first coat of epoxy is applied at the maximum temperature of the day. As the hull warms during the day, air is expelled from small gaps and staple holes. As the hull cools later, the air is sucked back into those same openings. If you start glassing in the early morning, the escaping air will make hundreds of tiny bubbles on the resin surface. Starting the glassing as the temperature has peaked will cause the resin to actually be sucked into the openings. This is not an ideal situation, because you would like to apply three coats of resin, a couple of hours apart, to avoid having to sand between coats. If you only get the second coat of resin on the first day, you'll have to wipe the hull with a wet sponge, dry it to remove the greasy residue called "blush" left by the curing epoxy, and hand sand it with 120-grit sandpaper before applying the last coat.

Start at the middle of the hull, and work toward the ends, applying the resin with a big 3" (75mm) natural bristle brush, or a roller covered in thin sponge. Special sponge rollers are available from epoxy dealers. Don't use the cheap, disposable glue brushes, as they will continuously lose their bristles.

After applying several batches of epoxy, use a plastic squeegee to remove the excess. Start from the keel, and run the squeegee down the fabric to the gunwale. Have a can or paper cup to catch the excess and to clean the squeegee. Do not reapply this resin, because it will be filled with air bubbles. Squeegeeing is a very important step, because the fiberglass cloth tends to float up in the resin. If the resin is allowed to cure in this way, some of the fabric will be sanded away at the high spots. When properly squeegeed, the fabric will have a matte, not shiny, appearance.

One thing worse than too much resin is too little. If the fabric looks whitish, you may have removed too much epoxy, and you'll have to brush on some more. Planking joints, staple holes, and end grain can all absorb extra epoxy and starve the fabric.

Don't apply the epoxy, squeegee, and walk away, or you'll definitely end up with starved areas. Stay close by, and keep examining the hull from every angle.

When the first coat of epoxy has just set up so that it can no longer run or be wiped off on your finger, apply another coat with the brush or foam roller. The biggest mistake you can make is trying to apply a heavy coat. Epoxy isn't like paint—it will continue running for a long time. Apply only enough to fill the weave of the cloth, and allow it to cure. The third coat is applied in the same way. Stand by with your brush as the epoxy cures so that you can smooth out the inevitable runs. Additional coats may be applied if you feel that the cloth has not been adequately covered, but be sure to clean and sand the hull first if it has cured for more than eight hours. Hardened runs are best removed with a sharp cabinet scraper. A scraper can be used over the whole hull if you wish and has the advantage of better surface fairing and no sanding dust.

If you have a helper to speed things up, you can put the fiberglass on both sides before applying any filler coats of epoxy. You can go ahead and lay the fabric on the opposite side, overlapping the keel. Glass the opposite side of the hull in the same way, being sure to sand areas of the previously glassed side that will be overlapped if they have already cured hard. If you've had problems getting the glass to wrap smoothly around the stem, trim off the unacceptable parts with a knife or sandpaper, and prepare some strips of fiberglass cut on the bias. Strips of fabric cut at a forty-five-degree angle will wrap around a tight radius much easier than the straight weave. Use small, round patches of fabric on corners, like a knuckle on the stem.

Trim the excess cloth along the gunwale with a sharp knife. I recommend wearing leather gloves to do this, as the cut glass edge is very sharp. Run some fine sandpaper along the edge to avoid getting cut later.

The hull sanding can be done now or later, but the surface will be less contaminated if you leave the sanding until just before varnishing. At least sand a strip along the sheer, where the outer gunwale will be attached. Start with 80 grit on a random orbital

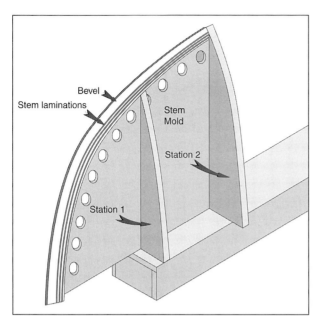

FIGURE 5-14. Laminated stem on a T2 stem mold. Note the holes for clamping the strips to the mold.

sander, and finish with 120 grit. Sand just enough to get rid of the shiny surface. If you sand into the fiberglass cloth, you can paint on some more resin and carefully block-sand it the next day.

LAMINATING

Laminating is the process of gluing together several thinner strips or layers of timber to make a thicker member, such as a stem or a curved cross beam. Laminating has the advantage of minimizing any weakness from poor grain orientation, or small knots and defects, by distributing them throughout the member. It also allows you to optimize the strength-to-weight ratio of a cross beam by using a harder, stronger timber on the outside layer and a lightweight timber for the inner layers.

Stems for strip-planked hulls use a temporary *stem mold* to determine their shape. The edge of the stem mold is first covered with two layers of plastic tape to prevent the stem laminations from bonding to the edge. The thin layers of timber are then coated with glue and clamped to the stem mold by using the row of holes in the mold to take the clamps. After the glue has cured and the clamps have been removed, put a couple of temporary screws through the stem into the mold, and one through the back side of station two into the end of the stem, to hold the stem in place while it is shaped with a plane. Leave some of the screws in until the planking gets to that point, and then remove them.

The other major laminating projects are the curved beams (iakos) on some of the designs. Draw the curve on a flat table, using the offsets shown in the plans. Screw blocks of wood to the table every 6" (150mm) or so along the line on the inside of the curve. Use a sheet of plastic, or a double layer of waxed paper, and hold it in place with a few staples to keep glue away from the table and the blocks.

Cut the timber strips to the thickness shown on the plans. The strips can be ripped on a table saw with a smooth cutting blade, or run through a thickness planer, for a very smooth joint. Mix the epoxy and glue filler powder, and coat one side of all but one piece. Bundle them together, and lay them up against the blocks. Use sliding bar clamps or "C" clamps to hold the bundle of strips loosely against the blocks, working from the straight end toward the curved end. Tighten the clamps gradually, and use a putty knife to remove excess glue that has squeezed out. If gaps exist between the layers, use additional clamps where needed. If a gap won't close completely, use the putty knife to force glue into the opening.

When the glue is hard and the clamps have been removed, you will observe a bit of spring-back or straightening of the curved beam. This is normal and is taken into account in the design. Use a disc or belt sander to remove most of the hardened, squeezed-out glue, being careful not to sand too far into the wood. You can finish it completely with a sander, or

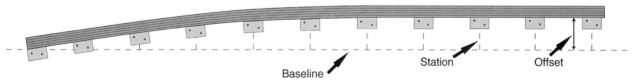

FIGURE 5-15. Curved cross beams consist of thin layers of timber glued together and clamped against a series of blocks screwed to a flat surface. Begin by drawing a baseline on the flat surface and measuring out the intervals between stations. Measure and mark the offset vertically from the baseline at each station. Connect the offset marks with a drawn fair curve. Screw down 2" × 2" (50mm × 50mm) blocks at each offset mark.

run it through a table saw or thickness planer to clean the surface. Allow for this extra needed width when cutting your strips. Finish the edges with a plane and sanding board, or run a round-over router bit along the edges.

BONDED FASTENERS

Using *bonded fasteners* is a great way to increase the holding power of wood screws and machine screws. Epoxy is used to increase the strength of the wood fibers adjacent to the metal fastener. The most basic way is to coat the inside of a screw's pilot hole with a pipe cleaner, toothpick, or syringe.

For highly loaded structural fasteners, the pilot hole can be as large as twice the diameter of the fastener. The greater the amount of epoxy resin around the fastener, the greater the strength, due to the increase in contact area with the wood.

For a wood screw, start with a normal pilot hole, then re-drill it to a larger diameter, but not to the full depth. This allows the screw to bite into some of the wood and hold its position while the resin hardens. Machine screws also can have the very end of their holes be a smaller diameter so that they will bite into some of the wood.

Mix epoxy without any thickeners, and pour the hole almost full of resin. Wait several minutes for the epoxy to soak into the wood. Put the wood or machine screw into the resin, and allow it to harden. Do not use thickeners unless you are forced to bond a fastener on a vertical surface, in which case it will still be better than not doing it at all. Bonded fasteners can be removed at a later date by holding a hot soldering

iron on the head of the fastener. The heat will soften the epoxy resin enough to allow it to be removed.

PAINTING AND VARNISHING

There is a huge range of choices available when it comes time to paint or varnish your canoe. Epoxy has little resistance to sunlight and will quickly deteriorate into a yellowish, cloudy material. It must either be covered with paint or at least five coats of exterior-grade or spar varnish. Spar varnish contains filters to prevent the sunlight from damaging the epoxy but still requires frequent recoating if left in the sun uncovered.

Varnish comes in either one- or two-part mixtures. Both have equal amounts of resistance to sunlight, but the two-part polyurethane varnishes cure much harder and will do a better job at resisting scratches.

Paint is also available in one- or two-part formulations, with an even wider variety of choices. Undercoats can be two-part epoxy, one-part oil based, or one-part water-based acrylic latex. Finish coats range from the very expensive two-part polyurethanes, to one-part polyurethanes, to acrylic latex house paint.

Two-part polyurethane finishes are hazardous to your health and require a piped-in, fresh-air system to the space suit that you should be wearing.

You can apply your finish with a spray gun, bristle or foam brush, or foam roller. Brushing is the most commonly used method, and some of the new one-part polyurethane marine enamels flow out so well that they look like they were sprayed.

The keys to a fine finish are preparation and cleanliness. Small defects in the surface will become much more obvious when they are coated. This is easy to fix with a painted finish, because filling and sanding can still be done between undercoats.

Sand a fiberglassed or bare wood surface with 120-grit sandpaper, but use 220-grit paper between coats of paint or varnish. A surface to be painted should be wiped down with a clean cloth slightly dampened with thinner. For a varnished surface, clean it with a *tack-rag,* which is a clean cloth that has been sprinkled with varnish. Also, be sure that the shop or painting area is not excessively dusty, or the wind will blow the dirt around. Don't apply any finish in direct sunlight.

Use a large, 3" (75mm) minimum brush, and take long, sweeping strokes, first horizontally, and finishing vertically to avoid sagging and runs. Keep a

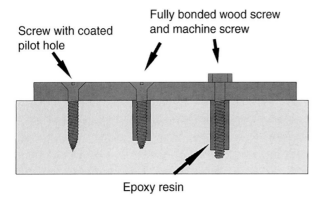

Screw with coated pilot hole

Fully bonded wood screw and machine screw

Epoxy resin

FIGURE 5-16. Epoxy bonding greatly increases the strength of mechanical fasteners. Fasteners with large, loose pilot holes full of epoxy glue are stronger than simply coating a normal-size pilot hole.

wet edge and work as quickly as possible. The ambient temperature and the type of paint you're using will have a great effect on how fast you have to work. If you haven't used a particular product before, practice on some scrap material rather than your hull. Finishes applied with a foam roller can be lightly finished with a good brush to smooth the bubbles left by the roller.

Spray painting with a compressor and spray gun is a whole subject on its own and can be done with great success if you have a clean area, some previous experience, and a good breathing apparatus.

Any non-water-based finish will emit strong fumes, so always wear a good respirator, designed to filter out organic vapors.

METAL WORK

In all of my designs, I have minimized the use of metal parts. I've reduced the use of metal fittings down to blocks for running rigging. You can buy the blocks, or make them from wood with plastic sheaves.

If you're building a leeboard, the aluminum reinforcing plate shown can be cut from a ⅛" (3mm) plate with a jigsaw or hacksaw.

WORKSHOP HEALTH AND SAFETY

Traditional boatbuilding, before the days of resins and electric sanders, was a much healthier experience. Almost every material we use for modern boatbuilding has some health hazards that must be guarded against.

Building a strip hull from western red cedar will expose you to the sanding dust, which can be harmful to the lungs. It's not something that waits for years to appear; it can cause breathing problems immediately. Be sure to wear a dust mask with *two* straps when sanding, and use a sander with an attachment that catches the dust in a bag or a vacuum system. Any fairing that you can do with a sharp plane or scraper will save on the dust problem. Other wood species are not as toxic as red cedar, but I would still use protection against inhaling the dust.

The sanding of cured epoxy can be reduced by the use of a sharp scraper. Skin exposure to uncured epoxy (especially the hardener) can cause an allergic

reaction in some people, resulting in a bad skin rash. Once you are sensitized to it, you may never be able to get near epoxy again. It's important to wear gloves at all times while mixing or applying epoxy. The disposable latex gloves used by doctors work well and are economical to buy in a dispensing box. Rubber dishwashing gloves are also good and hold up better if you're having problems tearing the thinner surgical gloves.

Always wear safety glasses when mixing resin, and wear your dust mask when mixing in glue fillers, because they will form a cloud around your head.

If you do have to remove epoxy from your skin, try using vinegar or plenty of soap and water. Using epoxy thinner or acetone only thins the resin so that it can better penetrate your skin.

Painting with two-part polyurethane paints or varnishes produces fumes that are carcinogenic, so be sure to wear at least an organic vapor respirator, and ideally a system that pumps fresh air into a full face mask. Cover your hands, too, because the thinner is also toxic.

Power tools of any kind have their own set of dangers. When using your table saw, always push the stock with a pusher stick, kept handy for that purpose, and always use a feather board when ripping thin stock to avoid kickback. Don't wear loose sleeves or baggy clothing around a table saw or router, or else you risk being pulled into the blade.

Router bits have been known to grab clothing and take off parts of fingers. And again—always wear safety glasses.

MAINTENANCE AND REPAIR

Maintaining the beauty and integrity of your creation will ensure that it lasts a long time. Traditional canoes in the Pacific and Indian oceans quite often have their own shelter on the waterfront. Curved, arched, A-framed, and thatched canoe houses protected the vessels from the ravages of sun and rain. At the very least, they were covered with palm fronds to protect them from rapid drying and warping. Shade and good ventilation are still today the best ways to preserve your canoe.

A strip-planked canoe hull that has been fiberglassed with epoxy resin will deteriorate very quickly if it is not protected by several coats of spar varnish or paint. Epoxy resin, while very waterproof, has no resistance to ultraviolet light from the sun. Without the protection of spar varnish (containing UV inhibitors) or paint, it will very soon turn hazy yellow and deteriorate if left exposed to sunlight.

Of the two coatings, varnish requires the most maintenance, with recoating required every six months if the craft is left out in the weather. Two-part polyurethane varnishes are much harder than the single-part mixture but have no greater resistance to the sun. They will require recoating just as often if they are left exposed. Paint will last many years depending on how much money you want to spend. Two-part polyurethanes can last up to ten years even when the boat is left in the sun.

The easiest way to extend the life of a varnished finish is to simply cover it. From the cheapest blue tarp to a custom made acrylic cover, anything is better than just leaving the boat exposed. Storing the canoe under a roof is even better, because it allows better ventilation and doesn't trap moisture, which can produce mildew in the hull.

Plywood hulls, like on the Wa'apa, can be built without the fiberglass sheathing on the outside if the plywood is of high-quality marine grade. Douglas fir plywood, however, will develop "checking" if it is not sheathed in fiberglass cloth. Checking is indicated by many fine cracks in the outer laminate of the plywood. A plain resin coating or any kind of paint won't prevent checking.

Sails should always be stored within a cover or bag, or indoors when not being used. Polytarp sails will deteriorate quickly from sunlight, and even the best commercial sailcloth will degrade but at a slower rate.

Most damage to canoe hulls consists of surface scratches, which can be very disturbing to the builder who has spent many hours acquiring a perfect finish. In most cases, these will disappear when the hull is recoated with varnish. If you can see a whitish blemish with the fiberglass weave showing, then you need to take more immediate action. The fabric may be delaminated from the hull and will require some surgery with a razor blade to remove it. After removing the loose fiberglass, use fine sandpaper to feather back the edges to allow a new patch of fiberglass to be laminated in place.

If the planking has been gouged or splintered, you can remove the damaged timber with a sharp razor knife, leaving a forty-five-degree, angled edge. Carve a piece of timber to fit and glue it in place. Don't expect an invisible repair, since the edge of the old and new fiberglass will probably be visible. In most cases, this type of damage happens below the waterline and the repair won't be noticed.

Major damage may require the replacement of several plank sections, but since you built this hull originally, you won't have much trouble figuring out how to do it.

If you're a long way from civilization when serious hull damage occurs, there are some precautions you can take. A roll of duct tape has saved more than one cruise. Duct tape won't stick to damp, salty surfaces, so spend some time cleaning the surface.

Large offshore vessels have escaped sinking by pulling a sail or canvas under the hull with lines holding it to the gunwale. The water pressure will hold the fabric against the damage and keep most of the sea outside of your hull.

There are underwater epoxy putties available, although they will stick better if you dry things out as much as possible. My favorite Third World solution involves using Styrofoam (expanded polystyrene, or eps) scraps found on any beach in the world and some gasoline. I've heard of this being done in locations that are thousands of miles apart, so I suspect that it is widespread. When the foam pieces come in contact with gasoline, they melt into a sticky goo that seems to bond to just about anything. This sticky goo combined with vegetable fibers like dried leaves, vines, or cotton cloth can be used to make a reasonably secure fiberglass-like patch.

Another kind of damage that is likely to occur is damage to the sailing rig, including broken masts, booms, and torn sails. Broken spars are difficult to jury-rig in a small canoe, but if you can get to the beach, repair materials can be found. Spars can be "fished" where another stick or short piece of spar is tightly lashed alongside the break. Wooden spars can be "scarfed" with the use of a sharp knife and a tight lashing. Note that almost all rig repairs require string or light lashing line. A supply of small, strong line and some imagination will take care of most situations.

A torn sail can be sewn if you have a needle and thread and some scrap fabric. Tears in the middle, unstressed portion of a sail can be patched with contact cement and a piece of fabric. Only the solvent-based contact cements are strong enough to hold a sail together.

If it is too difficult or impossible to repair a broken spar or sail, a smaller rig lashed together from what remains will usually get you back to shore. Again, that roll of light line will prove to be very useful.

Damage to a rudder may be difficult to repair away from a workshop. I always recommend that you carry a steering oar as a backup system. It is easily stored out on the beams and can add its weight to the ama. A steering oar can also be used as a righting pole in the event of capsize. You will always have a paddle, and that is also available for steering.

CHAPTER 6

Building the Ulua and T2 Strip-Composite Hulls

DO A PRACTICE SESSION

Strip-composite construction is a technique whereby thin strips of wood form the core of a sandwich panel. Applying fiberglass cloth and epoxy resin to both sides of the wood strips forms a very stiff and strong panel. If you need to be convinced about the integrity of this method, I suggest that you make up a small 12" (300mm) by 12" flat test panel using ¼" (6mm) by ¾" (19mm) strips, edge-glued with yellow carpenters' glue. Short staples bridged between adjoining strips will hold them together until the glue dries. When the glue has dried, remove the staples, sand the top surface smooth, paint on a coat of epoxy resin, and lay a square of 6-ounce (200-gram) fiberglass cloth into the wet resin. Apply additional resin until the cloth becomes transparent. Take a plastic spreader or rubber squeegee and gently squeeze out the excess resin, being careful not to remove so much that the cloth weave turns whitish. Allow it to cure, turn the panel over, and do the same to the other side. Apply one or two additional coats of resin to fill the weave pattern of the fiberglass cloth.

When this has cured, you'll have a very light and stiff panel that you can destruction-test if you wish. Not only that, but you have now experienced most of the operations needed to build a strip-composite hull. Place it across a pair of supports and stand on it. Hit it with a hammer or a rock, just like you may have happen in an actual hull. You could measure all of these forces, and all of that's been done by others, but the real benefit is in showing you just what kind of abuse a strip-composite hull will take.

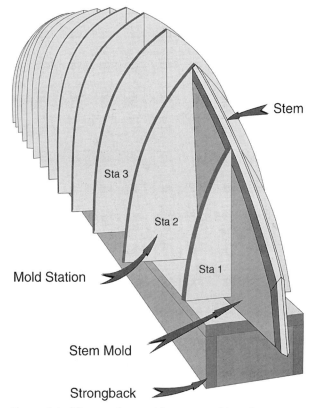

FIGURE 6-1. Ulua station molds, stem mold, and stem mounted on the strongback.

The Ulua and T2 hulls are built in the same way but have quite different hull shapes. The shape of the hull is determined by the *molds* and the *stems*. The molds are temporary and will be removed. The *stem* itself will be left in place, although the *stem mold* will be removed.

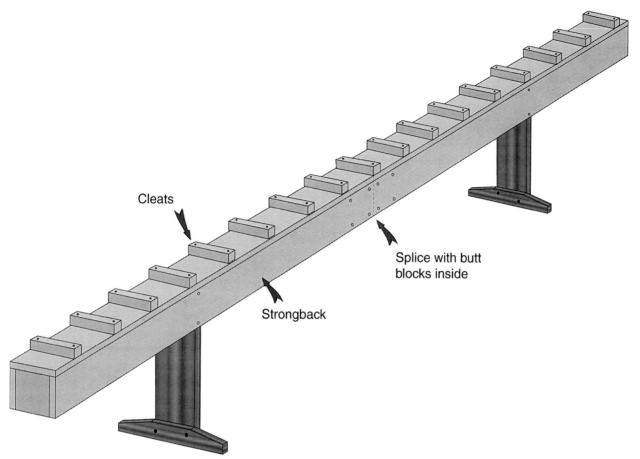

FIGURE 6-2. Completed strongback with cleats to locate mold positions.

THE STRONGBACK

The strongback is a firm, flat, level, and stable surface upon which the molds will be mounted. You won't regret spending the time to give it those attributes.

The strongback is a box beam, constructed from ¾" (19mm) particle board or plywood. It has a top and sides but no bottom and has bulkheads inside spaced every 16" (400mm). Two heavy timber legs support it at a convenient working height, or you can attach it to a pair of sawhorses. Thirty inches (760mm) is a good height for the top surface of the strongback.

Take one ¾" (19mm) sheet of particle board or plywood and cut it into six strips a little less than 8" (200mm) wide. By splicing the side panels end to end, you will have a 16' (4800mm) long strongback. This is shorter than the hull but actually makes it easier to work on the ends of the hull without the strongback getting in the way. Splice up two side panels and the top panel by joining two sections end to end, and making a butt block 8" (200mm) by

12" (300mm) and gluing and screwing it over the joint. Make seven rectangular bulkheads to fit inside at 16" (400mm) intervals.

Stretch a string tightly along the center of the top surface, held at each end by a small nail. Make

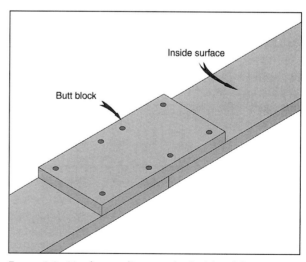

FIGURE 6-3. Use butt splices on the inside of the strongback sides and top to achieve the required length.

small pencil marks along it to be joined by a straight-edge, or use spray paint over the string to make a straight centerline. Measure, draw, and label the station interval lines, as shown on the plans in Figure 1-5 for the Ulua and in Figure 2-7 for the T2, at right angles to the centerline. At each station line, install an 8" (200mm) piece of 2" × 2" (50mm × 50mm) timber cleat. Examine the drawing carefully, because the cleats are not all on the same side of the station lines.

MOLDS

Molds can be cut from ½" (12mm) construction-grade plywood or particle board. I don't recommend using medium-density fiberboard (MDF), because you'll have difficulties with the staples either pulling out too easily from the edge or not at all from the face.

If you are lofting the molds directly onto the plywood or particle board, be sure to draw all of the waterlines and a centerline on both sides of the mold to aid in alignment later.

If you have purchased full-size paper patterns from the author, you can stick them to the plywood with spray adhesive, or with some other type of glue that doesn't wrinkle the paper. Make copies of any patterns that are in bulkhead or frame locations, and pick a pair of mold shapes to make a cradle later. If you're working from offsets, draw the mold shapes on paper to make patterns, or directly onto the plywood.

Cut the molds out with a jigsaw or band saw, being careful to stay just outside the line. Use a small block plane, a belt sander, or a stationary disc sander to get close to the line.

The Ulua uses *mold extensions*, but the T2 does not require them; therefore, the T2 molds can be screwed directly to the strongback cleats. The mold extensions are rectangular pieces of plywood that are screwed flat onto the mold, making the connection to the timber cleat at each mold station line. Cut these out and screw them to the molds, being careful to align them exactly with the indicated waterline.

The bow and stern stem molds are drawn and cut in the same way as the station molds. Cut a series of holes along the curved edge to allow the use of clamps when laminating the stem. The first mold at each end of the hull has to have a strip removed from its centerline in order to straddle the stem mold. The width of

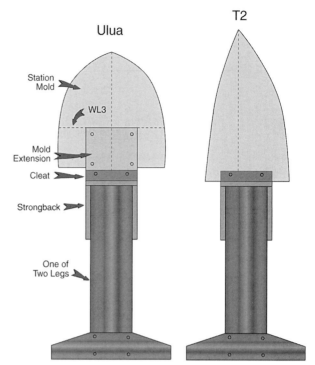

FIGURE 6-4. A station mold and mold extension for an Ulua mounted on the strongback. The T2 does not use mold extensions.

the strip to be cut out should be exactly the same as the thickness of the stem mold. Attach the split molds to the stem molds with a couple of screws driven in a forty-five-degree angle.

Mount the stem molds on the strongback first, along with the split mold already attached to it and the mold that attaches to the vertical edge of the stem mold. When both ends are plumb, square, and screwed into place, attach an extension stick on each stem mold and stretch a string between them so that the string is exactly plumb above the line drawn on the strongback and high enough to clear all of the intermediate molds.

Mount the intermediate molds with screws into the cleats on the strongback, aligning them at the top and bottom with the two centerlines. Hold the molds vertical by using scrap sticks and screws to angle-brace them against the strongback.

The permanent stems can be made in two ways. The Ulua stem is made up of two pieces that are straight enough to be sawn from a board. The T2 requires you to laminate several thin strips together, using the stem mold as a form. Making the stem longer than necessary will allow you to fasten it to the strongback while keeping the fastener away from the beveled portion. The permanent stem can be held in place with clamps, temporary screws, or thin nails while the bevel is being cut on its sides. The degree of beveling is not shown on the plans but is determined through the use of a *fairing batten*.

Draw a centerline on the outside of the stem, and use a plane, spokeshave, or rasp to bevel it until a fairing batten lies flush. A fairing batten is a strip of wood that is at least as stiff as one of the planks. Hold it along several of the molds with the end touching the stem. By looking at how it fits against the stem, you'll be able to tell how much more beveling is necessary. It is also possible to bevel as the planking proceeds, as long as the glue joints between the planks and the stem have cured. Shape enough bevel for the first six planks or so, and do the rest as the planking proceeds up the stem. Be sure to allow enough space for your tool or the planking could become damaged.

You may also build without permanent stems, in which case you would cut the stem molds to the outside line on the pattern, as shown in Figures 1-5 and 2-7. Plane a bevel on the stem mold itself, tape over the edge with plastic packaging tape, and bevel the end of each plank to match and adhere to the plank from the opposite side. The ends of the planks glued together will be the only thing holding the hull halves together until you sheath it in fiberglass. Before glassing the inside, put an epoxy fillet along where the inner stem would have been.

Stand back and walk around your setup, looking for misalignment of the vertical centerlines and horizontal waterlines. Take a straight, 6' (2m) strip of planking or your fairing batten, and lay it against the molds with your arms spread out wide, making sure it touches all the molds. If one mold seems high or low on one side, check the opposite side to make sure that

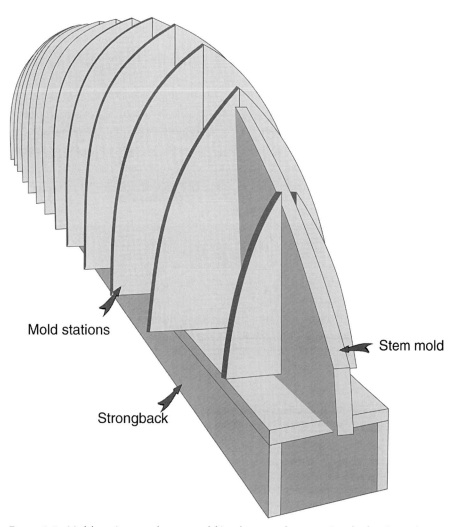

FIGURE 6-5. Mold stations and stem mold in place, ready to receive the laminated stem.

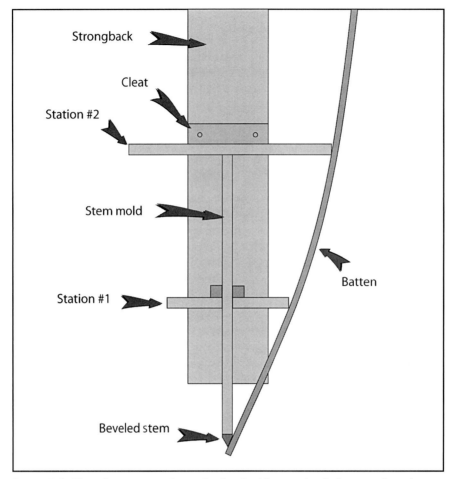

FIGURE 6-6. Use a batten or a piece of strip planking to check the stem bevel.

it isn't displaced to one side of the centerline before taking any action. If you wear strong glasses, rely on measurements rather than your eye, because the glasses can distort the shape of a straight line or curve.

High spots can be taken down with a block plane, rasp, or sander. Low spots can be filled by gluing and stapling on thin strips of timber to be shaped down when the glue cures, or if you want faster results, you can build up a a mold edge with polyester auto-body putty. The putty will harden in ten minutes, and you can plane or sand it to shape. Staple temporary planks at many different locations on the mold, and sight down them. This is a good practice all through the planking procedure. Shaving, filling, or shimming with thin scraps can be done at any stage in the planking.

When everything is shaped and aligned to your satisfaction, cover the edges of all the molds with plastic packaging tape to avoid gluing the planks to the mold. Do not cover a permanent stem, because the planks will be glued to it.

PLANKING

For this stage, you'll need some new tools. The Arrow T50 stapler is a good, reliable tool and can be field-stripped and cleaned when glue has frozen it solid. Use the 9⁄16" (14mm) staples. You'll spend a lot of time with your staple puller. When pulling a staple, hold a small putty knife against the planking next to the staple to avoid making dents in the planking with the puller. I highly recommend using a Japanese pull saw for cutting planks and doing careful surgery. When new, these are very sharp, so try to keep the bloodstains off of the hull.

Because a strip-composite hull is sheathed in epoxy and fiberglass on both sides, it is unnecessary to use a completely waterproof glue between the plank edges. The yellow, aliphatic carpenters' glue is most commonly used and causes the least mess. In the past, I've successfully used plastic resin, epoxy, and polyurethane glues. Epoxy is only normally used on large hulls.

82

Begin planking at the sheer line. A fair curve with the first plank is important, because the remaining planks will follow any unfairness in the vertical direction. The first plank is stapled to the molds and is glued only to the stems. Inspect the first plank from every angle. Sometimes just removing one staple will snap everything into a sweet curve. Trim the ends of the first plank with the pull saw.

If you have a permanent stem, trim the plank end exactly at the edge of the stem. If you have no permanent stem, leave an inch (25mm) of plank extending past the edge of the stem, and cut a bevel at its end with a saw to receive the plank from the opposite side.

Install the second sheer plank on the opposite side, and compare them from every angle. Apply glue to the top of the first plank and stem, and rest the next plank on top of it. Again, staple it to each mold, starting at the middle and working toward both ends.

If you're using square-edge planks and not cove and bead, you'll need to check the edge alignment of the planks in between the molds. If the edges are not aligned, or if the planks need pulling together, load some ¼" (6mm) staples and fire the staple with one leg in each plank while holding the planks tightly together. If you didn't remove all of the long staples from your gun, they will go all the way through the planks and into your fingers. If the molds are widely spaced in order to build a longer canoe, you may want to install some "cheater" mold strips in between the plywood molds. Cut some 1" (25mm) wide strips of 6mm (¼") plywood in the cross-grain direction in order to make them easier to bend. Wrap the strip in waxed paper and hold it inside the planking while stapling through the planking from the outside.

Continue with the first five or six strips on one side, but do not go any further until you've put an equal number on the other side of the hull. If the glue at the stems hasn't cured yet, you must be very careful when trimming the ends of the planks with the pull saw.

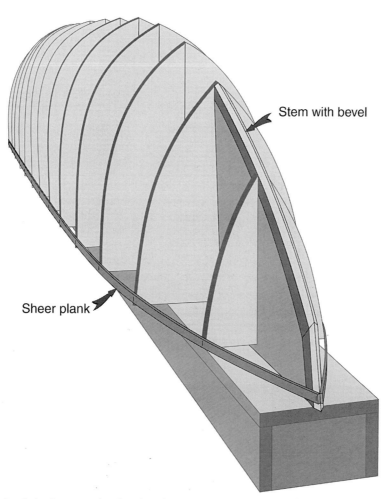

Stem with bevel

Sheer plank

FIGURE 6-7. The first pair of planks are only glued to the stem. Apply no more than six planks to one side at a time to prevent misalignment of the stem.

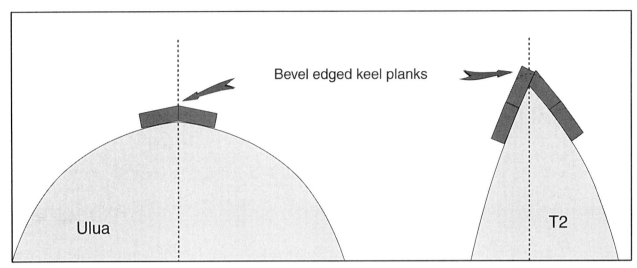

FIGURE 6-8. After planking has proceeded as high as the inner ends of the stems, install a pair of beveled planks to define the keel.

If you plank too much of one side ahead of the other, it can pull the stem mold out of alignment. It's always a good idea to sight down the stems often as planking proceeds. Just the act of pushing the end of the plank against the stem during stapling can be enough to move it out of line.

Once the planking has proceeded as far as the inner end of the stems, you have several options for finishing up. My favorite method is to stop the planking at a point that leaves just enough space for one more plank at the inner end of the stem. I then install two planks together straddling the keel line. You'll need to bevel the edges of these two keel planks where they bear against each other.

You can fill in the last open areas by one of several ways. You can continue planking up from the side planks, continue planking straight along the keel planks, or alternate with a resultant herringbone pattern. If planking up from the side is resulting in hard lateral bends, you can either switch to straight keel planks or taper the ends of the planks to ease the bend.

THE OUTER STEM

Plane, rasp, or sand a flat surface where the planks attach to the stems, to receive an outer laminated stem. Laminate thin strips of timber in place and clamp them down with waxed screws and washers. Sometimes you can clamp strips in place with tape or string wrapped right around the hull and strongback. Test it all before you apply the glue. Plane it down fair with the hull after the glue has cured. Fill the screw holes with wooden plugs.

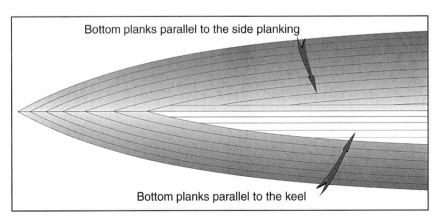

FIGURE 6-9. Planking to cover the bottom area can be installed parallel with the keel or parallel to the previous planks.

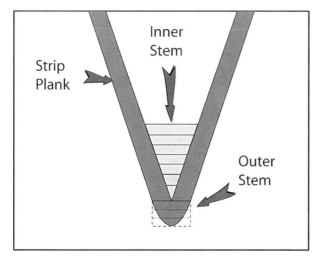

FIGURE 6-10. The outer stem is laminated over the ends of the strip planks.

FAIRING AND SMOOTHING THE HULL

A sharp plane or spokeshave is the best tool for initial smoothing of the hull. A sharp paint scraper is also useful. Shavings are much more manageable than sanding dust that goes everywhere in the work space. After doing all you can with the plane or scraper, begin sanding with 80-grit aluminum oxide sandpaper. The round random orbital sander is the best tool for this job. A soft, foam-backed pad will sand curved surfaces better than a stiff, rubber pad. Hold the sander flat to avoid gouging the surface.

After the coarse sanding is complete, vacuum the dust from the hull and look for gaps between the planking that may need filling before the fiberglass is applied. If the gap goes all the way through the hull, it should be filled. Mark the locations by putting masking tape along both sides of the gap. Mix sanding dust with your glue and force it into the gaps with a putty knife. In most cases, no filling is necessary. The sheathing of the hull with epoxy resin and fiberglass will fill in any small cracks.

Use 120-grit sandpaper for the final sanding. Do not sand it any finer than 120 grit, because this will provide the best base for the epoxy resin. Be careful when you are sanding close to edges at the stems and keel; it is best to sand these areas with a long sanding board, like those used in automotive body shops. You can sand the entire hull with a long sanding board if you wish. The hard fact is that this is the only way to get near-perfect fairness.

To see what the hull will look like when it is fiberglassed, wipe a damp sponge or rag over the hull surface. This will raise the grain and also expose any scratches remaining from earlier coarse sanding. Allow the hull to dry, and sand it again to smooth the raised grain and remove any visible scratches. Allow the hull to dry overnight before applying any epoxy resin.

Sheath the exterior with one layer of 6-ounce (200-gram) woven fiberglass cloth as described previously. Apply three fill coats of resin, but leave the final sanding until you are ready to varnish the hull. Sand any area that will be bonded to later, such as along the gunwale.

REMOVING THE HULL FROM THE MOLD

Before you remove the hull from the mold, you'll need to build a cradle to hold it securely upright. Use the mold pattern copies that you saved for this, and make a pair of cardboard patterns first to check for fit. Be sure to allow for some carpet or foam padding on the inside edges of the cradle. Make the cradle from ½" (12mm) plywood or particle board.

You can either remove the screws holding the molds to the strongback, and roll the hull and molds all together, or just try lifting the hull off with the molds still attached to the strongback. Hopefully you haven't left any inaccessible screws holding the permanent stem to the stem mold. If it won't lift off, remove the mold to the strongback screws, and disassemble the mold from within after the hull and mold are righted.

Set the hull upright in its cradle, and take some time to congratulate yourself. The hull sides are quite floppy at this stage, but have no fear, because they'll be extremely rigid when everything's finished.

Rip a pair of ⅝" × 1½" (16mm × 38mm) straight timber strips for temporary gunwales. These do not need to be the full length of the hull and are best if they just go past the watertight bulkhead positions. Attach them to the outside of the hull with screws driven from the outside, just short enough to prevent them from sticking through the inside surface. They'll just be biting into the fiberglass surface to hold.

Attach the temporary gunwales so that the upper edge is ¼" (6mm) higher than the edge of the hull. Now you can screw on a couple of spreader sticks on top of the temporary gunwales from one side to the other, holding the hull sides at the correct spacing. Measure the correct spacing from the molds.

It is a good idea to keep a couple of spreader sticks until the interior of the hull is glassed in place to prevent any warping or distortion in the hull from changing humidity or weather conditions. The sticks can be removed temporarily while you are sanding the interior.

GLASSING THE INTERIOR

Rough shaping of the interior is best done with a sharp scraper that you've ground or filed to a curved working edge that will fit into the tightest areas of the hull. Follow the scraping with the random orbital sander. A soft, foam-backed pad will help to prevent you from digging into the surface. Fill the area along the edges of the stem with lightweight epoxy filler to enable the fiberglass to fit without voids.

The interior can be glassed in the same way as the exterior, except that you only need one fill coat of resin after the fiberglass is bonded into place. You can either lay the glass in lengthwise, as on the exterior, or use shorter lengths and glass from gunwale to gunwale, overlapping the edges for each new section of fiberglass. This will leave rib-like ridges on the interior of the hull, but the fiberglass will be easier to install. Don't try to fit the end of the glass into the narrow stem area. Just cut it short of the stem and add a bias-cut strip separately.

Be careful when squeegeeing the interior, because it is very easy to pull the fabric away from the surface in concave areas and not notice it until it's too late.

FITTING THE INTERIOR STRUCTURE

Remove the temporary outwales and sight down the sheer. Use a plane to fair the sheer line if needed. Install the inwale or inner gunwale with clamps and glue, or use screws from the outside. Leave a millimeter or so of hull above the gunwale strip.

Don't let a stiff inwale distort the shape of the hull. The tight bend at the ends can be relieved with many thin saw cuts across the grain of the inwale on the side that doesn't touch the hull. Epoxy glue soaked into the cuts will restore the strength of the inwale.

Make the two watertight bulkheads, the waes (spreaders located below the cross-beam positions), and the ring frame if you're building the Ulua. Cut holes for access panels and drains before installing bulkheads. Clean the hull surface with water to remove any epoxy residue, and sand the surface before bonding parts to it. Fillet the joints between the bulkhead and hull with epoxy filler, and install a single 3" (75mm) bias-cut strip of fiberglass over the fillets. The rows of staple holes on the outside are a good indicator for locating the station lines.

Make plywood saddles for the ends of the waes, and bond them into place with epoxy glue. Make up seat support stringers, in the case of the Ulua, and bond them into place with epoxy glue. If you have a self-bailing cockpit, as in the T2, install the cockpit floor now with thick glue followed by a fillet on top. When you are glassing the T2 cockpit floor, lap the

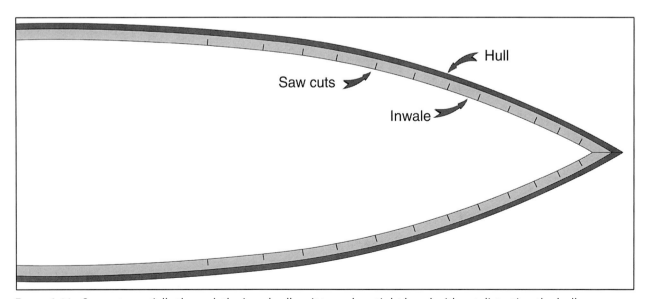

FIGURE 6-11. Saw cuts partially through the inwale allow it to make a tight bend without distorting the hull.

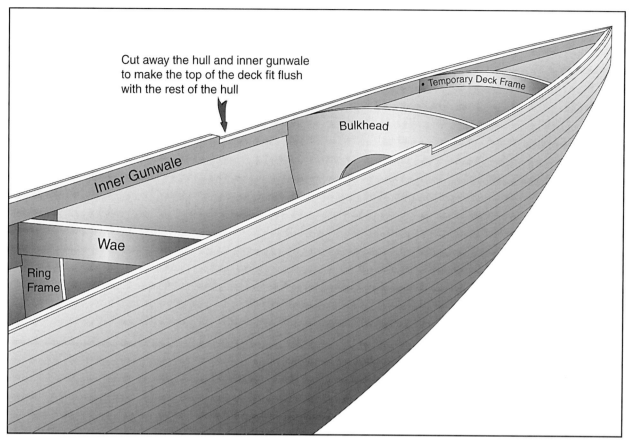

Cut away the hull and inner gunwale to make the top of the deck fit flush with the rest of the hull

Temporary Deck Frame

Bulkhead

Inner Gunwale

Wae

Ring Frame

FIGURE 6-12. A temporary deck beam is necessary if you are strip-planking the foredecks. A narrow strip of hull and inwale is cut away to allow the deck to fit flush with the rest of the hull.

glass up over the fillets and onto the interior hull sides. Cut any access holes in the floor before installing it.

The mast step for the Ulua must be very strongly attached to the hull and ring frame. Unstayed masts exert quite powerful forces at the base. Bevel the underside of the flat base to fit against the hull sides, and glue it in place with epoxy glue, being sure to clean and sand the interior surface of the hull first. Also, have one edge of the flat base glued tightly against the ring frame. For additional security, I'd recommend a layer of fiberglass over the flat base and lapping onto both the hull sides and the ring frame.

FORE AND AFT DECKS

The fore and aft decks can be strip-planked like the hull or made of plywood. Mark the inwale and hull edge where the fore and aft decks begin. You'll need to cut a narrow strip of hull and inwale away to the depth of your deck thickness. Use a jigsaw, and finish up with a coarse sanding board that is long enough to allow you to sand across both inwales.

If you are having a strip deck rather than a plywood one, install some temporary deck beams cut to a circular arc. Put packaging tape over the top of the temporary frames, the inwale, the hull, and the top of the bulkhead. Strip and glass in the normal way, being sure to make the deck slightly larger than the edge of the hull. Remove the deck, put it in a shaped cradle, sand it smooth, and glass the underside.

Before you glue the deck to the hull, be sure to check that the hull is sitting level and untwisted. Lay a level across the hull at the wae locations, and make sure that they are the same. Any twist will be locked in once the deck is glued down. The deck can be clamped into place with masking or other tape wrapped around the hull. When the glue has cured, trim the deck edge very carefully with a plane and sanding block. Use a short scrap of outer gunwale material held up against the hull and deck edge to check your accuracy.

Install the outer gunwale with clamps or screws and glue. The ends are under a lot of tension when

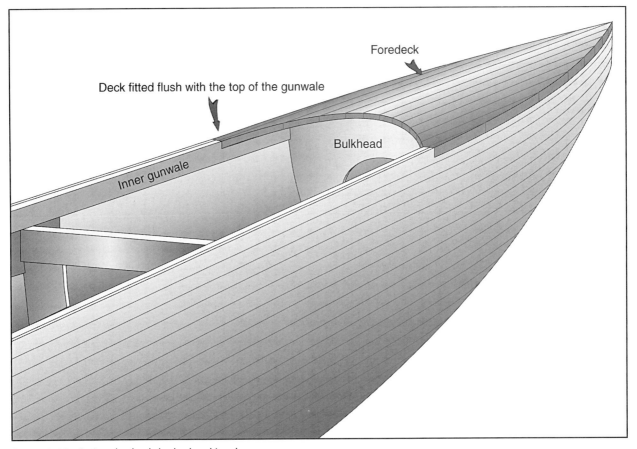

FIGURE 6-13. Strip-planked deck glued in place.

they are bent into place, and sometimes a lot of ingenuity is necessary to hold them in place for the glue to cure. Screws are a good solution, and even if they're removed later, the holes can be drilled out to a standard size and filled with a wooden bung or plug. Do a dry run first to make sure that your method works.

I wouldn't even try to do a miter joint at the ends, since it's very difficult to get the joint perfect. I cut both gunwale pieces off square to the hull's centerline and glue on a short piece of wood across their ends. I then round it all off to a radius when the glue has cured.

MANUS, SPLASH GUARDS, AND DASHBOARDS

The Ulua's manu is a carved projection often seen on the extremity of the bow and stern of traditional canoes. There is a lot of latitude for individual expression here that makes every canoe different. "Manu" translates as "bird" in Polynesian, and in many cases the carving will be of a bird's head or tail. It is probably

safest to do the carving on the workbench and then glue the manu in place to avoid damaging the deck while shaping and sanding. You may also consider the option of extending the length of the laminated stem before planking and using this as part of the manu.

A splash guard should be mounted on the Ulua's foredeck and will do a good job keeping water out of the hull if you bury the bow in a wave. The splash guard shown in Figure 6-14 is made from a flat piece of plywood or solid timber that's been cut to a scimitar shape. Make a cardboard pattern, holding it raked forward about forty-five degrees, until it fits closely to the deck camber. It may take several patterns before you get what you like. Trace the pattern onto the plywood and cut it out. Hold the wooden splash guard against the deck, and bevel the mating edge until it fits closely to the deck. Glue it in place with epoxy, with masking tape holding it in position. A two-piece, "V"-shaped splash guard can also be made in the same way.

With the T2 design, there is no manu, but rather a set of "dashboards" that act as a bulwark and increase the freeboard over the very fine bow

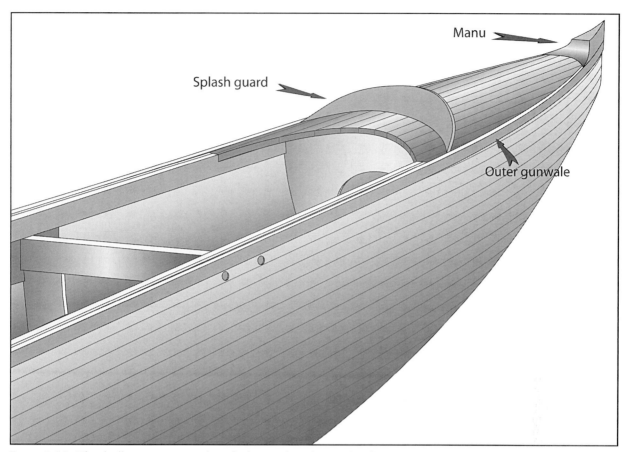

FIGURE 6-14. Ulua hull—outer gunwale, splash guard, and manu in place.

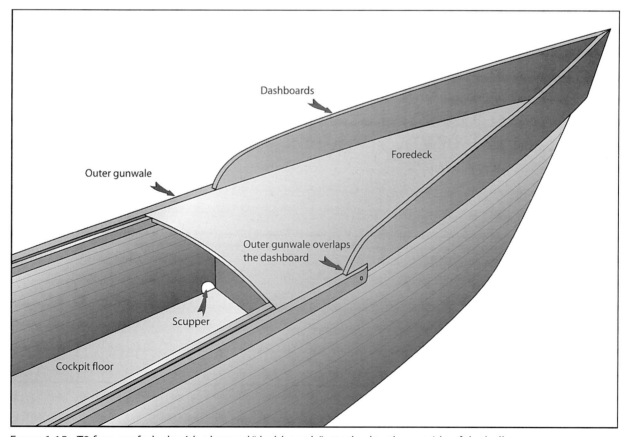

FIGURE 6-15. T2 fore or aft deck with plywood "dashboards" attached to the outside of the hull.

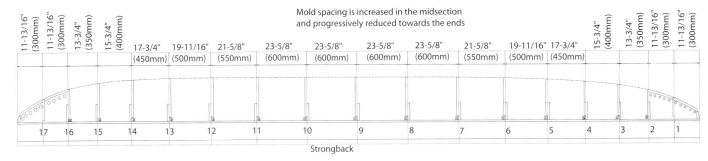

150% Ulua

FIGURE 6-16. To build a 150 percent Ulua hull, the molds are spaced wider apart. The spacing is doubled in the middle of the hull, but the increase in spacing is progressively reduced toward the stems to avoid changing the shape of the bow and stern.

sections. The dashboards are plywood and are screwed and glued to the outside of the hull. The end of the outwale is undercut to overlap the dashboard by 2" (50mm). The "V" shape forms a trap for the end of the yard when you are using a lateen or crab-claw rig.

STRETCHING THE ULUA

You can stretch the Ulua hull to a longer overall length without altering the depth or width. Increasing the hull length by 50 percent (i.e., *scaling* the boat by 150 percent), for example, results in a four-person, 27' (8.1m) hull. At 150 percent, the planking

thickness and fiberglass weight can remain the same. Stretching the hull is easily accomplished by increasing the spacing interval between the molds on a longer strongback. The stem molds with their attached section molds can remain the same. For a 150 percent scaling, double the spacing between the four center intervals and progressively reduce the spacing toward the ends. Refer to Figure 6-16, which shows typical spacing for a 150 percent scale Ulua.

Doubling the interval to 2' (600mm) requires that you use more care when planking in that area. Because there is less support for the planks, use "cheater strips" described earlier to ensure that the plank edges are not offset from each other.

FIGURE 6-17. Marc Termonia's partially planked Ulua hull. (Photo courtesy Marc Termonia)

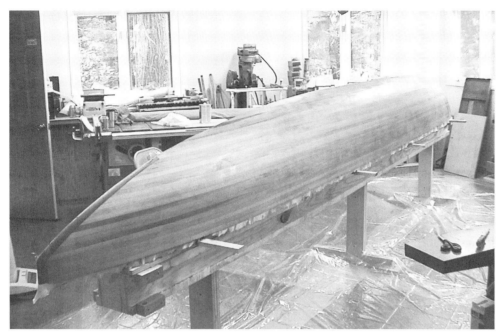

Figure 6-18. Kent Robertson's planked and glassed Ulua. (Photo courtesy Kent Robertson)

Figure 6-19. Clay Ghylin's partially planked T2, with clamps being used rather than staples to hold the planks in place. (Photo courtesy Clay Ghylin)

FIGURE 6-20. Fairing a T2 hull before glassing. (Photo courtesy Clay Ghylin)

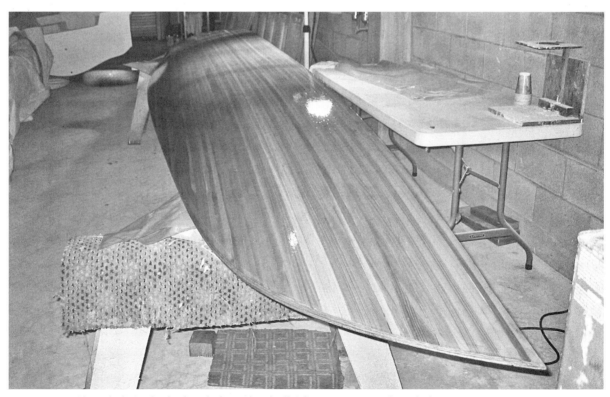

FIGURE 6-21. Clay Ghylin's planked and glassed T2 hull. (Photo courtesy Clay Ghylin)

FIGURE 6-22. T2 bulkheads and cockpit floor support structure in place. (Photo courtesy Clay Ghylin)

Figure 6-23. T2 deck being glued to the hull. (Photo courtesy Clay Ghylin)

FIGURE 6-24. Guy Rinfret's T2 with dashboard, manu, and painted graphics. (Photo courtesy Guy Rinfret)

FIGURE 6-25. Kent Robertson's Ulua with a traditional Hawaiian manu and splash guard. (Photo courtesy Kent Robertson)

CHAPTER 7

Building the Wa'apa Plywood Hull

◈ The Wa'apa consists of a three-piece hull that can be configured as a 24' (7.2m) hull, or, by leaving out the midsection, a 16' (4.8m) hull. It can alternatively be built as a one- or two-piece hull. The layout for scarfing full-length panels is shown in Figure 3-9. The hull sections are joined with four bolts at each bulkhead.

This method of building a flat-bottomed plywood hull is about as simple as can be devised. A hull section consists of two side panels, a bulkhead at one end, a stem timber at the bow, and a bulkhead or frame approximately midway between the two ends.

A pair of identical side panels are attached to the station 2 bulkhead, bent around the station 1 bulkhead, and attached to the stem timber. The side panels already have their gunwales and chines attached before they are bent around the bulkheads. The bottom panel is added last.

Choose the best-quality plywood that you can afford, and you won't regret it. Check the dimensions of the panels before you buy them. Most plywood sheets are 8' (2440mm) × 4' (1220mm), but there are some metric sheets that are only 94½" (2400mm) × 47¼" (1200mm). The smaller sheets won't allow for a 2" (50mm) scarf joint on the side panels if you wish to have a one-piece hull. Your only option with the smaller sheets would be to use a butt splice with fiberglass strips on each side.

Examine Figure 3-9, which shows the cutting layout on the sheet of plywood. There isn't much wasted space, so lay the pieces out carefully. You will need two stems, two of bulkhead number 1 (watertight), four of bulkhead number 2, and one of frame number 3. Number 3 will not be cut from plywood, but rather made up of a timber perimeter with plywood gussets reinforcing the corners. The stems are cut from ¾" (18mm) solid timber.

Draw the side panels on the plywood sheets. Draw the curved lines with a straight timber batten held between thin nails. Be sure to use the stiffest batten possible to make the curves fair and identical. Cut out the side panels with a jigsaw or small circular saw, being careful to stay slightly outside the line. Stack the matching panels together, and finish up

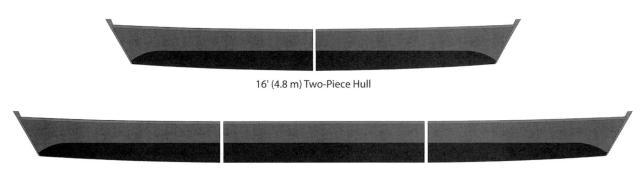

16' (4.8 m) Two-Piece Hull

24' (7.2 m) Three-Piece Hull

FIGURE 7-1. The Wa'apa can be configured as a two-piece, 16' (4.8m) hull, or as a three-piece, 24' (7.2m) hull.

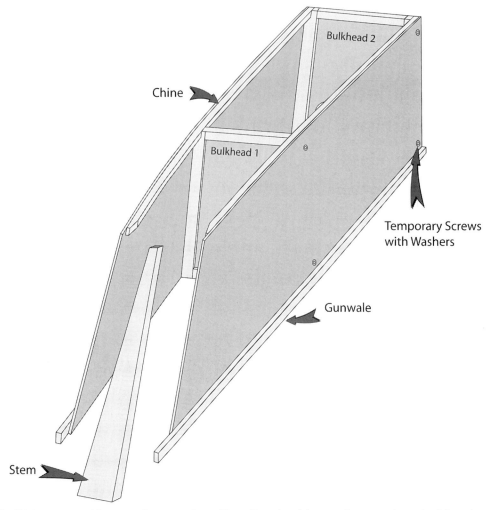

FIGURE 7-2. The Wa'apa assembly procedure consists of bending the side panels around two bulkheads and joining them to the stem.

with a sharp block plane or sanding block to make them identical. *Because this hull is assembled without any building base or strongback, any mismatching of panels or bulkheads could result in a twisted hull.*

Glue and clamp, or nail, the gunwales and chine to the side panels. You have the choice of using many small spring clamps or nailing with ¾" (18mm) bronze ring nails, screws, or narrow-crown staples. The chine and gunwale will be beveled later, after the sides are joined, so attach this piece to the panel with ⅛" (3mm) of it extending past the edge of the panel. This will allow enough material for beveling later.

Glue and fasten the timber perimeters to the bulkheads with nails, screws, or narrow-crown staples. Check the completed similar bulkheads against the plan and each other to be sure that they are as identical as possible. Use a sharp block plane

or stationary sander to trim the edges. Bulkhead numbers 2 and 3 require no beveling. Bulkhead number 1 could take a slight bevel but it's not entirely necessary, as the gap will be covered with an epoxy fillet later. Cut the round holes for the watertight bulkhead access panels to fit a plastic screw-out access panel.

Ideally, all of the bolt holes joining the hull sections will be drilled exactly square to the bulkhead. If you are drilling with a handheld drill, the following procedure will ensure that everything fits in both size configurations.

1. Drill the 5/16" (8mm) bolt holes through the stacked pair of number 2 bulkheads that will be used at the ends of the two end hull sections. This will ensure that the holes will line up for a 16' (4.8m) version hull.

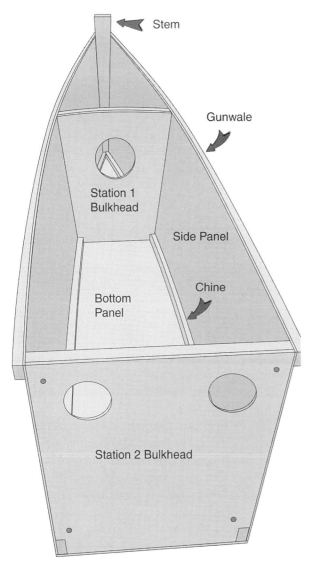

FIGURE 7-3. One 8' (2.4m) section of the Wa'apa hull with the bottom panel in place.

2. Take the number 2 bulkheads that will be used for the center hull section, stack the mating (already drilled) bulkhead over it, and drill through the existing holes into them. That will ensure that the center section holes will line up with the end sections for a 24' (7.2m) hull.
3. Mark the bulkheads so that the correct ones will be bolted together later.
4. Cut the stems from solid timber or ¾" (18mm) plywood if you wish. Bevel the edges at ten degrees.

On the interior of the side panels, draw the station 1 line where the watertight bulkhead is located. Trim the bow end of the chines to fit each other in a miter joint. Perfect miter joints are difficult, but epoxy putty can fill the gap.

With the chine and gunwale bonded to the side panels, you can now assemble one of the hull end sections. Do a dry run first, without any glue in the joints. Screw the side panels to the number 2 bulkhead with two temporary screws through flat washers. Install more temporary screws at the top and bottom of the number 1 bulkhead, and bend the sides together toward the stem. This is the most difficult procedure of the whole project, and it is important that you work out exactly how you'll proceed before you apply any glue. Long, sliding bar clamps can be useful at the bulkhead end. Holding the stem end together is very tricky, but temporary screws through flat washers seem to work the best. A helper is also useful at this stage.

After you determine how you'll hold the sides and bulkheads together, take them apart and apply

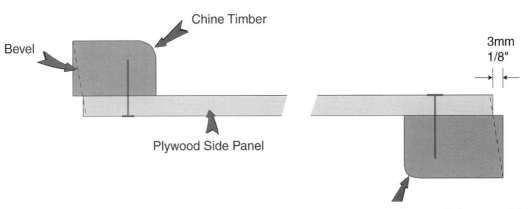

FIGURE 7-4. Chines and gunwales are fastened to the side panels while they're still flat on a table.

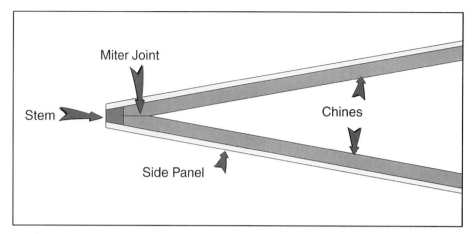

FIGURE 7-5. A miter joint is used where the chines meet the base of the stem.

thickened epoxy to the joints. Reassemble them, and take diagonal measurements as shown in the drawing. Use a bevel gauge or any angle-measuring device to match the panel-to-bulkhead angles. Put additional nails into the bulkheads and stem between the temporary screws. Tack on some diagonal sticks to help hold the hull shape until the glue hardens.

After the glue is cured, install a thickened epoxy fillet around the watertight bulkhead on both the forward and aft sides. Also fill any gaps at the stem and bulkhead number 2.

With the hull upside down, bevel the chine with a sharp plane, constantly checking the angle with a straightedge from chine to chine. Make some marks on the outside of the side panels at the watertight bulkhead location so that fasteners can be put through the bottom panel into the bulkhead. Lay the ¼" (6mm) plywood sheet on the chines, and trace around the sides for cutting. Cut the bottom

panel slightly oversized, and glue and nail it to the chines, bulkhead 1, and bulkhead 2. After the glue has cured, trim the edges flush with the sides. Finish with a long, coarse sanding board to ensure that the edge is a fair curve, and round over the edge to a ¼" (6mm) radius.

Use a couple of temporary screws to laminate an extra ¾" (18mm) of soft timber on the outside of the stem, covering the edges of the side panels. After the glue has cured, remove the screws and plane this "false stem" down to a rounded shape. Taper the ends of the gunwales to blend into the stem. If you intend to hang a kick-up rudder on the aft stem, you can omit the extra timber and leave it flat for easier installation of rudder fittings.

Before fitting the fore or stern deck, glue in a small beveled ledge or cleat for the deck to fasten to on the inside face of the stem. The deck panels are easier to make if you make a cardboard pattern first. Plane the bevel on the top of the gunwale to fit

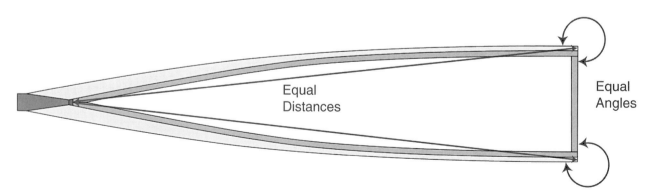

FIGURE 7-6. Measure equal angles and equal distances to ensure that the hull is properly aligned before the glue cures.

tightly to the deck panel. Note that the deck will take the curve of the top of bulkhead number 1 at its aft end, and it will flatten out as it gets closer to the stem. Cut the panel slightly oversized, and trim the edge after it's been glued and nailed down. If you're opting for the shunting crab-claw rig, install a ½" (12mm) thick plywood pad under the deck panel right up close to the stem. This will provide a fastening point for the end of a guide rail if you choose to use one.

When the two end hull sections have been completed, install the bolts in the predrilled holes to join the two sections. Use a plane or long sanding board to correct any mismatch between the sections. Some filling with epoxy fairing putty may be needed. Use a batten to check for fairness.

The seats are cut from ¼" (6mm) plywood with a timber stiffener under the unsupported edge. Plywood saddles shown on the drawing are glued to the inside hull surface to support the ends of the stiffeners. Plane the bevel on the top of the gunwales, and check with a straightedge spanning across the hull.

Glue and nail the seats to the top of the gunwale and bulkheads as shown in Figures 3-4, 3-5, 3-6, 3-7, and 3-8. One or more seats will have a thick, plywood doubler glued on the underside where the mast passes through the seat. Bevel all of the remaining gunwales the same, and glue a ¼" (6mm) strip of timber or scrap plywood to the top surface of the gunwale between the seats and foredeck, making it flush with the seats and deck. Round all of the edges, and finish with a long sanding board.

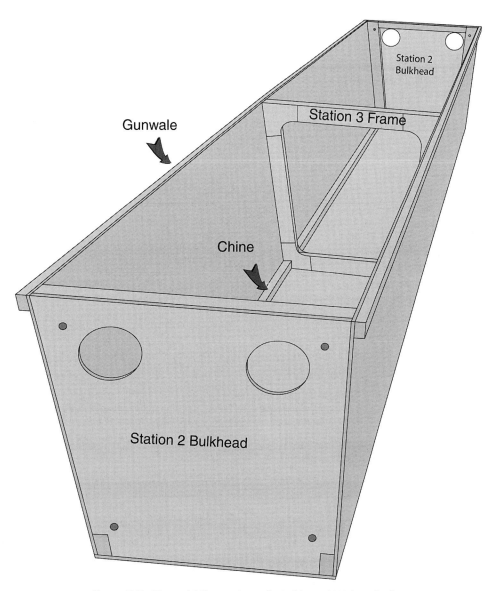

FIGURE 7-7. The middle section of a 24' (7.2m) Wa'apa hull.

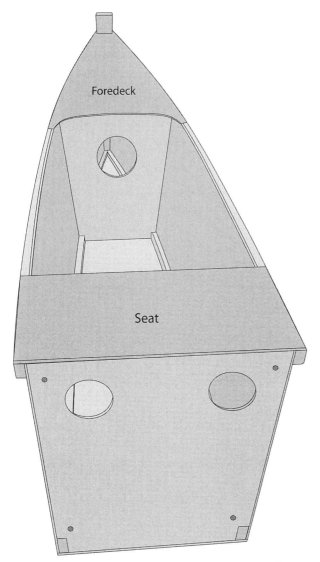

FIGURE 7-8. Forward hull section with foredeck and seat installed.

HULL MIDDLE SECTION

The central hull section is almost a rectangle, but not quite. Straight edges never look right on a hull, so there is a slight curve along the gunwale and the chine.

Assemble the center hull section by attaching the side panels to bulkheads number 2 at each end and frame number 3 in the middle. Again, check the diagonal measurements and panel-to-bulkhead angles. If you have space, it is possible to assemble the center section with the number 2 bulkheads clamped to the completed end hull sections. Put a sheet of thin plastic between the bulkheads to prevent gluing it all together. Install the bolts to hold the bulkheads together during assembly. This method has

FIGURE 7-9. Bulkheads, side panels, and stem ready for assembly.

the advantage of giving your eye an opportunity to check the overall fairness and alignment of the hull sections.

A string stretched from stem to stem is a good reference if you have the hull right-side up. The middle hull section can also be assembled upside down.

FIGURE 7-10. Side panels are fastened to the bulkheads and bent together at the stem.

Glue and nail the side panels to the bulkheads and center frame. Before cutting out the bottom panel, be sure that the diagonal measurements are equal, and that the amount of curvature along the gunwale and chine is the same on both sides. Install the bottom panel and round the edges. Install the seats and finish the gunwales, as was done for the end sections.

If you are going to sheath the bottom with fiberglass, you must also round over the edge where the hull sections meet, because fiberglass cloth will not go over a sharp edge. After the glassing is finished, form a sharp edge with epoxy putty, and sand it fair with the adjoining hull section.

FIGURE 7-12. An outer stem is glued in place and shaped round and fair with the hull panels.

FIGURE 7-11. Hull section with bottom panel installed.

FIGURE 7-13. Three hull sections bolted together, complete with foredecks and seats.

CHAPTER 8

Amas

◆ The ama is what differentiates the outrigger canoe from all other types of watercraft. It is required to perform as flotation and ballast at the same time. Traditionally, amas are carved from the lightest wood available. Breadfruit, hau, and wiliwili wood are commonly used in Oceania. In other areas, cedar, poplar, balsa, paulownia, or any lightweight wood would work. Modern recreational canoes use either a hollow, female-molded fiberglass ama made of two halves or a solid, foam core shape with a fiberglass skin. Plywood, strip planks, or PVC pipe have all been successfully used to build amas.

A shunting proa, which has to sail with either end forward, will of course also require a two-way ama. Weight is less of a detriment to a shunting ama, since it will almost always be used as ballast. Buoyancy is valuable, however, if the canoe is caught aback and the ama is forced under water. A shunting ama should have enough buoyancy to withstand going aback, especially if you sail in cold water.

A tacking outrigger is better served with an ama that has its buoyancy concentrated more forward, to reduce the chance of a diagonal capsize. A buoyant ama out to leeward must support the sail forces both sideways and forward. Therefore, the best place to concentrate the ama's buoyancy is as far to leeward and forward as is practical. In some cases, the bows of the main hull and ama will be extended the same distance forward from the iako. In Indonesian double outriggers, bamboo amas sometimes extend beyond the bow of the main hull. Ama buoyancy aft of the aft iako is less important, and the ama is usually cut short at that point. If the ama has a transom, it should normally ride above the water's surface in order to reduce drag.

Builders sometimes ask about *toe in* or *toe out*, and its effect on handling and performance. Hawaiian paddling outriggers sometimes align their amas with the bow closer to the big hull than the stern. I've experimented with this on the Ulua but haven't noticed any effect from it. Indonesian double outriggers toe their ama bows outward and claim that it is faster.

Amas can also be tuned by installing wooden shims under the iakos where they cross the gunwale. If you mostly sail alone and sit aft with no weight forward, the stern of the ama may be dragging up more of a wake than is desirable. By shimming under the starboard (right) forward lashing, the ama's bow will be pushed down, lifting the stern of the ama and reducing its drag-inducing wake. Shimming under the port (left) aft lashing will have the same effect.

Traditionally, in places such as Tahiti, where tacking outriggers are the most common type, the forward iako is extended outward on the non-ama side to allow a crew member to hike out and prevent the solid-timber ama from sinking when it is to leeward. On larger outriggers and some catamarans, the forward iako was sometimes doubled up with an identical beam a short distance away and parallel to it to support a narrow deck. The mast was also stayed to the end of the iako on the non-ama side and gave the hiking crew something to hang on to.

With modern materials, it is now possible to build an ama that is buoyant enough to make hiking out unnecessary, although hiking out is still useful for speed enhancement to un-weight the ama and reduce its drag.

In Hawaii, amas with a pronounced "banana" shape are seen. Due to the extremely rough conditions encountered there, a highly rockered shape evolved that gives better stability to a canoe as it passes through steep waves. And to make it really confusing, traditional, nearly straight Samoan amas have their bows turned down slightly. The only logic I can see for this is that it ensures that the ama will be "wave piercing." Wave-piercing shapes can have lower drag because of a reduction in pitching over the surface of waves.

FOAM AND FIBERGLASS AMAS

Other than an ama made from a solid log, the foam and fiberglass ama is, in my opinion, the easiest to build. I recommend using the method employed to build tens of thousands of surfboards since the 1960s.

You may wonder why a lightweight construction method is used to build an ama that is partially used for ballast. My philosophy is that, if you build it light, you can always add weight in the form of lead dive weights, water ballast, or gear stowed out on the outrigger platform. If you build it heavy, you have no options. In very light winds or when paddling, you don't want to be moving any unnecessary weight.

You have the choice of using polyurethane foam or polystyrene foam. There are two main types of polystyrene foam available. The most common type seen is used in packing materials and cheap ice chests. When this polystyrene foam is crushed, you will see individual beads. I don't recommend that you use this type, as it is open celled and water can migrate through it if the outer fiberglass skin is punctured.

The other type of polystyrene foam is closed-celled, extruded foam that will not absorb water. The one I'm experienced with is the light, blue-colored Styrofoam made by Dow. It comes in several thicknesses, and you may have to glue layers together to reach the required thickness. I've glued it with either polyurethane glue or epoxy resin mixed with lightweight quartz microspheres. White or yellow carpenter's glue doesn't seem to cure between layers of polystyrene foam.

Polystyrene foam *must* be glassed with epoxy resin. Polyester or vinylester resin will dissolve the foam on contact.

Another option is the more expensive polyurethane foam. The brown foam produced when mixing two liquids together, or purchased in sheets, is quite fragile and requires extra layers of fiberglass to be durable enough. The white polyurethane foam used for surfboard blanks is exquisite to shape. The bare foam can be decorated with water-based paint and glassed over with the clear polyester surfboard resin. The advantage of using polyurethane is that it can be glassed with either the less expensive polyester or vinylester, although epoxy resin will also work. Note that anything you glass with epoxy resin must be protected from the sun by either paint or a minimum of five coats of spar varnish.

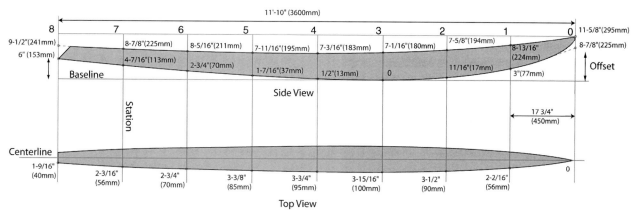

Ulua Ama

FIGURE 8-1. A plywood *shear web* determines the profile shape of a foam-cored ama. Draw a horizontal baseline, measure and mark station locations, and measure vertical offsets at each station. Tack a batten along the marks and draw a fair curve. The plywood shear web is then cut out with a jigsaw, and slabs of foam are glued to both sides. Use the offsets in the top view to make a half pattern that can be traced onto the top of the foam blank.

103

Begin building the foam and fiberglass ama by cutting out a ³/₁₆" (4mm) plywood shear web drawn to the side-view profile of your ama design. You can use thicker ply if you wish, but the ama will be heavier. Because the ama will most likely be longer than the plywood sheet, butt the panels together, and laminate a patch of fiberglass cloth over the joint on each side. Use the plywood shear web as a pattern to draw shapes on the foam. In most cases, you will need at least 3" (75mm) of foam glued to both sides of the web. Stack the layers together with wet glue, and weigh them down until the glue sets.

Make a cardboard half pattern of the topview shape shown in Figure 8-1, and draw around it onto the foam with a marking pen.

Roughly shape the blank with a handsaw, being careful to cut well outside the line. A Japanese pull saw is particularly good at this (and everything else).

The remainder of the shaping can be done with several different tools. The pros use an electric hand planer, and it works very well. A hot wire cutter will do a very clean job of rough shaping without making any dust. You can also use a random orbital sander with 36- to 40-grit paper, but keep it moving to prevent gouges. Draw long, straight or curved lines or chines with the marking pen for guidance. A long sanding board like the ones used in automotive shops will also do the job. The whole job can be done with the hand sanding board and will ensure professional results, because you are more likely to get an unfair shape with a power sander. Shape everything in a multichine shape first, and round over the edges last. This helps to ensure a fair shape, because you can sight down the chines and sand them into a fair curve.

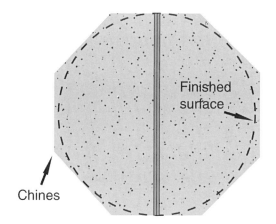

FIGURE 8-3. The foam blank is roughly shaped with a handsaw or electric planer and is finished to its rounded shape with a long sanding board.

Finish sanding with 80-grit paper wrapped around a block or piece of foam. You will find it difficult to avoid gouging the soft foam when shaping. Don't worry about it, since microsphere filler was invented for this problem.

When you're satisfied with the shape, lay the ama on its side in foam cradles, and cut the 10-ounce (330-gram) fiberglass cloth to glass one side at a time. If you only have 6-ounce (200-gram) fiberglass cloth, use two layers of it applied wet on wet. Cut the fabric to overlap the ply web by at least ½" (12mm). Don't try to get it to form over the ends,

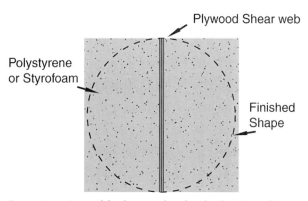

FIGURE 8-2. Foam blocks are glued to both sides of the shear web.

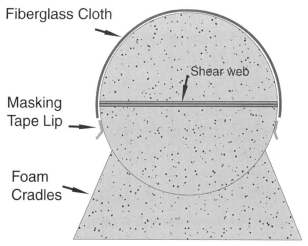

FIGURE 8-4. Fiberglass cloth and epoxy resin are applied to the first side, with a small overlap of the shear web.

because the fabric is too stiff for that. Stop ½" (12mm) short of the tip. Apply a masking-tape drip lip a little beyond the edge of the fabric to prevent resin from running down over the foam. Resin drips are difficult to remove from foam without gouging the surface.

If you have gouges to fill, fold or roll up the fabric, mix a stiff batch of resin and microspheres, and fill the gouges with a putty knife. Don't overfill, because you're not waiting for it to harden. Spread the fabric back onto the foam and begin wetting it with the resin. Use either a brush or a foam roller, followed by a plastic spreader or squeegee to remove all excess resin.

Allow the first side to cure, roll it over in the cradles, and carefully block-sand the edge of the cured fiberglass to allow the next piece to overlap without air bubbles. If you have some really ugly spots, you can fill them with the stiff microsphere mixture before you glass the second side. Repeat the steps from the first side, again using the masking tape to stop the runs. After the second side has cured, apply additional coats of resin with a brush to one side at a time. Thin coats are best because the resin runs easily.

If you intend to mount a leeboard on the ama, double up the layer of fiberglass between the iako attachment points to address the extra load.

To avoid the difficulty of wrapping glass around the sharp ends, cut about ½" (12mm) of the ama off with a hacksaw. Dig out some of the foam and mix a batch of stiff epoxy filler. Use the harder microfiber additives to make a strong mixture. Fill the end and build it out to the original length. Shape it down fair with the ama when it hardens. This will give you a tougher end to deal with impact damage.

A direct connection between the ama and cross beam (iako) usually requires a curved beam to get the ama low enough. A *pylon* for direct attachment is used on the Ulua design. Begin with a 1⅜" (40mm) thick piece of wood for the center of the raised pylon. Cut the wood to the shape shown in Figure 8-5. Glue it to the top of the ama with epoxy, and fit foam fairings in front of and behind the center wooden piece. An easy way to get the bottom of the foam fairings to fit perfectly is to tape some coarse sandpaper to the top of the ama and move the foam back and forth over it until it matches the surface of the ama. Glue the fairings in place, and after curing, shape them with coarse sandpaper wrapped around a dowel or tube. Cover the entire pylon with two layers of fiberglass cloth large enough to spread out at least 2" (50mm) onto the ama. The use of many small, round patches of fiberglass cloth will greatly simplify getting around the angular shape. After curing, fill and fair with epoxy fairing compound.

The dowel passing through the iako protrudes about ½" (12mm) below its bottom surface, and it fits into a loose hole drilled in the top of the pylon.

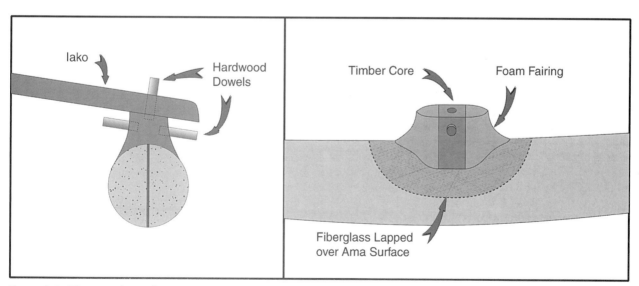

FIGURE 8-5. The wooden pylon core is glued to the fiberglassed surface, and foam fairings are added. Fiberglass is lapped over the pylon and down onto the finished ama surface and faired in with epoxy fairing compound. Hardwood dowels are glued into drilled holes after glassing is completed.

The joint is lashed together with strips cut from a tire inner tube. It's quick and easy to rig and allows the very important small degree of flexibility that prevents stress concentrations and structural failure. The rubber lashings loop around the transverse dowels glued into the pylons.

Indirect connections are most common throughout the Pacific region. They have the advantages of keeping the ends of the cross beams high and out of the waves, and the beams don't have to be built curved. They range from the incredibly complex to the simple forked stick, as shown later in this chapter.

Attaching struts to the ama is as simple as cutting a loose-fitting hole, pouring in some microsphere mixture, and inserting the strut. To ensure that everything will fit, have your cross beams attached to the main hull and lashed to the struts before bonding the struts in place. Install all of the struts at the same time, including any diagonal members. After curing, form a small epoxy fillet around the strut where it passes through the fiberglass skin.

When applying a painted finish to the ama, be aware that high temperatures, caused by sun exposure, can soften the epoxy enough to cause blisters between the foam and the glass skin. White is ideal, but a lighter shade of any color will be better than a heat-absorbing dark color. If you do get some blisters, drill two small holes in each one and inject epoxy resin with a disposable plastic hypodermic syringe. Cover the blister with plastic sheeting, and weigh it down until it has cured.

BUILDING A PLYWOOD AMA

The two-piece ama construction described here applies to the ama shown on the Wa'apa drawings. It is a simple, square, cross-section box, oriented so

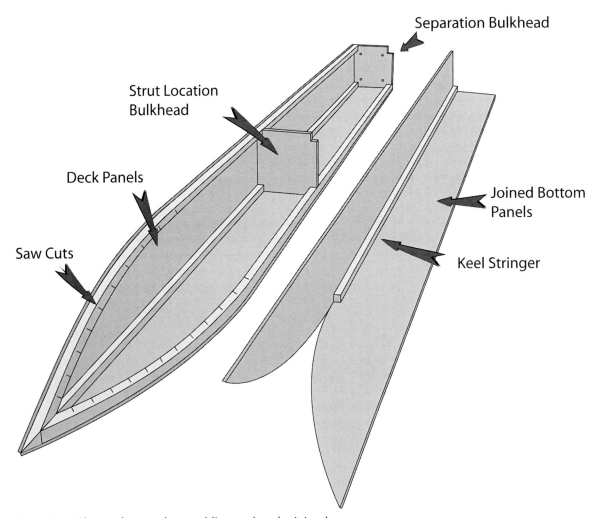

Figure 8-6. Plywood ama subassemblies ready to be joined.

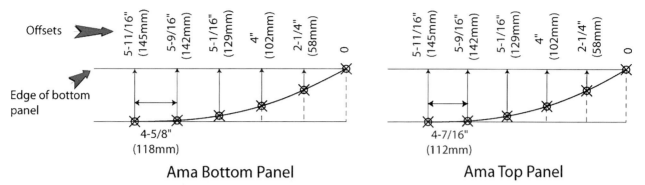

Ama Bottom Panel   **Ama Top Panel**

FIGURE 8-7. The curved ends of the ama deck and bottom panels can be laid out by measuring offsets from the straight edge of the panel. Refer to Figure 3-9. Note that the bottom panel is slightly longer than the deck panel because it has to bend along the curve of the bow.

that it effectively has a "V" bottom and a "V" deck. It is the simplest possible plywood shape, with the pointed ends not even requiring any bevels. All joints are ninety degrees. The short, curved section under the forefoot is joined by the "stitch-and-tape" method, where the plywood edges are pulled together with wire or monofilament nylon, edge-glued with thickened epoxy, and covered with a strip of fiberglass tape on the outside only.

A 16' (4.8m), two-piece ama can be built from a single sheet of ³⁄₁₆" (4mm) or ¼" (6mm) plywood. Use a straight board as a cutting guide to cut eight 5¾" (145mm) wide panels from the sheet of plywood. You can use either a circular saw, a jigsaw, or a table saw if you have plenty of space. One end of each panel is cut to a curve. The offsets for drawing the curve are shown in Figure 8-7. Note that the offsets for the deck and bottom panels are the same, but the spacing between the offsets is greater for the bottom panels. The two bottom panels are 1¼" (30mm) longer than the two deck panels.

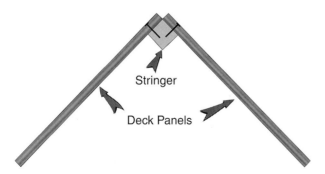

FIGURE 8-8. Plywood ama deck panels joined with a stringer.

If you decide to have a one-piece ama, you'll have to scarf or butt-splice the plywood panels to the full length. The heavy separation bulkheads can be replaced with a single lighter one.

Join the two pairs of deck panels with the timber stringer along the top ridge, as shown in Figures 8-6 and 8-8. Use glue with small nails. Install the two chine stringers along the bottom edge of the deck panels. Make saw cuts halfway through the chine stringers every ¾" (20mm) along the area that follows the curved ends of the deck panels to enable them to bend to the tight curve.

Install the ½" (12mm) bulkheads at the strut locations with epoxy glue and small fillets, since these will be watertight bulkheads. With a bulkhead at the strut locations and the paired bulkheads at the separation joint, the ama has four separate, sealed compartments, with access panels into the middle two compartments.

Install the ¾" (18mm) plywood bulkheads at the separation joint. Stack the two bulkheads together before installation, and drill the bolt holes.

If you are using an ama-mounted shunting leeboard, install two ½" (12mm) plywood backing blocks under the inboard side of the deck up against the separation bulkhead to take the mounting bolts.

Cut a ½" (12mm) wide notch into the end of the hardwood strut so that it can straddle the strut bulkhead. Cut a rectangular hole in the deck panels to allow it to be epoxied and filleted to the bulkhead.

Join the two pairs of bottom panels with the keel stringer. The keel stringer is shorter than the ones used on the deck panels and stops where the curved portion of the panels begins.

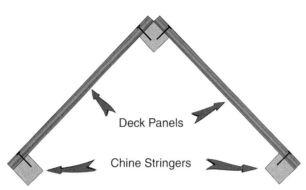

FIGURE 8-9. Chine stringers are installed on the edges of the deck panels.

Fit the assembled bottom panels to the assembled deck panels. Check the fit carefully, planing or sanding off any high spots.

Drill matching pairs of small stitching holes along the curved edges of the bottom panels. Nail and glue the bottom-panel assembly to the deck-panel chines. Bend the curved ends of the deck panels down while pulling the open edges of the bottom panels together with copper wire or monofilament nylon. Fill the curved, stitched joint with thickened epoxy.

Use a plane or long, coarse, sanding board to round the edges. It is not necessary to fiberglass the entire ama, but it is structurally necessary to at least put a strip of fiberglass cloth along the outside of the stitched joint. Cutting the strips on the bias at a forty-five-degree angle will put twice as many fibers across the joint. The rest of the keel joint should also

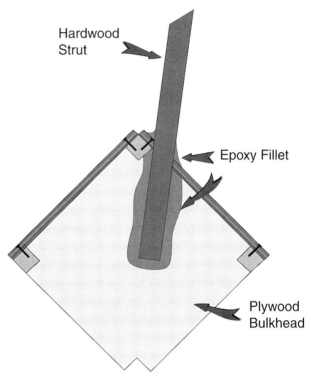

FIGURE 8-11. The strut has a slot cut into its end to straddle the bulkhead, and it is bonded to it with epoxy fillets.

be covered with a fiberglass strip to increase abrasion resistance.

Cut holes near the separation joint for the plastic screw-out access panels. Locate them on the outboard side (away from the main hull) of the ama deck panel if you will be mounting a leeboard on the inboard side. The access panels allow access to the bolts and inspection for leakage. A worthwhile option with any hollow ama is to fill some of the interior with empty soft-drink bottles or blocks of foam for emergency flotation.

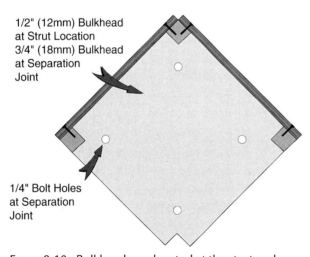

FIGURE 8-10. Bulkheads are located at the strut and separation joint. The separation bulkheads have their bolt holes drilled before assembly.

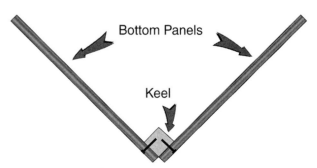

FIGURE 8-12. The bottom-panel subassembly is joined with a keel stringer.

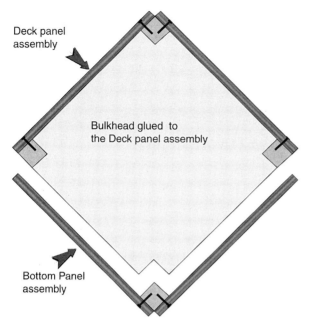

FIGURE 8-13. Bottom-panel assembly ready to attach to the deck assembly.

STRIP-PLANKED AMAS

While strip-planking an open hull is relatively simple, building a closed ama is more difficult. It can be done in one of three ways.

1. Strip planked over a mold with the molds left inside. No fiberglass is used on the interior. The interior molds make this the heaviest option.
2. Strip planked over a mold, one-half shell at a time, where the mold is discarded but the inside surface of the half shells is fiberglassed.
3. Strip planked into a female half-shell mold.

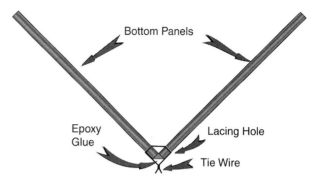

FIGURE 8-14. The keel joint at the curved end sections doesn't have a stringer, but is bonded with thick epoxy glue and overlaid with strips of fiberglass cloth and epoxy resin.

The first option is the easiest approach, where you set up a series of thin, plywood mold sections spaced every 12" (300mm) to 16" (400mm) and connected together by a ½" × ½" (12mm × 12mm) stringer running along the top spine of the deck and along the keel. The end shape is defined by plywood stems.

You'll have to precoat the strips on their inside with epoxy resin, because you won't be able to access or fiberglass this surface later.

Clamp or screw the frame to a solid base to keep it straight for the first few planks. Begin with a strip at the midpoint of each side so that, with the stringers on the top and bottom, the frame will now remain rigid. Continue planking in both directions away from the first plank by applying glue to each previous plank, and stapling the next plank tightly against it. Alternate sides to avoid distorting the frame. Sand and fair the outside, and sheath it with fiberglass cloth.

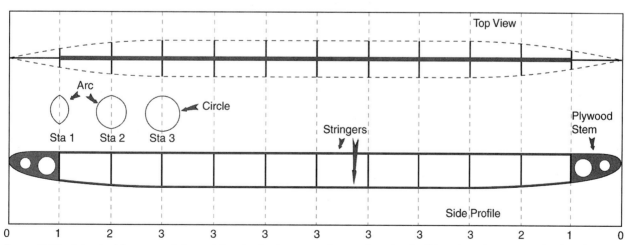

FIGURE 8-15. A typical framework for a strip-planked ama made up of station bulkheads, stringers notched in the top and bottom, and plywood stem molds at the ends.

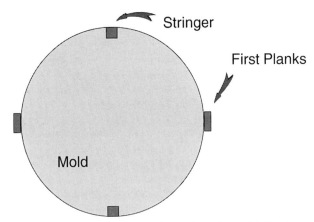

FIGURE 8-16. Cross section of a male strip mold. The first pair of planks act to stabilize the shape of the mold.

The second option begins with the same mold components, but you must tape the edges of all the surfaces with plastic packaging tape before you begin planking. Plank one complete side, sand it, fiberglass it, and remove it to a fitted cradle. Fiberglass the inside of the half shell and set it aside. Plank and glass the other side, and remove it for interior glassing. Fit and glue the two halves together, and laminate a narrow strip of fiberglass over the joint along the deck and keel.

The third option uses a female strip mold. This mold seems to take the most work to construct, but if the ama design is cigar-shaped symmetrically end to end and top to bottom, you can get away with a half mold to do both half shells. Both ends of the mold must be accurately identical to ensure that the two halves fit when they are glued together.

Tape the mold surfaces as usual, and staple the strips in place, edge-gluing them to adjacent planks, and trimming the ends where they extend beyond

the mold edges. Sand the interior surface, sheath the interior with fiberglass, and remove the half shell to a shaped cradle to avoid distortion. Strip and glass the second half shell, glue the two halves together bound with masking tape, and glass the entire exterior after the joint has cured.

AMA CONNECTIONS

Connecting the ama to the iako or cross beam can be approached in several ways. Throughout the Pacific and Indian oceans, you can literally see dozens of methods. Modern western-designed multihulls almost invariably use a *direct* connection. With this method, the beam, or iako, is generally curved down toward the ama and bolted or molded directly to it. The Hawaiians and Indonesians also use this method.

Because of the very rough nature of surf landings in Hawaii, a robust direct connection is favored, but with lashings made of rubber inner-tube strips for that important stress relief.

In most of the Pacific region, indirect connections are still favored in almost all other locations. Probably the most simple is the forked stick, as is used in Kiribati.

Indirect connections can use a straight beam or iako rather than a curved, laminated one. The indirect connection keeps the end of the iako higher above the surface of the water for reduced drag in waves.

Another widespread technique uses a series of straight sticks. This can vary from three to six straight struts per connection. Tahitian tacking canoes use a mixed system with a four-stick connection on the stiffer forward beam, and a direct connection on the light and flexible aft beam.

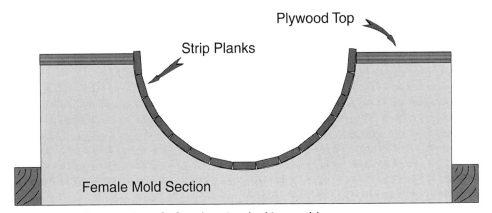

FIGURE 8-17. Cross section of a female strip-planking mold.

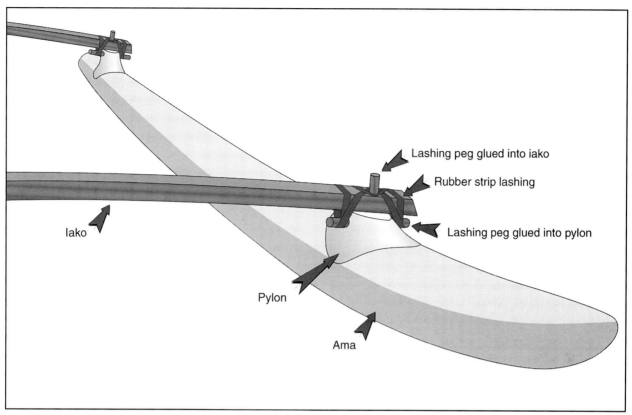

FIGURE 8-18. A typical Hawaiian-style connection, as used on the Ulua.

A type of ama connection that has been seen in the Marquesas Islands and in the Indian Ocean uses a flat sawn board. This is the original "quick-connect" system that requires less time than most other methods to put together and take apart. It also allows the ama to pitch without any undue stress on the joints. When the lashing line is tightened, the end of the beam jams itself securely into the loose-fitting hole. I use this method on the Wa'apa design. The hollow at the top is used to hold fishing poles or spears and is optional.

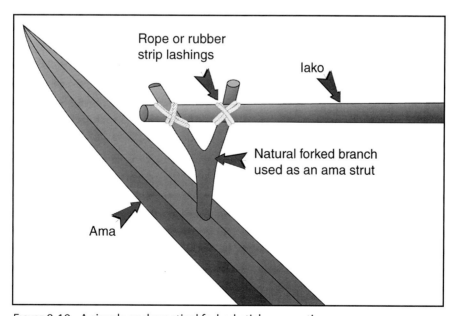

FIGURE 8-19. A simple and practical forked-stick connection.

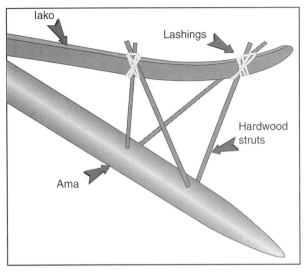

FIGURE 8-20. A Tahitian-style connection at the forward cross beam.

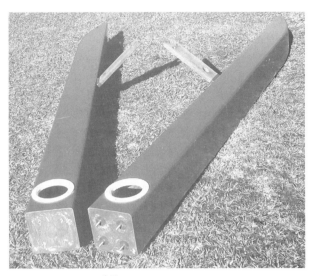

FIGURE 8-23. Four ¼" (6mm) bolts connect the two-piece plywood ama.

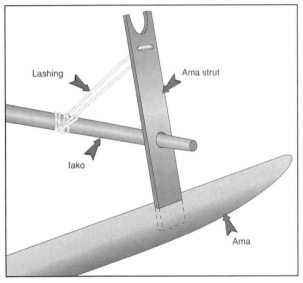

FIGURE 8-21. A Marquesan "quick-connect" strut. A modified version is used on the Wa'apa.

FIGURE 8-24. Tarawa's original foam-filled ama has an inverted "V" plywood deck.

FIGURE 8-22. Foam blocks being glued to a plywood shear web. (Photo courtesy Marc Termonia)

FIGURE 8-25. The Wa'apa connection method allows limited movement of the ama in the pitch axis.

CHAPTER 9

Cross Beams and Hull Connections

In a small canoe, the most practical beam or *iako* to connect the ama to the hull is a simple, solid laminate. Larger canoes such as the Wa'apa can use hollow beams to save weight. The iakos used with a tacking rig must be strong enough to resist the bending force generated when the ama is to leeward and is being forced down in the water, whereas iakos used with a shunting rig can be lighter because they are normally only on the windward side.

A configuration sometimes used in modern Hawaiian sailing canoes is called the *broken wing*. A second *safety* ama is mounted opposite the main ama and reduces the possibility of capsize in severe conditions. A safety ama is also a useful addition to a shunting proa.

Another option is the double-outrigger or trimaran configuration. While this is a very attractive option to beginning sailors, be aware that the additional weight of an extra ama and increased beam length will cut into the payload. It is desirable with a double outrigger to have both amas mounted higher so that when the craft is fully loaded at rest, only one ama is touching the water. This will make tacking quicker and will also reduce overall drag.

Quite often in traditional outriggers, the gunwale, or side of the hull, is raised between the iakos so that the beams can be mounted higher to clear the waves. Modern Hawaiian racers add blocking under the iako to raise their height above the water. The double-outrigger option shown in Figure 3-8 incorporates a raised gunwale on the middle section for this purpose.

A straight or slightly curved hollow box beam can also be used with larger canoes. An 18' (5.4m)

canoe's beams are almost too small to make this practical, but a straight hollow beam is shown as an option with the Wa'apa.

BUILDING A SOLID LAMINATED IAKO

Draw the shape of the curved beam on a flat table or sheet of plywood, using the offsets shown on the plan. Screw down a 1½" × 1½" × 3" (40mm × 40mm × 75mm) block of wood at each offset location.

Choose the timber carefully, using only pieces with straight grain and very small, tight knots. Use the best pieces on the top and bottom lamination, or use a harder, stronger timber for the top and bottom, with softer timber in the middle, because most of the stress occurs in the two outer layers. The strips can be cut with a table saw and laminated as they are, or you can run them through a thickness planer if the saw cuts are too rough. In any case, epoxy glue will fill most gaps and result in a strong beam.

Put a double layer of waxed paper along the form blocks. Apply adhesive to the strips and bundle them together along the blocks. Start adding clamps from the straight end, and keep going until the curved end is pulled down. Put additional clamps between the blocks if the glue isn't squeezing out in some locations. Clean up the excess glue with a putty knife.

After removing the iako from the form, grind off the excess glue. The easiest way to finish the iako is with a thickness planer, but if you don't have one, you could run the iako through a table saw or just sand it smooth. Round the edges with a router or a plane and sanding board.

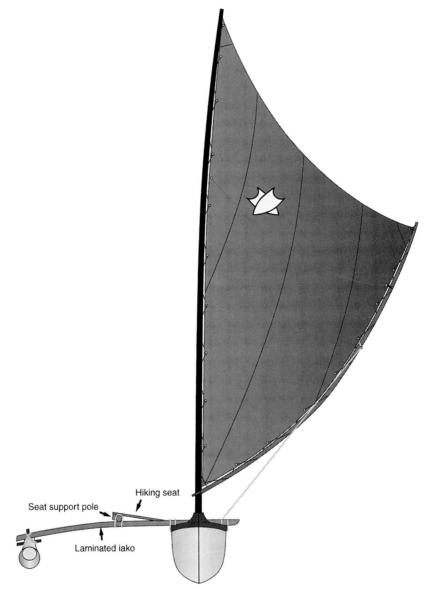

FIGURE 9-1. A solid laminated iako is used on the Ulua.

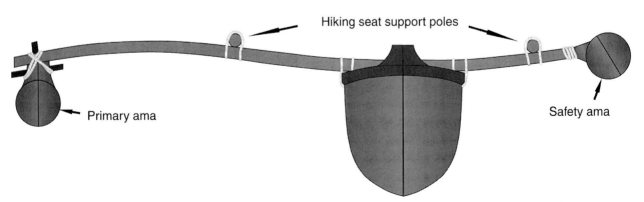

FIGURE 9-2. The broken-wing configuration uses a "safety ama" opposite the main ama. It doesn't touch the water unless capsize is imminent.

Figure 9-3. A double outrigger or trimaran.

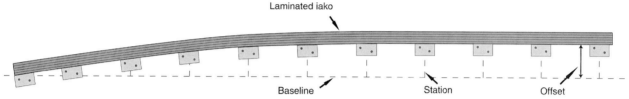

FIGURE 9-4. A solid laminated iako is constructed by gluing and clamping thin layers of timber up against a series of blocks attached to a flat surface. The curved shape is determined by measuring a series of offsets from a baseline.

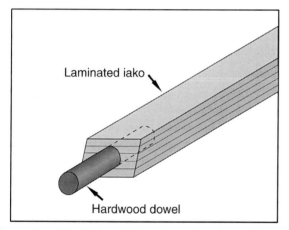

FIGURE 9-5. The Wa'apa's iakos have a hardwood dowel glued into a hole in the end of the beam, with a fiberglass wrapping to prevent splitting.

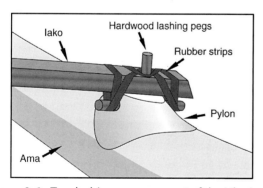

FIGURE 9-6. Two lashing pegs are part of the Ulua's ama pylon. A third peg is part of the iako and extends out of the bottom of the iako for ½" (12mm), and fits into a shallow hole drilled into the top of the pylon.

In the case of the Wa'apa, use a flat spade bit to drill a hole into the outboard end to take the hardwood dowel. Wrap the end of the iako with fiberglass tape to prevent splitting.

The Ulua iako ends require that a dowel be glued in vertically on the top of the outboard end to hold the elastic lashings.

BUILDING A HOLLOW, BOX BEAM IAKO

The straight, hollow beam shown with the Wa'apa double outrigger consists of a ¾" × 2¾" (18mm × 70mm) top and bottom chord with ¼" (6mm) plywood sides.

Cut out the plywood sides using a stiff batten to draw the curved top edge. Splice the plywood together with butt blocks or scarf joints. Block the bottom chord straight along a bench top. Insert and glue solid blocking at the locations shown in Figure 9-7, and bend the top chord along the blocking, gluing it in place. Use small nails and glue, or many clamps, to attach the ply web to the bottom and top chords. After the second side is attached, round the edges and sheath the entire beam with fiberglass or just paint it. A fiberglass sheathing is not necessary for strength, but it will provide a more durable finish. Drill the ends to take the hardwood dowels.

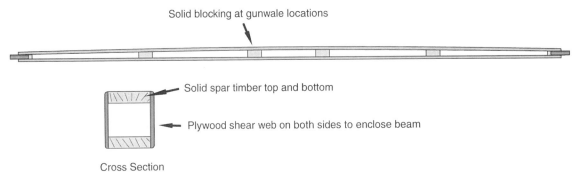

Solid blocking at gunwale locations

Solid spar timber top and bottom

Plywood shear web on both sides to enclose beam

Cross Section

FIGURE 9-7. A hollow, box beam iako is specified for the Wa'apa double outrigger. Beams with gentle curves can also be built with this method.

ALUMINUM TUBE BEAMS

Aluminum tubing with a minimum diameter of 2"(50mm) and a wall thickness of ⅛" (3mm) is suitable to use for iakos with the T2 and Ulua designs. If you wish to have curved beams, it is best to take the tube to a specialist company to have this done. The stiffest alloy, such as 6061-T6 (which is used for spars on all sizes of sailing craft), is the best for this application but may be too stiff for bending into a curve.

The alloy beams can be left bare, painted with special primers and paint, powder coated, or anodized. Anodizing is probably the best treatment, but care must be taken to insulate any stainless-steel hardware from contacting the aluminum surface to prevent corrosion through electrolytic attack. Plastic gaskets or silicone sealant will separate the dissimilar metals and prevent corrosion of the aluminum.

Where the round tubing crosses the gunwale of the canoe and attaches to the ama, it is best to have hardwood cradles to support them.

CONNECTIONS

The structural joints between the iakos and the hull and ama are an important consideration, since most failures will occur in these areas. Bolts with metal brackets or straps have been used in many cases, but I feel that it is the least desirable solution in the small canoes that we are considering. The high-stress concentrations around bolts or metal fittings will be the first source of failure.

Traditional lashings were made with sennit or coconut-fiber rope. These lashings are very elastic and require frequent tightening and replacement. The most frequently seen lashing material now in

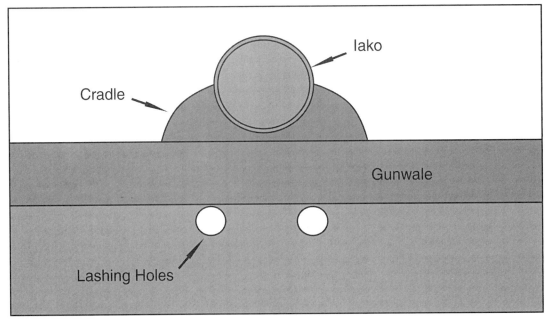

FIGURE 9-8. A hardwood cradle is used to support round, aluminum-tube iakos.

Oceania is large-diameter, nylon monofilament fishing line. For the designs in this book, I recommend ³⁄₁₆" (4mm) polyester rope.

Nylon rope can be used but does stretch when wet; therefore, perhaps it's a good idea to do the lashings while the nylon is already wet to prevent it from loosening. Cotton or a cotton/polyester blend is also used in modern Hawaiian canoes.

Another commonly seen lashing material used throughout Oceania is strips cut from rubber tire inner tubes. Either cut long lengths around and around the tube, or cross-cut circular rubber bands. I always use the rubber-band lashings on the iako-to-ama joint because it stays tight and gives just enough of the desired elasticity. I've bailed out of the Ulua in surf and seen the hull thrown airborne sideways and land on the ama in the shallow water. A subsequent inspection revealed no damage or visible stress to any of the connections.

When sailing a tacking canoe, I prefer rope lashings at the hull-to-iako joint. With the ama to leeward, very high stresses occur at the lashings, and I prefer the lower stretch of rope lashings.

A variation of the rope-lashing method uses a straight piece of timber (wae) below the cross beam that extends through the sides of the hull just below the gunwales. This allows lashing without leaving any open holes in the hull and is particularly useful where the area is decked over, or is a watertight compartment.

In order to prevent the iako from sliding out of its lashings, I use what I call a "locater block" screwed to the top of the iako directly above the gunwale. The locater block also allows you to assemble the canoe the same way each time, since it determines the spacing between the hull and the ama.

Beginning and finishing a simple lashing can be confusing, and if it is not done well, you may be returning to shore in several pieces. I use a very nontraditional, small plastic cleat at each location. The lashing line can start with a figure-eight stopper knot through the base of the cleat, and then, when all of the wraps are completed, it can be tied off at the same cleat. Without a cleat, you can use a series of half hitches to finish a lashing.

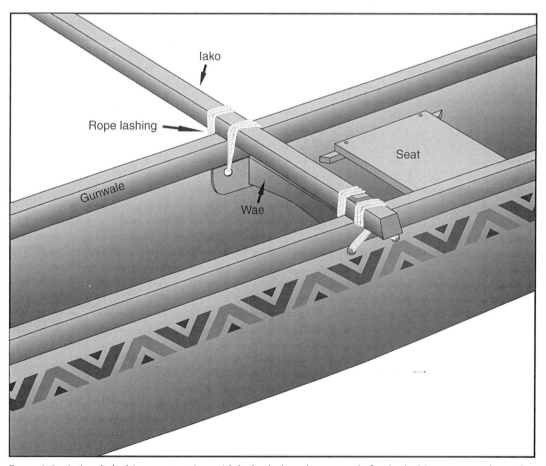

FIGURE 9-9. A simple lashing connection with holes below the gunwale for the lashings to pass through. A wooden spreader (wae) is centered below the cross beam. There is one lashing hole on each side of the wae. A small cleat can be screwed to the doubler pad inside to begin and end the lashing.

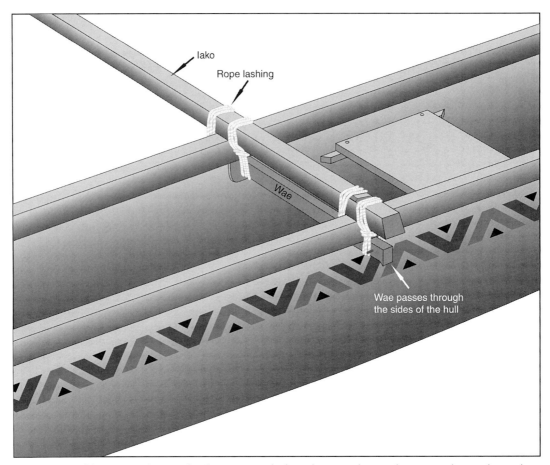

FIGURE 9-10. This connection method uses a wae below the cross beam that extends out through the sides of the hull. This can be used if you don't want lashing holes in the hull or if your cross beam passes over a decked area of the hull.

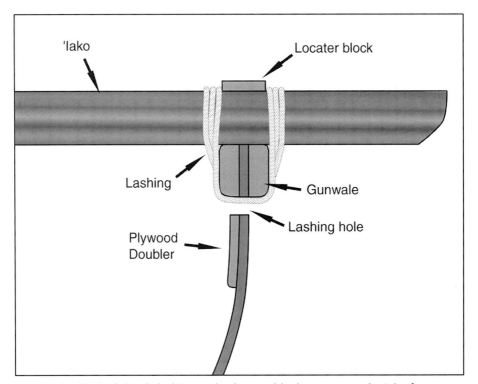

FIGURE 9-11. Typical simple lashing with a locater block to prevent the iako from slipping out of its lashings.

118

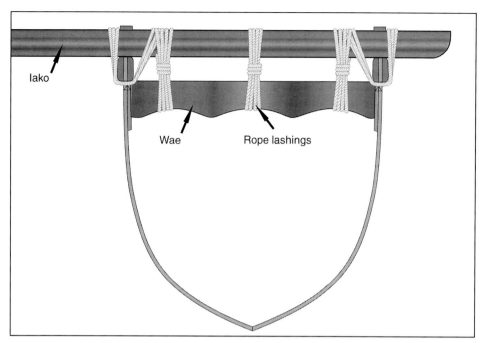

FIGURE 9-12. An elaborate, traditional-style lashing can be very impressive as long as you don't have to disassemble the canoe often.

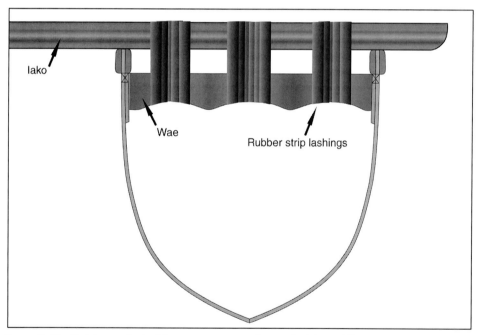

FIGURE 9-13. Rubber-strip lashings are commonly used with paddling canoes but allow too much stretch for a sailing canoe when used on the main hull.

FIGURE 9-14. (ABOVE LEFT) A laminating jig for solid iakos consists of a row of wooden blocks screwed to a flat surface. Note the waxed paper taped in place to prevent gluing the beam to the table or the blocks.

FIGURE 9-15. (ABOVE) Strips of wood glued together and clamped to the blocks.

FIGURE 9-16. (LEFT) Wa'apa beam ends with hardwood dowels and fiberglass wrapping in place.

FIGURE 9-17. (BELOW) A Wa'apa lashing straddles two hull sections, with one lashing hole in each section.

CHAPTER 10

Steering, Leeboards, and Accessories

STEERING

There are several ways to steer an outrigger sailing canoe, and quite often more than one method is used at the same time. The most common steering methods are as follows:

- Paddle
- Steering oar
- Rudder
- Dagger boards
- Crew weight shift
- Sail trim

The tacking outrigger has a somewhat simpler problem than a shunter, because a rudder or steering oar can be mounted at one end and left there. A shunting outrigger has to either move the rudder or oar during each shunt or have duplicates mounted at each end.

Steering with a Paddle

Steering with a paddle is almost always possible as long as you have a crew member to tend the sail. It is difficult to paddle-steer while single-handing, because the paddle requires two hands, and no hands are left to release the mainsheet in a gust. Paddle steering is a fine art that won't be learned quickly, but it is usually necessary when the canoe is being propelled only by paddlers.

A steering paddle generally has a larger blade area and a stronger shaft than an ordinary paddle. A skilled steersman can make it all appear quite easy, but your first times can be exhausting experiences.

Most of the time while you are sailing, the paddle can be used as a big skeg and simply be "poked" or held down below the hull on the side opposite to that which the boat is turning. A paddle in this position can also be used to lever water away from the hull or pull water toward the hull. Varying the depth of the poke will steer a canoe in a steady wind by changing the position of the underwater center of lateral resistance. If the steering seat is just forward of the iako, the handle of the paddle can be braced against the forward edge of the iako.

Steering Oars

The steering oar is a versatile tool and has been used to steer traditional craft up to 100' (30m) in length or more for thousands of years. Larger vessels used multiple oars deployed together, but in our case, a single, 8' to 10' (2.4 to 3.0m), ordinary oar will suffice. The pivot point of the oar needs to be attached to a cross beam or steering bracket with a standard full-circle oarlock, or to a simple lashing in an emergency.

The oar can be used in several different ways:

1. The oar can function as a rudder by immersing the blade and angling it to turn the canoe. This mode is most commonly used for course correction on broad reaches and for rounding up into the wind to drop the sail, or to tack.
2. Going aback is the biggest no-no with shunting proas and can necessitate dropping the sail. It can also cause a capsize. If you sail long enough, it will happen. Sailing up under headlands, or

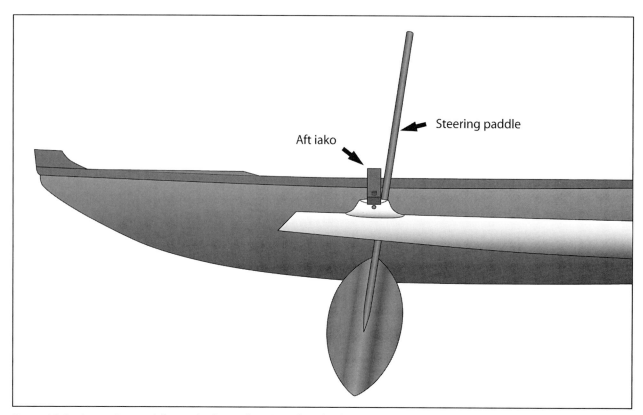

FIGURE 10-1. A steering paddle can be braced against the aft iako. In a well-tuned sailing canoe, immersing the paddle deeper into the water will cause the canoe to turn away from the wind direction. Lifting the paddle will cause the canoe to turn into the wind.

getting a sudden wind shift, can put you into an embarrassing situation. This is where the steering oar has saved me from difficulties on several occasions. Using it as an oar with a powerful sweeping motion will kick the stern of the canoe around instantly. This is something you can't do with a rudder.

3. I also use the oar as a movable source of lateral resistance by simply trailing it like a skeg parallel to the boat's centerline, but varying the amount of immersion. If I'm beam-reaching and want to bear off, I'll angle the oar deeper into the water and the canoe will turn downwind. The greater water pressure at the increased depth of the blade holds the stern of the canoe firmly and allows the bow to fall away from the wind direction. This produces less drag than using the oar as a rudder and is readily apparent by the lack of turbulence.

4. The oar can also be used with a sculling stroke to propel the canoe in calms. This works amazingly well, and you'll get better with practice.

A fully rigged sailing canoe is rarely well set up for paddling, and the seamless transition from control to propulsion is a real delight.

So after all the good stuff, what's the downside? Steering oars are fine for day sailing in good weather. They can become a handful in strong conditions, or where you'd like the canoe to self-steer for short periods. Just letting go of the oar, or lifting the blade, can cause the canoe to round up into the wind.

As a rule of thumb, I would recommend that steering oars be approximately one half the length of the canoe. Scaling the steering oar up to larger canoes can turn into real oceanic he-man stuff. Pacific museums contain huge steering oars that take several men just to lift. This is all very well on an afternoon sail, but not what you want on an ocean passage with your mate.

To make shunting quicker when sailing single-handed, I found that having an oar rigged at each end of the hull was much better. The unused forward oar is simply retracted inboard in its oarlock until it is needed on the other tack.

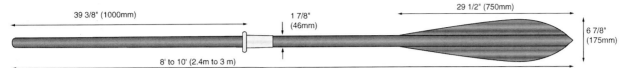

39 3/8" (1000mm) 1 7/8" (46mm) 29 1/2" (750mm) 6 7/8" (175mm) 8' to 10' (2.4m to 3 m)

FIGURE 10-2. A typical steering oar that can be used to steer a canoe or to propel it by sculling.

You will note that on my shunting canoe designs, the oar is located on the windward side of the hull, whereas on traditional canoes it is always to leeward. A leeward position allows the water pressure to hold the oar against the side of the hull and makes steering easier. Unfortunately, if you are single-handing and have to sit out on the windward rail, you won't be able to reach a steering oar mounted on the leeward side.

Rudders

Rudders as we know them were not widely used in Oceania. A quarter rudder lashed to the side of the hull is used on some Micronesian proas. Viking ships had a similar rudder location. It can be difficult to mount a rudder on an outrigger canoe, because they seldom have transoms, and a fixed, underhull rudder is damage-prone in the shallow water that canoes frequent. The Ulua's rudder mounts on the outboard motor bracket that is clamped to the aft iako. Any standard kick-up rudder such as is found on beach cats or sailing dinghies can be used.

It is important to mount the rudder and leeboard on the same side of the hull. Small amounts of change in heeling angle will require constant steering correction if the rudder and leeboard are on opposite sides. The port (left) side of the hull is preferred, because if you use the single pivot-bolt attachment shown in Figure 10-5, the nut will loosen if the rudder or leeboard kicks up. Mounting the boards on the starboard (right) side

FIGURE 10-3. A steering oar in position and pivoting on a hardwood spreader lashed to the gunwales. The lashing holes, which are securing the steering bracket, are those used for the cross beams when the hull is in the 16' (4.8m) configuration.

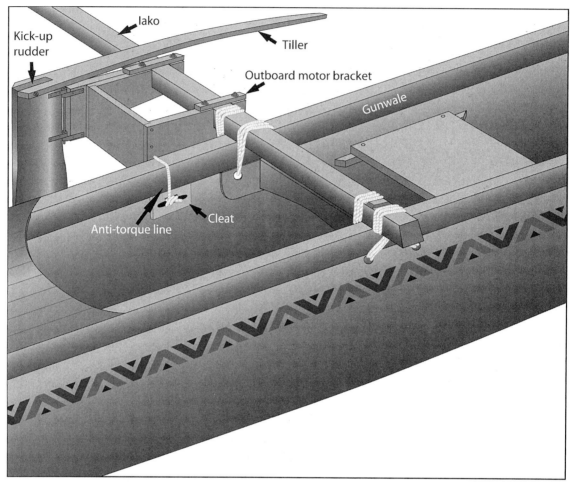

FIGURE 10-4. A kick-up rudder mounted on the outer side of the Ulua's outboard bracket. Note the "anti-torque" line, which is attached to the bottom corner of the outboard bracket and terminates at a small cleat on the inside of the hull to prevent the iako from twisting when an outboard motor is being used.

has the opposite effect and tightens the nut if they kick up.

While you are sailing, a tiller with an extension is normally used to control the rudder. If the wind dies and you have to paddle for a long distance, you can make your paddling more effective by leaving all of the steering to the rudder rather than trying to do it with the paddle. Foot pedals, such as those used in kayaks, are an effective way to steer the Ulua while paddling. The hard-chined hull of the Wa'apa tracks well enough without a rudder while paddling. Manufactured foot pedals can be purchased, or made from scrap timber and plywood with a pair of stainless-steel or brass hinges. The control lines are ⅛" (3mm), low-stretch rope passing through small blocks located as shown in Figure 10-6. The tiller can be removed by pulling

a single pin, or swung over aft to prevent it from interfering with your paddle.

Dagger Boards

A unique way to steer a sailing canoe is with a dagger board, either by raising and lowering the dagger board to change direction, or using a dagger board that incorporates a movable flap. Raising or lowering the dagger boards a small amount offers very precise steering and can be controlled via lines or cables led to any location onboard.

With a shunting rig, two boards are needed, with the forward one retracted or partially showing, for precise trim. Dagger-board steering becomes less effective running downwind, but as proas seldom sail that course, it's rarely a problem. Some shunting

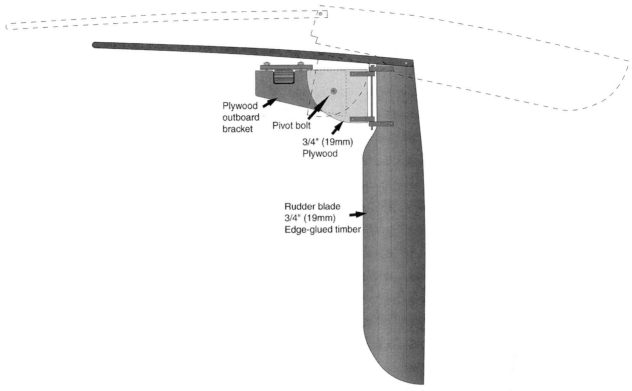

FIGURE 10-5. The Ulua kick-up rudder is mounted on the outer side of the outboard motor bracket.

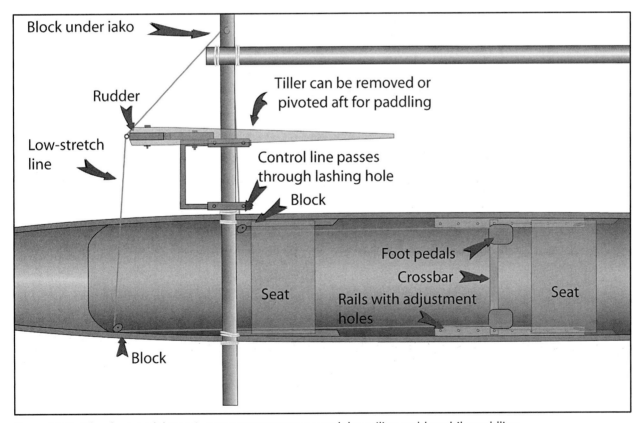

FIGURE 10-6. Ulua foot-pedal steering arrangement to control the sailing rudder while paddling.

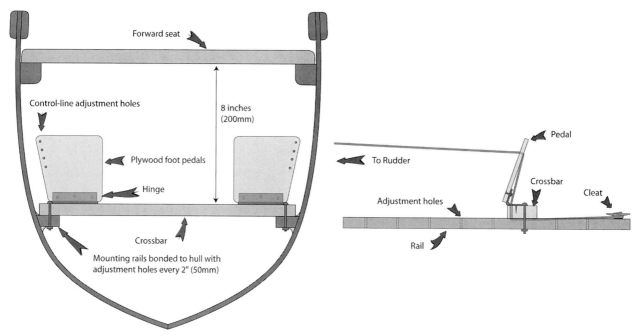

FIGURE 10-7. Cross section of the Ulua's foot-pedal installation. Commercially available kayak foot pedals can also be used.

designs even incorporate all moving spade rudders mounted in dagger-board cases. These are mostly seen on larger, oceangoing canoes.

The necessary control lines rigged to precisely raise and lower two boards is extensive and make more sense with larger canoes. The board and case must also be as friction-free as possible to allow easy adjustment under high side loads.

Raising or lowering a steering dagger board changes the underwater profile of the hull and moves its center of lateral resistance (CLR; see Chapter 12). Pushing the aft dagger board deeper shifts the CLR aft, and the canoe turns away from

the wind direction. Retracting it into the hull will cause the canoe to turn into the wind.

Weight Shift

Shifting the weight of the crew or helmsperson can have a profound effect on the underwater profile of the canoe (CLR) and therefore on the sailing trim. Move some weight aft, and you will develop lee helm, or the tendency for the canoe to turn downwind. Shifting weight forward will generate weather helm, or the tendency to turn into the wind. Moving more weight out toward the ama will generate more

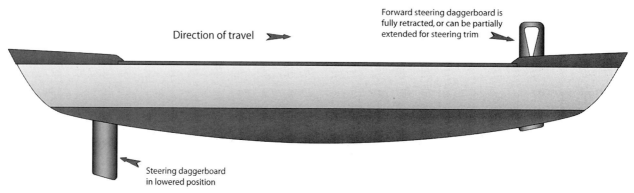

FIGURE 10-8. A shunting proa can be steered with a pair of simple dagger boards by raising and lowering them with control lines.

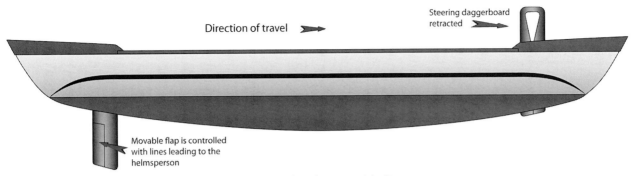

Direction of travel ➤

Steering daggerboard retracted ➤

Movable flap is controlled with lines leading to the helmsperson

FIGURE 10-9. Dagger rudders are sometimes equipped with a movable flap.

drag on that side and turn the canoe toward the ama. The T2, with its narrow, deep, "V" hull, is more sensitive in this regard than the more rounded hull of the Ulua. The placement of weight and sail trim, combined with the principal steering device, will all contribute to an easily steered canoe. There is nothing simple about trying to analyze the forces resulting from small changes in rudders, leeboard angles, hull shape, sail trim, or a myriad of other factors.

Sail Steering

The Oceanic lateen or crab-claw sail found universally in Micronesia has the ability to maintain lift under very high angles of attack. In other words, if you oversheet it, it won't stall and lose drive like a more conventional sail. This is a very useful trait and can be used to steer a canoe on beam-reaching and close-hauled courses. Sheet in hard, and the canoe will start to bear away; ease the sheet to stop it or to head back into the wind. With practice, you can use this to do most of the steering on those courses without any input from the steering oar. This effect is due to the very long boom that moves the center of effort well out to leeward when the sheet is eased. Once you are on a broad reach, you'll need the help of a paddle, oar, or rudder.

LEEBOARDS

The leeboard is an important factor in any round- or flat-bottomed canoe's sailing performance. While traditional Oceanic canoes did not have a mounted leeboard, crew members would hold their paddles along the side of the hull to achieve the same effect. Since many canoe sailors prefer to sail single-handed, the leeboard takes the place of that extra crew.

Traditional, mono-hulled canoes usually have a pair of leeboards, and they are sailed with the leeward board down and the windward board pivoted up. Because of its greater hull beam and heeling angle, a board on the windward side is lifted too far out of the water to be effective. Outrigger canoes have a narrow beam and small heeling angles so that only one board is necessary.

Note the cross-sectional shape difference between a tacking leeboard and a shunting leeboard shown in Figure 10-10. The shunting board will be going both ways, but always with the same side to windward and leeward. This allows you to leave the leeward side almost flat, with most of the curvature on the windward side generating lift more effectively.

The Ulua and Wa'apa designs use a single pivoting leeboard. Not only does the board provide lateral resistance, but by pivoting it fore and aft, you can ease the load on the steering or rudder by moving the center of lateral resistance to the best position. Normally, the leeboard would be positioned vertically when you are sailing to windward, and it is gradually angled aft as your course changes to a reach or run.

The Ulua's leeboard is mounted on a single pivot bolt just below the gunwale. The bolt passes through an aluminum angle bracket inside the hull on top of the forward seat and transfers the load to the seat. A fixed leeboard is best used in combination with a kick-up rudder. If you choose to steer with an oar or paddle, the movable clamp-on bracket will allow better adjustment of the balance between the sail and the hull.

The Wa'apa's tacking-rig leeboard pivots on a single bolt that passes through the hull just below the seat, and passes the load into a plywood, gusseted angle bracket. A Wa'apa rigged with a shunting sail, however, has the leeboard mounted on the inboard side of the ama. This is an important distinction, because an ama-mounted leeboard will aid in keeping the ama to windward while the canoe is undergoing

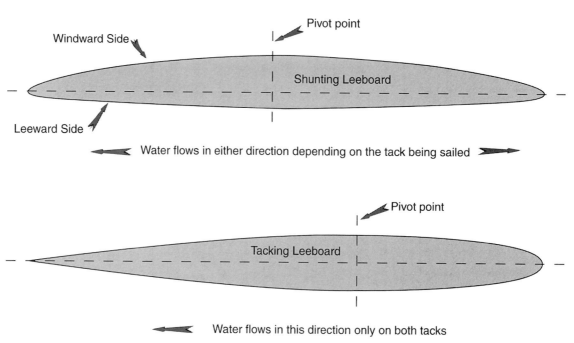

FIGURE 10-10. Shunting and tacking leeboard cross-sectional shapes. Shunting and tacking leeboards are not interchangeable.

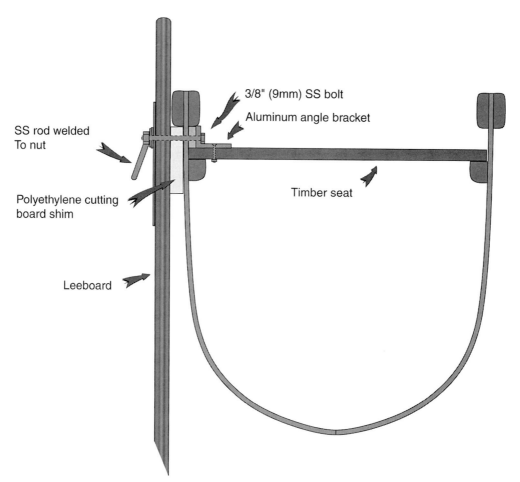

FIGURE 10-11. A through-bolted, pivoting leeboard mounting on the Ulua hull. Note how the load is transferred to the seat through the metal bracket to prevent the side of the hull from being twisted.

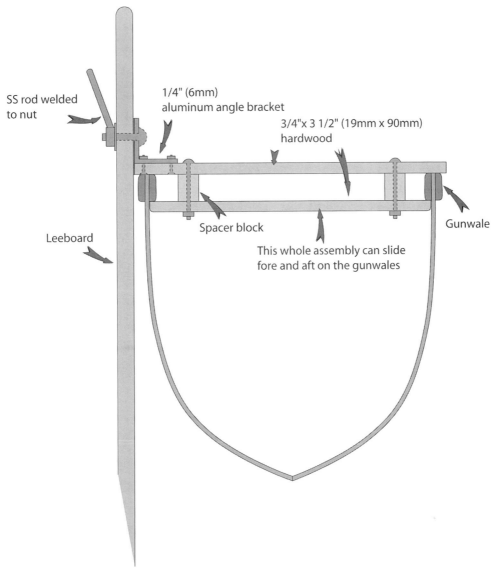

SS rod welded to nut

1/4" (6mm) aluminum angle bracket

3/4"x 3 1/2" (19mm x 90mm) hardwood

Spacer block

This whole assembly can slide fore and aft on the gunwales

Gunwale

Leeboard

FIGURE 10-12. Movable clamp-on leeboard brackets are recommended for canoes with oar or paddle steering, and enable precise location of the center of lateral resistance.

the shunting operation. A shunting rig with a leeboard mounted on the main hull can become directionally unstable during a shunt and possibly spin around and set the sail aback.

All of the leeboards that I have built are simple, edge-glued laminates of solid, straight-grained timber. To avoid warping, it is better to glue up several pieces rather than just use a wide board.

Laminate the blank for the leeboard by edge-gluing at least two boards with square, well-fitting edges. The narrower the strips that are glued together, the less chance there is of any warping later. Alternate the grain direction, as shown in Figure 10-16, to avoid warping. After the glue has cured, cut out the shape with a jigsaw. To achieve an

airfoil shape, use an electric hand plane or a disc sander with a foam-backed pad. These are both very powerful tools and can cause a lot of damage in the wrong hands. Finish shaping with a coarse sanding board. Fiberglassing the leeboard is optional. I usually just apply five coats of spar varnish.

ACCESSORIES

Outboard Motor Brackets

The outboard brackets shown in the plans for the Ulua and Wa'apa are used for more than just mounting an outboard motor. A rowlock mounted on the

129

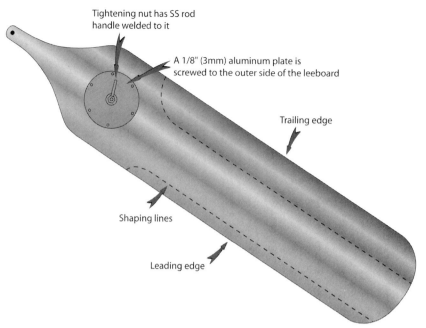

FIGURE 10-13. The outline shape of a tacking and shunting leeboard can be the same, but the cross-sectional shape must be different. The dotted line shows how a tacking board would be shaped.

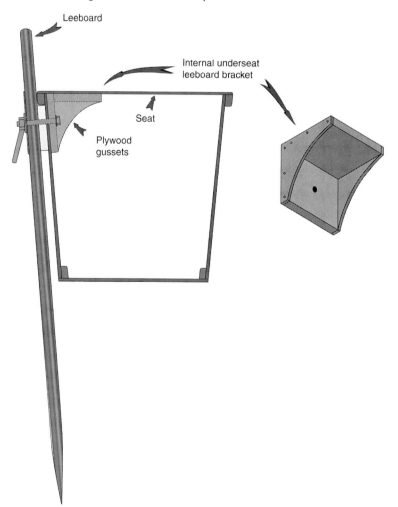

FIGURE 10-14. The Wa'apa tacking leeboard mount. The same bracket is used to support the mast step when the canoe is equipped with a shunting rig.

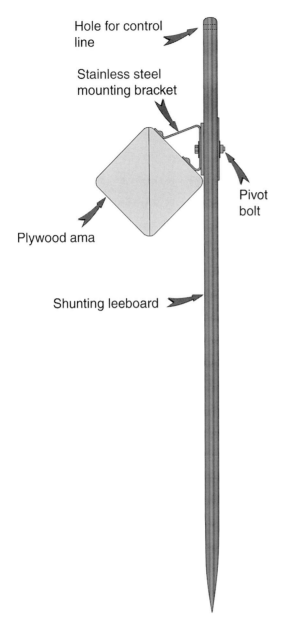

Hole for control line

Stainless steel mounting bracket

Plywood ama

Pivot bolt

Shunting leeboard

FIGURE 10-15. Wa'apa's ama-mounted shunting lee-board, mounted on the inboard side of the plywood ama. See also Figure 3-11.

FIGURE 10-17. The Wa'apa's outboard bracket is mounted below the iako with four ⁵⁄₁₆" (8mm) bolts.

bracket will take an oar for steering or sculling. A kick-up rudder can also be mounted on the bracket. Even if you never intend to use an outboard motor, the bracket is essential.

I've used a two-horsepower outboard motor to propel the Ulua and the Wa'apa. There is no need for a more powerful engine, and the extra weight of a larger engine would be undesirable. Note the "anti-torque line" in Figures 1-4 and 10-4 that is attached to the bottom corner of the bracket and leads up and over the gunwale to a cleat located

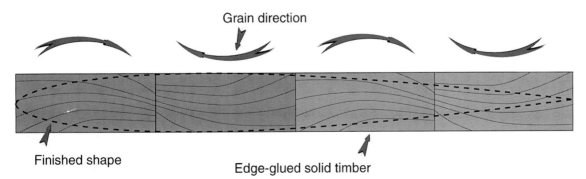

Grain direction

Finished shape

Edge-glued solid timber

FIGURE 10-16. Alternate the grain direction when gluing up a rudder or leeboard to avoid warping later on.

FIGURE 10-18. A kick-up rudder and outboard motor mounted on the Ulua's bracket. Note the anti-torque line coming from the bottom of the bracket, over the gunwale, and tied to a cleat.

inside the hull. The thrust from the motor will try to twist the iako out of its lashings, and the short line will prevent this from happening. Use a low-stretch line for this purpose.

Note in Figures 10-17 and 10-18 that the Wa'apa bracket is mounted completely below the iako, while the Ulua's bracket is notched to fit around the iako. The different mounting height is necessary, because the iakos are higher above the water in the Wa'apa, and the outboard motor must be immersed enough to prevent the propeller from ventilating.

Because there can be a lot of stress on the bracket from either a motor or the steering device, be sure to build it strong. If you are not confident about your joinery, install aluminum angle brackets on the interior corners to reinforce the joint.

Hiking Seats

All three designs show seats that extend outboard from the hull to allow one or more crew members to hike out and prevent the ama from lifting or sinking. The shunting T2 uses one large, slatted seat on the ama (windward) side, while the Ulua and Wa'apa tacking rigs can have seats on both sides of the hull.

The T2's seat bridges across the two iakos, while the smaller hiking seats on the Ulua and Wa'apa are supported by the gunwale on their inboard edge and a fore and aft pole on their outboard edge. A loose lashing around the pole allows the seat to be pivoted outboard for paddling, where it rests against a second pole.

I've come to prefer a slatted, wooden seat over a canvas or netting trampoline, due to the difficulty of getting a trampoline out of the way when you need to paddle.

FIGURE 10-19. The hiking seats on the Wa'apa pivot outboard for paddling and rest against a second bamboo pole.

FIGURE 10-20. A windward-side hiking seat on the T2, with a wooden knob bolted in place to snub the sheet. Note the leeside guide rail to aid in shunting an Oceanic lateen sail.

CHAPTER 11

Spars, Spar Specifications, and Sails

SPARS

Several choices of materials are available for making masts, booms, and luff spars or yards. Fiberglass, timber, aluminum, and bamboo are all good materials for spar-making.

A mast used for an un-stayed tacking rig is stepped in the bottom of the hull and experiences mostly *bending* loads, with the greatest concentration being at deck level. Masts for shunting rigs, such as the Oceanic lateen and the Gibbons/Dierking rig, are stepped at deck level and are supported by stays and a shroud. Shunting masts experience mostly *compressive* loads.

Fiberglass

I recommend windsurfing masts for the tacking rigs. Fiberglass windsurfing masts, made for wave jumping, are incredibly resilient and will bend off to leeward in gusts, eliminating the need for reefing in many cases. Carbon masts are somewhat more delicate and shouldn't be used unstayed if they contain more than 50 percent carbon fiber. Where the mast wall contacts the hole in the canoe seat or partners, wrap it heavily with tape or inner-tube rubber to avoid damage. The masthead requires only a solid, wooden plug with a hole to attach to the head of the sail. Seal the ends of the mast with foam to keep water out and allow them to float.

The luff spar for the T2 Gibbons rig is ideally tapered equally from both ends. It can be made from two cut-down windsurfing masts, with their larger ends joined in the middle with a metal tube, a fiberglass tube, or a timber dowel. The sail will hold it together in compression, so there's no need

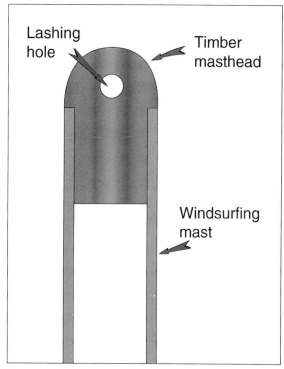

FIGURE 11-1. A fiberglass windsurfing mast with a wooden head. The head of the sail is lashed to the hole, or a halyard can be led through it.

to make this a permanent joint. A well-fitting joint is important.

Solid or Hollow Timber

Masts, booms, and yards can be made from either solid or hollow timber. The hollow spars will be much lighter, with only a small increase in diameter. Spar timber for hollow or solid spars should be carefully chosen for its straight grain, light weight, and an absence of all but the smallest tight knots. Sitka spruce is your first choice, but Douglas fir or

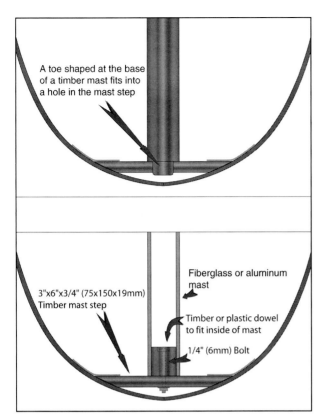

FIGURE 11-2. Mast steps for a hollow or solid mast. The step must be securely glued or glassed into the hull.

pine can be used with a weight penalty. Cedar can be used to make booms but is too weak for unstayed masts.

Solid Spars

Solid spars clearly require less labor than hollow ones. If you're very lucky, you may find a single piece of light, clear timber of adequate dimensions for the spar you are building. In most cases, however, you'll have to laminate two or more pieces together. If the pieces are too short, scarf them before laminating the layers, and stagger any scarfs over the length of the spar. A table saw with the blade set at forty-five degrees can be used to take the square corners off the stock and make it eight-sided. Use an electric or hand plane to make it round.

Hollow Spars

Unstayed, hollow, straight or tapered masts and booms can be made with the birdsmouth method.

Most birdsmouth spars use eight strips of wood with a forty-five-degree notch cut into one edge. The required finished diameter of the spar

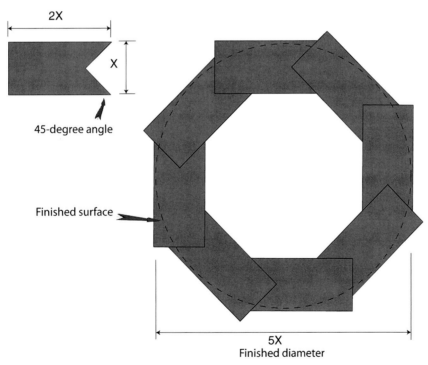

FIGURE 11-3. To construct a birdsmouth spar, determine the required diameter of the spar, and divide by five to obtain the dimension "X" (thickness of the staves). The width of the staves is 2X. Cut the staves, scarf them to obtain the full length if necessary, cut the forty-five-degree notch in the edge of each stave, and glue them all together.

determines the width and thickness of the individual strips. Refer to the birdsmouth cross-sectional diagram (Figure 11-3). For a 2½" (63mm) diameter spar, X = ½" (12.5mm), so that an individual strip would be ½" (12.5mm) thick and 1" (25mm) wide.

If the timber stock is not long enough for the spar, scarf it to the full length before cutting the notches. The angled notch in the birdsmouth strips can be cut with a table saw set at forty-five degrees, or with a special router bit. Make solid inserts for the ends and any other place where attachments will be made later. If the spar is to have a constant diameter (untapered), you are ready to assemble the spar.

After a dry test fit, apply epoxy or resorcinol glue and use cable ties, tape, hose clamps, or short lengths of plastic line to bind it together. Do not use resorcinol glue unless your fit is perfect and you can apply high clamping pressure.

Rest the spar on a series of level blocks or a flat surface. Use a string line or a straight line drawn on the surface for a reference. Sight down the length of the spar after it's clamped to ensure that it is straight. If you are building a curved spar, it is easy to bend it to the desired amount at this stage.

A tapered spar can have its largest diameter at one end (like an unstayed mast) or at its midpoint (yards or loose-footed sail booms). Material is removed from the square, un-notched edge over the distance that you want to taper the spar. While you are removing material from the square edge with a plane or saw, be sure that the edge remains square. To determine the maximum amount that you need to remove at the small end, take a scrap piece of notched strip sawn a little narrower, and cut it into eight short pieces. Trial-fit the pieces together to determine if you've removed enough. You can also work this out on paper, but a quick trial in the workshop is just as fast.

After the glue has cured, use an electric or hand plane to remove the ridges on the spar, gradually working toward a round shape. Finish with a long sanding board and electric sander. A minimum of five coats of spar varnish are needed for a clear finish.

Bamboo

Bamboo can provide an excellent spar material. If you have access to large-diameter, long-length bamboo, by all means try it. Use the same diameter bamboo spars as are specified for hollow timber construction.

If the bamboo is green and freshly cut, it is best to soak it in the sea or a river for a few weeks to get rid of the insects that can shorten the life of the spar. Another two months of drying will result in a light, resilient spar. The drying can be accelerated by scraping the thin, outer surface from the bamboo. The thin, outer membrane also inhibits any gluing or paint bonding. In tropical countries, bamboo is often seasoned by passing the green shafts through the flames of a fire. This treatment also gets rid of insects and glazes the surface. If the bamboo is already dry, you can use a sander to remove the outer surface. Painted bamboo will have a longer life than if it is left bare. The hollow ends should be plugged with a wooden dowel. A heavy string seizing wrapped around the ends and soaked in epoxy will prevent splitting.

Aluminum

Aluminum tubing has a long history as spar material and is the dominant material in use today. Aluminum windsurfing masts are too fragile to use as unstayed masts, but could be used as booms or spliced together for yards.

If you are buying aluminum tubing that is not already advertised as spar material, be sure of the alloy number; 6061-T6 is the most common spar grade and is much stiffer than household varieties.

There are standard fittings available for the ends of aluminum spars, but you can make your own by simply fitting a solid timber dowel into the end and drilling one or more holes through it for the rigging. Put a couple of screws through the aluminum into the wooden dowel to prevent it from moving.

The mast steps used with the tacking rigs for an aluminum spar are the same as are shown in Figure 11-2 for a hollow windsurfing mast. The step for a shunting mast can be a simple wooden socket or a pad eye to take a spinnaker pole end on the base of the mast.

Boom Jaws

Boom jaws are an ancient and simple way to terminate the inboard end of the boom. They can be fitted to hollow metal or bamboo booms by attaching the jaws to a short, timber stub that fits inside the end of

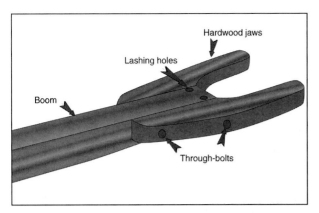

FIGURE 11-4. Hardwood boom jaws should be through-bolted at the inner end of the boom.

the boom. The jaws themselves should be made of a hard and strong wood, glued and through-bolted to the stub or spar. The opening between the jaws should be at least ¾" (19mm) wider than the diameter of the mast at the contact point. The extra width allows the boom to rotate to a limited degree and prevent excessive stress on the jaws.

Leather can be glued or tacked to the inner contact surface of the jaws to prevent abrasion of a timber mast.

SPAR SPECIFICATIONS

Ulua

MAST
Mast length = 15'0" (4600mm)
Fiberglass windsurfing masts: Tougher wave-jumping masts are best.
Aluminum mast:
Diameter = 2¼" (57mm)
Wall thickness = ⅛" (3mm)
Tapered solid timber mast:
Base diameter = 2⁷⁄₁₆" (62mm)
Head diameter = 1⁷⁄₁₆" (36mm)
Tapered hollow timber mast:
Base diameter = 2¹¹⁄₁₆" (68mm)
Head diameter = 1⁹⁄₁₆" (40mm)

BOOM
Boom length = 13'9½" (4200mm)
Curved timber boom length = 13'9½" (4200mm).
The boom is laminated from two pieces of ¾" × 1⅝" (19mm × 42mm) timber, bent along a jig as shown in Figure 11-3.

T2: Oceanic Lateen Rig

MAST
Length = 11'8" (3550mm)
Fiberglass windsurfing masts can be used by cutting off the smaller end.
Aluminum mast:
Diameter = 2¼" (57mm)
Wall thickness = ⅛" (3mm)
Solid timber mast (untapered):
Diameter = 2¼" (57mm)
Hollow timber mast (untapered):
Diameter = 2¼" (57mm)

YARD
Length = 16'5" (5000mm)
Two fiberglass windsurfing masts can be joined at their bases to make a fiberglass yard.
Aluminum yard:
Diameter = 2" (50mm)
Wall thickness = ³⁄₃₂" (2mm)
Tapered, solid timber yard:
Midpoint diameter = 2⅜" (60mm)
End diameters = 1³⁄₁₆" (30mm)
Tapered, hollow timber yard:
Midpoint diameter = 2⁹⁄₁₆" (66mm)
End diameters = 1⁵⁄₁₆" (33mm)
Bamboo: Same size as hollow timber

CURVED BOOM
Length = 16'11" (5150mm)
This boom is laminated from three pieces of ¾" × 1⅝" (19mm × 42mm) timber bent along a jig.

T2: Gibbons/Dierking Rig

MAST
Length = 9'7" (2925mm)
Aluminum mast:
Diameter = 2¼" (57mm)
Wall thickness = ⅛" (3mm)
Solid timber mast (untapered):
Diameter = 2¼" (57mm)
Hollow timber mast (untapered):
Diameter = 2¼" (57mm)

YARD
Length = 19' (5800mm)
Two fiberglass windsurfing masts can be joined at their bases to make a fiberglass yard.

Aluminum yard:
Diameter = 2" (50mm)
Wall thickness = ³⁄₃₂" (2mm)
Tapered, solid timber yard:
Midpoint diameter = 2⅜" (60mm)
End diameters = 1³⁄₁₆" (30mm)
Tapered, hollow timber yard:
Midpoint diameter = 2⁹⁄₁₆" (66mm)
End diameters = 1⁵⁄₁₆" (33mm)
Bamboo: Same size as hollow timber

BOOM

Length = 8'10" (2700mm)
The best material for this boom is 1¼″ (32mm) aluminum tubing.

Wa'apa: Large Tacking Rig

MAST

Length = 17'0" (5200mm)
Fiberglass windsurfing masts are available at this length.
Aluminum mast:
Diameter = 2¼" (57mm)
Wall thickness = ⅛" (3mm)
Tapered, solid timber mast:
Base diameter = 2¹³⁄₁₆" (72mm)
Head diameter = 1¹¹⁄₁₆" (43mm)
Tapered, hollow timber mast:
Base diameter = 3¹⁄₁₆" (78mm)
Head diameter = 1⅞" (48mm)
Bamboo can be used with the support of a stub mast.

BOOM

Length = 13'10" (4220mm)
Aluminum boom:
Diameter = 2½" (63mm)
Tapered, solid timber boom:
Midpoint diameter = 2⅜" (60mm)
End diameters = 1¾" (45mm)
Tapered, hollow timber boom:
Midpoint diameter = 2½" (63mm)
End diameters = 2" (50mm)

Wa'apa: Small Tacking Rig

MAST

Length = 14'0" (4300mm)
Fiberglass windsurfing masts are available at this length.

Aluminum mast:
Diameter = 2" (50mm)
Wall thickness = ³⁄₃₂" (2mm)
Tapered, solid timber mast:
Base diameter = 2⁵⁄₁₆" (59mm)
Head diameter = 1⁵⁄₁₆" (34mm)
Tapered, hollow timber mast:
Base diameter = 2⁹⁄₁₆" (66mm)
Head diameter = 1½" (38mm)

BOOM

Length = 11'10" (3600mm)
Aluminum boom:
Diameter = 2" (50mm)
Tapered, solid timber boom:
Midpoint diameter = 2" (50mm)
End diameters = 1½" (38mm)
Tapered, hollow timber boom:
Midpoint diameter = 2¼" (57mm)
End diameters = 1¾" (45mm)
Bamboo: Same size as hollow timber

Wa'apa: Large Shunting Rig

MAST

Length = 13'2" (4000mm)
Aluminum mast:
Diameter = 2¼" (57mm)
Wall thickness = ⅛" (3mm)
Solid timber mast (untapered):
Diameter = 2½" (63mm)
Hollow timber mast (untapered):
Diameter = 2½" (63mm)

YARD

Length = 19'8" (6000mm)
Two fiberglass windsurfing masts can be joined at their bases to make a fiberglass yard.
Aluminum yard:
Diameter = 2¼" (57mm)
Wall thickness = ³⁄₃₂" (2mm)
Tapered, solid timber yard:
Midpoint diameter = 2⁹⁄₁₆" (65mm)
End diameters = 1⅜" (35mm)
Tapered, hollow timber yard:
Midpoint diameter = 2¹³⁄₁₆" (72mm)
End diameters = 1½" (38mm)
Bamboo: Same size as hollow timber

BOOM

Length = 19'8" (6000mm)

This curved boom is laminated from three pieces of ¾" × 2" (19mm × 50mm) timber bent along a jig.

Wa'apa: Small Shunting Rig

MAST
Length = 11'8" (3556mm)
Aluminum mast:
Diameter = 2" (50mm)
Wall thickness = ³⁄₃₂" (2mm)
Solid timber mast (untapered):
Diameter = 2¼" (57mm)
Hollow timber mast (untapered):
Diameter = 2¼" (57mm)

YARD
Length = 14' (4267mm)
Aluminum yard:
Diameter = 2" (50mm)
Wall thickness = ³⁄₃₂" (2mm)
Tapered, solid timber yard:
Midpoint diameter = 2" (50mm)
End diameters = 2" (50mm)
Tapered, hollow timber yard:
Midpoint diameter = 2" (50mm)
End diameters = 2" (50mm)
Bamboo: Same size as hollow timber

BOOM
Length = 14'0" (4267mm)
Aluminum boom:
Diameter = 2" (50mm)
Wall thickness = ³⁄₃₂" (2mm)
Tapered, solid timber boom:
Midpoint diameter = 2" (50mm)
End diameters = 1½" (38mm)
Tapered, hollow timber boom:
Midpoint diameter = 2¼" (57mm)
End diameters = 1¾" (45mm)
Bamboo: Same size as hollow timber

The Wa'apa double-outrigger sail plan, shown in Figure 3-8, requires a stayed mast. This is a very conventional dinghy rig with the side stays attached to the fore and aft poles supporting the hiking seats. These fore and aft poles will have to be extra stiff, and will need strong lashings to carry the loads from the mast shrouds. They can be made of any of the materials used for spar construction.

I have not provided specifications for this rig, as it is assumed that it will be a secondhand rig taken from a sailing dinghy or beach catamaran.

Fore and Aft Hiking Seat Support Poles: Wa'apa and Ulua

These specifications apply to both the Wa'apa and Ulua.
Support pole length = 8'7" (2600mm)
Aluminum tube support poles: 2" (50mm) diameter
Solid timber support poles: 2¼" diameter
Hollow timber support poles: 2½" diameter
Bamboo: Same size as hollow timber

SAILS

You have the choice of having your sail made by a professional sail maker or making it yourself. Figures 11-5 through 11-14 have enough information for the sail maker to go ahead, and he will no doubt have good advice on building in some shape. A sail maker can do a better job if you already have the spars that you're going to use.

You can purchase polyester sailcloth (i.e., DuPont Dacron®), or use one of the less expensive alternatives like polytarp. I don't recommend the lightweight material commonly sold as blue tarp. It will stretch out of shape quite soon if you use it in strong winds and will impair your windward sailing ability. I recommend the heavier grade that has a lot more reinforcing fibers. It can be purchased from canvas supply companies and is sometimes used for tent floors. It is commonly available on a roll in a 6' (1.8m) width. All inexpensive grades of polytarp do not have much resistance to sunlight, but if you keep it stored out of the sun, you will get many years of service.

I always sew my sails together, but some people use strong, adhesive tapes such as 3M Super Seam tape, or they use an iron to melt layers of polytarp together.

A convenient way to lay out the sail is to cut long sticks (like leftover strip planks) to the exact length of each side of the sail, clamp the ends at the corners, and lay the sticks on top of the fabric, noting the alignment of the seams shown in Figures 11-7 through 11-13. Use double-sided tape or silicone sealant to stick the panels together, overlapping about ¾" (19mm) to form a slightly oversized, blank piece of fabric. Be sure to allow enough extra fabric for the luff and foot curve. Allow an extra ¾" (19mm) along the leech to fold over. Use one of the long sticks to draw the luff curve, and if you are using a curved boom, use the boom to draw the foot curve. The hollow leech curve can be whatever pleases your eye.

Sew two rows of stitching at each seam. After the blank is sewn, carefully cut the luff and foot to a fair curve.

Any built-in shape from broad-seaming or edge curves depends on the stiffness of the spars being used. A bendy mast will require more curvature in

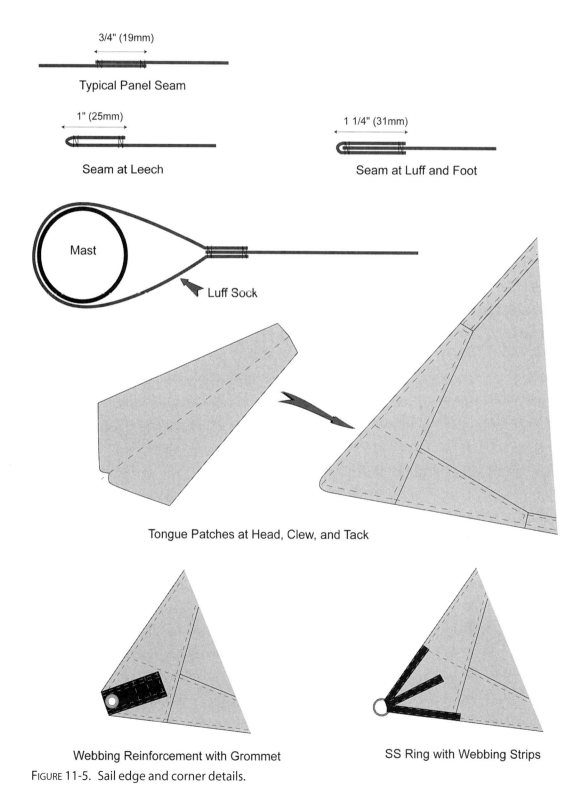

3/4" (19mm)

Typical Panel Seam

1" (25mm)

Seam at Leech

1 1/4" (31mm)

Seam at Luff and Foot

Mast

Luff Sock

Tongue Patches at Head, Clew, and Tack

Webbing Reinforcement with Grommet

SS Ring with Webbing Strips

FIGURE 11-5. Sail edge and corner details.

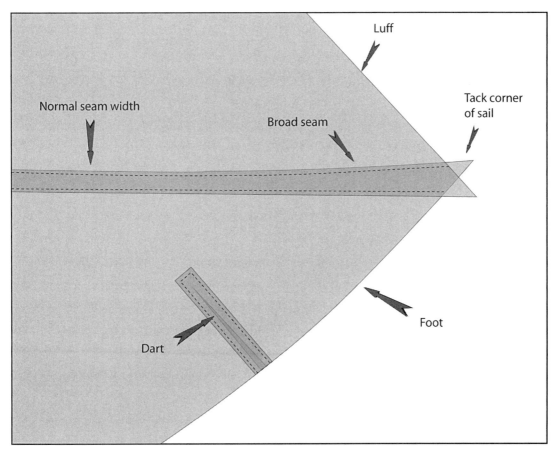

FIGURE 11-6. Increasing the seam overlap at the edge of the sail is called broad-seaming and will build in a three-dimensional shape.

the luff, whereas a stiff carbon spar will require very little. In Figures 11-7 through 11-13, I've shown the average amount I use with 100 percent fiberglass windsurfing masts.

Broad-seaming is a technique that builds in a three-dimensional shape to the fabric. In the old days when the sails were made from cotton or other stretchy fabrics, luff and foot curve was enough to give the sail its desired shape. Modern sailcloth stretches very little and requires additional help like broad-seaming to give it the desired three-dimensional shape. While a normal seam has a constant width of overlap, broad-seaming widens the overlap gradually as it gets closer to the edge (usually the luff) of the sail.

I don't normally add any broad seams along the luff if I'm using stretchy fabric like polytarp, but one at the tack of the sail is good, along with a dart or tuck along the curved foot of the sail. Sails with foot curvature set better with a tuck or dart about one third of the way along the foot from the mast. Just cut the fabric for about 16" (400mm), overlap by the

indicated amount (see Figures 11-7 through 11-13), and sew a 2" (50mm) wide strip over it on both sides.

Fold over and crease ¾" (19mm) of the leech, and apply double-sided tape and two rows of stitching. Cut strips of fabric 2½" (63mm) wide, crease them in the middle, and fold them over the luff and foot edges. These strips don't have to be full length; you can piece together shorter strips, overlapping them by about 3" (75mm). Apply two rows of stitching.

Make the corner tongue patches, fold them over the corners, stick them with double-sided tape, and stitch them in place. If you wish to have a large grommet at the corners, reinforce the area with wide webbing folded over the corner, as shown in Figure 11-5.

Install small grommets along the luff and foot for lacing or cable ties. Cable ties are plastic straps made to hold bundles of electrical wiring together. They work very well for attaching a sail to its spars. Black ties are usually intended for outdoor applications.

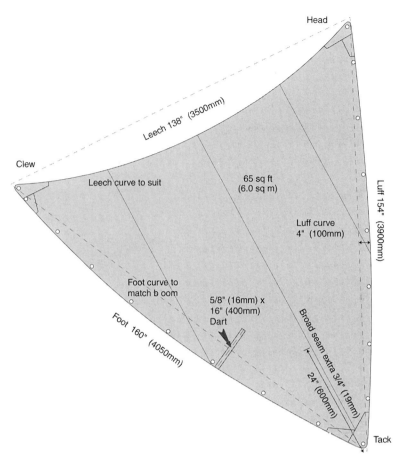

FIGURE 11-7. Sail layout for the Ulua tacking rig. Note that a luff sock can be substituted for grommets and lacing along the luff.

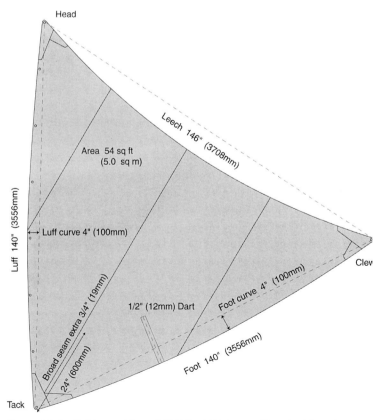

FIGURE 11-8. Sail layout for a 16' (4.8m) Wa'apa with a tacking rig.

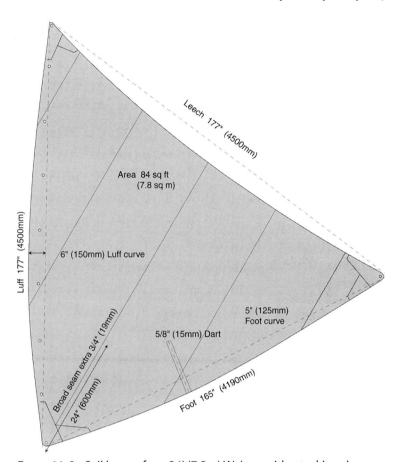

FIGURE 11-9. Sail layout for a 24' (7.2m) Wa'apa with a tacking rig.

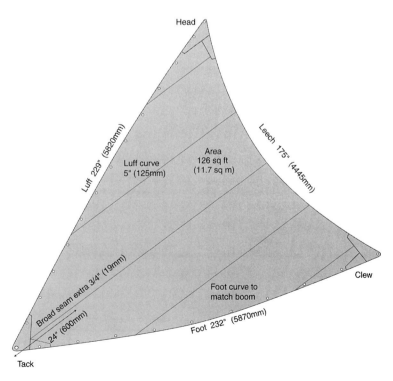

FIGURE 11-10. Sail layout for a 24' (7.2m) Wa'apa with a shunting rig.

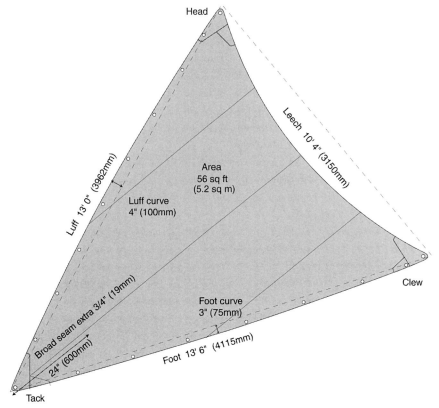

FIGURE 11-11. Sail layout for a 16' (4.8m) Wa'apa with a shunting rig.

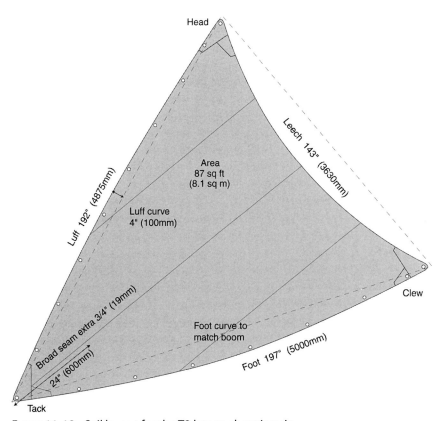

FIGURE 11-12. Sail layout for the T2 lateen shunting rig.

Making a Gibbons/Dierking Sail

The structure of the Gibbons/Dierking sail is similar to a windsurfing sail, with a sock along the luff and the necessity of aligning the warp of the fabric parallel with the leech to withstand the high tension there. Because there are actually two differently aligned leeches, you'll get the best results with a miter cut or a seam running parallel with the boom. The Gibbons sail is a flat piece of fabric; there is no need for broad seaming or darts. The halyard tension will control the sail's draft.

Begin by taking the yard, the boom, and some small line to rig up an oversized "bow and arrow." Draw the bow, while leaving 6" (150mm) of arrow (boom) extending past the bow. The bend taken by the yard will determine the luff curve and the basic shape of the sail and can be used to draw the shape onto the fabric blank. The fabric blank is a slightly

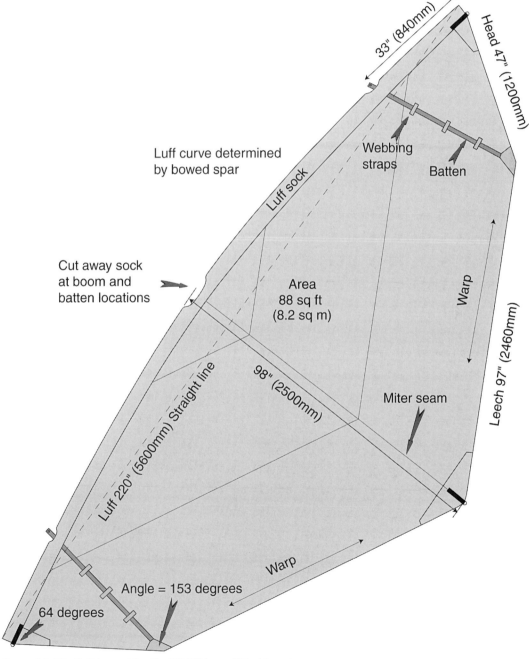

FIGURE 11-13. Sail layout for the T2 Gibbons/Dierking rig.

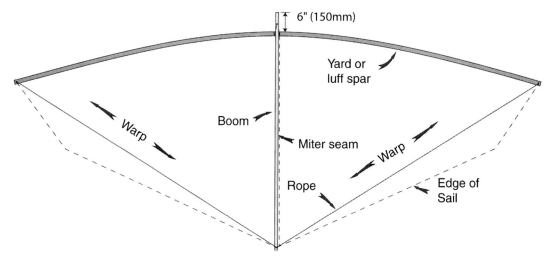

6" (150mm)

Yard or
luff spar

Warp

Boom

Miter seam

Warp

Rope

Edge of
Sail

FIGURE 11-14. Using the luff spar and boom to lay out a Gibbons/Dierking sail.

oversized piece of fabric that is big enough for the entire sail.

Align the warp of the fabric with the leeches, and join them with a miter seam parallel with the boom. Overlap the panels by ¾" (19mm), and stick the pieces together with either double-sided tape or silicone sealant. This will make sewing them together easier and will prevent puckering.

Lay the "bow and arrow" on top of the blank, and trace the luff curve from the inside of the bow (yard). The sock will be added later to wrap around the spar. Use two tape measures or sticks, cut to the length of the head and leech, to mark the aft edge of

the sail. Add another ¾" (19mm) to be folded over on the aft edge.

The single full-length batten at each end of the sail is mounted on the windward side with a short, sewn pocket only at the leech. Two or three intermediate fabric straps are sewn on the sail to hold the batten in place. Do not sew on a full-length batten pocket or you won't be able to furl the sail. The batten extends past the luff spar through a slit in the sock and is tensioned with a small line looped around the luff spar. This arrangement, which is the opposite to conventional practice, makes furling a lowered sail easier.

CHAPTER 12

Rigging, Tuning, and Sailing

RIGGING AND TUNING

CE and CLR

One of the most important concepts to understand when you are setting up any sailing craft is the relationship between the center of effort (CE) and the center of lateral resistance (CLR).

The CE is the geometric center of the sail, found by drawing lines between each corner of the sail and the midpoint of the opposite side. This does not necessarily indicate the *true* center of effort; it is only used for estimation purposes.

The CLR can be found by making a *scale* drawing on a piece of stiff cardboard of the underwater profile of the hull, including the leeboard. There is disagreement about whether a fixed rudder should be included in this, but I would say that a deep, high-aspect blade should be included, whereas a steering oar or shallow rudder should not. The cardboard scale profile is cut out and balanced with a pin to find the CLR.

The CE should always be at least even with, or forward of, the CLR, averaging about 5 percent of the waterline length forward of the CLR. This distance is called the *lead*. If the canoe has strong weather helm (tries to turn into the wind), the lead should be increased, whereas if steering is needed to keep the canoe from bearing away from the wind, the lead should be reduced. Weather helm will increase in a stronger wind, so be sure to test in all conditions.

An outrigger canoe has a few more factors to make it even more complicated. Weight distribution of crew and cargo also has an effect on this balance.

By sinking one end of the canoe more than the other, the underwater profile is altered and will affect the amount of steering input needed. A single person sailing and sitting in the aft seat will lift the bow and could cause lee helm, or a tendency to turn away from the wind. Too much weight forward can cause more weather helm. Narrow canoes are more sensitive to weight distribution than their beamier cousins.

The ama also has an effect on the sailing balance of a tacking rig. On one tack, the ama is to leeward, where its drag tries to turn the canoe downwind. On the other tack, it is unweighted, or flying, and causes very little or no drag. You can compensate for this by angling the leeboard fore and aft. With the ama to leeward, the blade of the leeboard would be angled forward to offset the effect of the ama drag.

There are several ways to change the balance of a tacking rig: You can move the mast step fore and aft along with the collar (the fitting at gunwale level); you can change the rake of the mast by altering the position of either the step or the collar; you can change the mounting position of the leeboard; or you can add or remove a permanent rudder.

The CE of an Oceanic lateen shunting rig can be shifted fore and aft by changing the halyard attachment point on the yard or by having alternative mast-step positions with the use of a sliding track or extra sockets or pad eyes. Traditional Kiribati canoes often used a row of extra mast-step sockets to change the CE for different courses sailed, similar to the effect gained with a modern Windsurfer's sliding mast track.

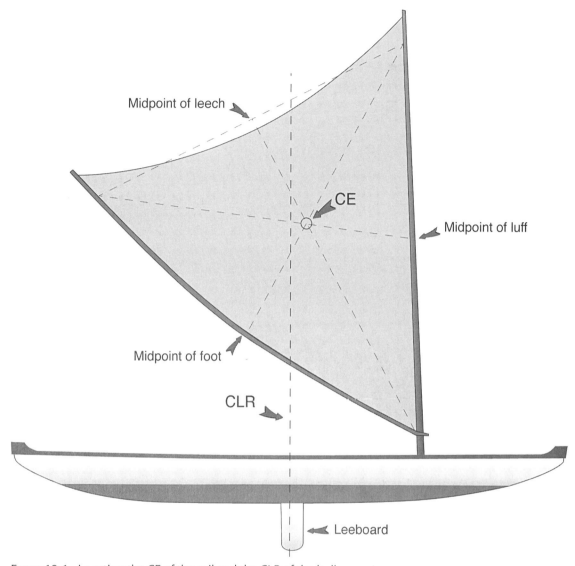

FIGURE 12-1. Locating the CE of the sail and the CLR of the hull.

Tacking Rig Setup

The Ulua is generally set up with a tacking rig. A single-part mainsheet begins with a loose bowline around the aft iako, leads up to the boom through a block, goes to another block hanging below the boom jaws, then to another block below the jaws attached to the wae, and on to a cam cleat mounted below the aft edge of the forward seat. This allows easy access from the aft hull seat and the hiking seat. A two-part mainsheet begins at the boom, goes down to a block attached to the aft iako, heads back to the block on the boom, and then goes on to the jaws, as in the single-part sheet.

This mainsheet system has the added benefit of tightening the luff of the sail when close-hauled and loosening it when reaching or running. A separate

downhaul is not necessary, but a safety lanyard from the boom jaws to the wae is recommended to prevent the mast falling out of the canoe in the event of a capsize.

The brailing/spiller line has a dual purpose. Since my tacking rigs don't use halyards, the brailing line is used to pull the boom up against the mast while bundling up the sail as it goes up. The brailing line begins by being lashed to a grommet about three quarters of the way up the luff of the sail. It then leads to another grommet that is an equal distance out along the foot of the sail. The brailing line then passes through and leads to a small block that is lashed to the same luff grommet. From there, it leads to the forward iako for tying off, or it can be led aft to within reach of the crew. The other purpose of this line is to spill wind and de-power the sail during squalls by partial brailing of the sail.

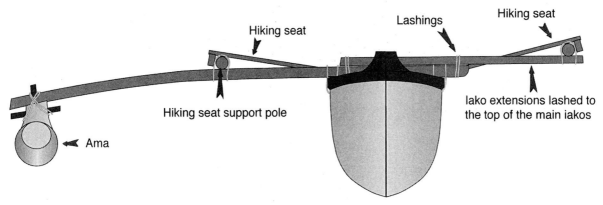

FIGURE 12-2. An Ulua with a second hiking seat opposite the ama.

Traditional Oceanic canoes didn't really have reefing methods as are used today. On larger vessels, a second smaller sail and spars could be carried on board, but small canoes either used a spiller line to de-power the sail, or they dropped the sail and waited out the squall. The sails in this book can all be reefed, but not quickly and conveniently while sailing. Simple reef points can be included when making the sail and tied in with the rig lying on the beach. This is about the only way to reef a sail with a curved boom. If you opt for a straight boom with a loose-footed sail, the sail can be partially wound up on the mast. The outhaul line will have to be readjusted to the new sail area.

I've recently experimented with installing a long zipper to remove a portion of the sail area. The aft edge or leech of the sail is normally hollow or curved inward. By sewing on a zipper into a much deeper, hollow curve, a significant area of sail can be removed. The corners of the sail at the zipper ends must each be reinforced with a pair of grommets and a lashing. The installation of the zipper is best left to a professional, because it can form an undesirable ridge in the sail if this process is not done right.

An unstayed windsurfing, mast-supported sail can profit from a forestay. This is simply a ¼" (6mm), low-stretch line leading from a loop around the hull's bow (an eye strap keeps it from slipping off) to a loop of webbing around the mast about two thirds of the way up, with the line continuing on to the masthead. As the sail is sheeted in hard to go to windward, the masthead will be bent aft. This has the effect of flattening the sail. Note that if you use a forestay, you won't be able to reef by winding the sail around the mast.

If you wish to make the Ulua go faster, you'll have to increase the sail area. This can be done with higher rigs and the necessity of a complete staying

system. To carry the increased sail area, you must increase the righting moment. In other words, you have to hike out. The hiking seat shown is adequate for the standard sail plan, but with a larger rig, you will want a second seat on the non-ama side, supported by iako extensions, which can be lashed in place. Hiking on the non-ama side will prevent you from sinking the ama if you're in a higher-powered rig. You may also need another pair of seats to allow additional crew members to hike out.

One advantage of an unstayed rig is that you can ease the mainsail entirely and let the boom go flying toward the bow. This is useful when you are approaching your destination while sailing downwind, because it allows you to slow down without brailing up the sail.

Shunting Rig Setup

The T2 and the Wa'apa have a choice of two quite different rigs that share a few common components. The masts of both the Oceanic lateen rig and the Gibbons/Dierking rig are supported by two backstays (leading from just below the masthead to each bow), a weather shroud (leading from just below the masthead to a bridle between the outer ends of the iako), and a mast prop (a shock-absorbing strut attached about one third of the way up the mast and stepped on a fore and aft spar running between the iakos two thirds of the way out to the ama). In both rig types, the mast is tilted toward the direction of travel. This is necessary to place the CE forward of the CLR.

All of the stays and shrouds are running rigging, enabling you to fine-tune the balance while underway. The weather shroud can be tightened to angle the mast to windward in strong winds, thereby reducing heeling angle and introducing a small lift component. In light airs, the mast is eased to leeward,

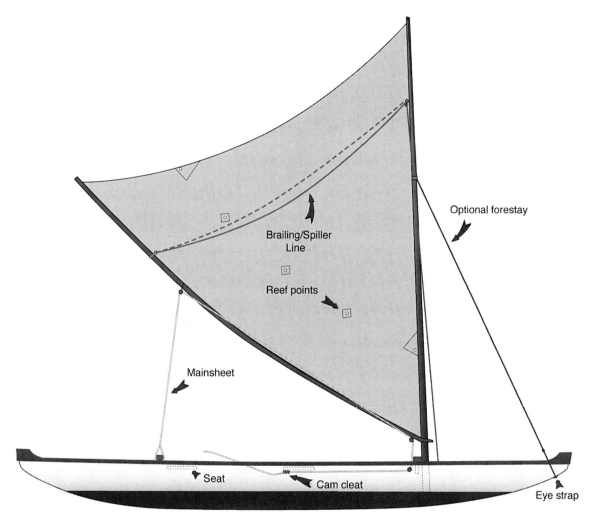

Optional forestay

Braling/Spiller
Line

Reef points

Mainsheet

Seat

Cam cleat

Eye strap

FIGURE 12-3. Ulua mainsheet, brailing line, and forestay leads.

where it makes shunting easier. The line from the weather-shroud bridle is led to within easy reach of the crew and can be fitted with a block and tackle so that it can be adjusted under load.

The backstays begin just below the masthead and lead to a block at the bow and back toward the nearest iako. A stopper knot or ball is placed along the backstay at the point where it will prevent the mast from tilting any further forward than is required. A further enhancement puts a powerful loop of bungee cord at the end of the backstay between the stopper and the iako. When set up correctly, the mast will be held vertical if the tack lines are released. Pulling the yard end toward either bow will stretch one of the bungees and loosen the other. The bungees make the backstays self-adjusting during the shunt.

The mast prop is also bungee-powered. The two parallel overlapping struts are pushing outward because of the bungee loop, and are holding the mast from falling to windward in light airs, or in the

event of getting back-winded. It will also allow the rig to lay over up to twenty-five degrees from vertical in a back-winding situation and help to prevent the ama from sinking.

The weight of bungee necessary for any given rig is dependent on the rig size and the weight of the mast. You can buy bungee cord by length from a roll at most marine-hardware stores or canvas-supply stores. I use three parallel lengths of ¼" (6mm) bungee cord for the T2. Add more lengths until the mast goes vertical when the tack line is released.

The sheet to control the sail and boom can be a single loop of line, with both ends attached to the same point on the boom. From the boom, the sheet leads to a block that is attached to the leeward dash-board. It then loops around to windward of the mast (and behind the sailor), to another block on the other dashboard, and back to the boom. Routing the sheet behind the sailor prevents the sheet from tangling with other lines in the hull.

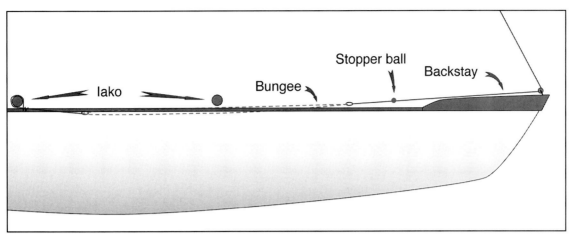

FIGURE 12-4. T2's bungee-powered backstay. A rope tail, at the end of the bungee, attaches to an iako and provides tension adjustment.

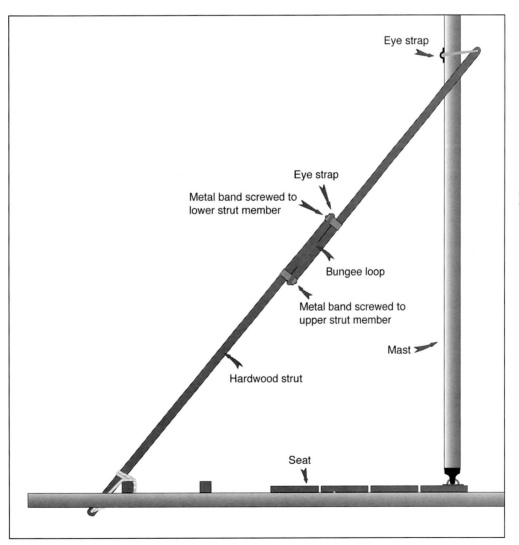

FIGURE 12-5. The shock-absorbing mast prop used with shunting rigs.

Attach blocks and stays to the dashboard by drilling a pair of holes and lashing the block in place with small line.

The Gibbons sail is essentially a flat piece of fabric. When the yard and sail are hoisted, the halyard tension will determine the draft or depth of the sail shape. The higher the halyard tension, the more the luff spar is bowed, which flattens the sail. In strong winds, the halyard should be very tight, and in lighter airs, it should be eased. You can easily see the effect; trial and error with marks on the halyard will allow you to tune the rig for maximum performance. It is important to have a stout, low-stretch halyard, or you will end up with a baggy sail in strong winds—just what you don't want. I'd recommend a 5/16" (8mm) to 3/8" (10mm) braided line for this purpose.

Moving the CE with the Gibbons rig is a matter of changing the vertical position of the boom attachment point at the masthead. This can be done with a series of attachment holes through the masthead or with a track and sliding car, like a boom gooseneck track. This car and track could even be controlled with small lines to the deck. Raising the boom attachment point tilts the sail more forward and reduces weather helm. Lowering the attachment point rakes the rig aft and increases weather helm. It is wise to make the mast a bit extra-long to allow a full range of adjustment to suit your sail and spars. Once you have found the best overall position, you may have to readjust the position of the stopper balls on the backstays.

SAILING BASICS

Tacking Rigs

Canoes that use a tacking rig are operated in the same way as the majority of small conventional sailing dinghies. I will describe a typical sail with the Ulua or Wa'apa.

I normally store the rig brailed up, with the boom folded up against the mast and the sail furled up between them. With the hull on the beach and aimed into the wind, pick up the brailed rig and place the mast base into the mast collar and down into the step. Release the brailing line and pull down on the boom to unfurl the sail. Feed the mainsheet through its blocks, and tighten the sheet to see how the sail looks. If you have a forestay, attach it to the loop around the bow or fitting at the stem. Release the sheet and allow the boom to weathercock into the wind.

For a beginner, it is easiest to start with the wind blowing parallel to the beach. With the leeboard and

rudder kicked up, push the hull into the water, and use a paddle to get into deep enough water to lower the leeboard and rudder. Pull in the sheet until the sail stops shaking, and you will start moving forward with the wind coming at a right angle to the hull. This point of sail is called a beam reach. If the wind is coming over the ama side, one person must be in the hiking seat. If no one is on the hiking seat, you may capsize. Because the ama is usually on the left (port) side, you are now sailing on a port tack.

Use the rudder to turn the canoe gradually toward the wind direction. The sail will start to shake, so pull in more of the sheet line. You will only be able to sail within about fifty degrees of the wind direction. If you steer too far into the wind, the canoe will stop and start drifting backward. If this happens, release the sheet and try to steer backward to an angle where the sail can fill once again. If you are completely stalled, use a paddle to orient the canoe.

Once you are moving at full speed again, use the rudder (or steering oar) to turn completely through the wind direction. This is called tacking and should involve a turn of about 100 degrees. The canoe will tack more reliably if the crew weight is toward the aft end of the canoe. It is best to turn a little past fifty degrees to the wind and allow the canoe to reach full speed; then gradually turn it back to your closest course into the wind. You are now on the starboard tack, with the wind passing over the right (starboard) side of the canoe. On this tack, the ama is to leeward and being pressed into the water by the force of the wind. You should change your location to the seat in the hull to relieve the pressure on the ama.

A canoe with a single ama will turn more easily in one direction than the other. Going from a starboard tack to a port tack is slower and more likely to stall, because you're dragging the ama around through the wind. Going from a port tack to a starboard tack is helped by the drag of the ama.

Use the rudder to turn away from the wind direction, easing the boom and sail out as you turn. Keep turning until the wind is about forty-five degrees from the stern of the canoe. This point of sail is called a broad reach. A broad reach is most enjoyable with good speed and dry sailing, but don't allow yourself to get too far downwind of where you started, because it's much slower and wetter work getting back.

Sailing straight downwind requires some caution. Steer with care to ensure that the canoe does not go past the wind direction. If you go past the wind direction, the wind can get behind the sail enough to slam the boom over to the opposite side. This is called jibing and can cause damage to the canoe and the crew if it is not controlled. Practice jibing in light winds, and remember to duck as the boom passes over your head. Pulling in and releasing the sheet as the boom is moving from side to side will help in controlling the jib. During a jibe, remember to be in the hiking seat before beginning the maneuver.

The brailing line can be used to reduce the sail area when you are broad-reaching or running in strong winds. It is also useful when approaching the beach, where the sail can be completely brailed up.

Shunting Rigs

Although a shunting rig is more complex than a tacking rig, it has an advantage in that you can train for the shunting event without actually putting the canoe in the water. I like to call this training "lawn shunting." During a shunt, a canoe will not be changing direction or moving much, so you can practice quite realistically on your lawn.

Orient the canoe with the wind passing directly over the ama (beam reach). Note that a shunting rig must always have the wind passing over the ama side. Have the butt of the yard pulled to one of the bows with the tack line. Hoist the sail with the sheet loose to allow the boom to pivot out to leeward and weathercock into the wind. As the yard gets closer to its final position, it will pull the masthead toward the bow. Pull in the sheet a little to see how the sail looks with some wind in it. If you pull in too much, you may experience your first "lawn capsize."

When shunting on the water, you will always orient the canoe in the same way, with the wind as close as possible to ninety degrees from the centerline of the hull. Too close to the wind or too far on a broad reach invites "back-winding" the sail. If the wind catches the back side of the sail, it'll lay it flat against the mast and stall the canoe. If the wind is strong, it can submerge the ama. If you are back-winded in light winds, you can usually turn the canoe with your paddle or steering oar. In strong winds, it may be necessary to brail up the sail or lower it before the canoe can be returned to its course.

With the canoe properly oriented to the wind direction, the first step in shunting is to release the sheet, allowing the boom to swing out to leeward with a completely loose sheet. If the wind is too light to hold the boom all the way out, lean the mast to leeward by easing the weather shroud.

After releasing the tack line, the mast will be pulled to the vertical (fore and aft) position by the bungees connected to the backstays. If you're rigged with an Oceanic lateen where the yard butt passes above the deck, pull the opposite bow's tack line and grab the yard with your other hand to guide it toward the new bow. As the yard butt approaches the new bow, the pull on the tack line will become greater, because you are stretching the backstay bungees on the new backstay. For an Oceanic lateen where the yard butt passes below the leeward gunwale, you don't need to grab the yard; just pull the yard along the guide rail with the tack line.

One difference resulting from the path of the yard butt is that you'll need two separate and identical mainsheets if the butt passes below the gunwale. If the yard passes above the gunwale, it can pass over a single mainsheet that can be used on both tacks.

After pulling the yard to the new bow with the tack line, secure it in a cam cleat, and pull in the mainsheet to move off in the opposite direction.

The procedure for the Gibbons/Dierking rig is very similar to that for the Oceanic lateen. The sheet is released, the tack line is released, the mast goes vertical, the yard goes horizontal with the sail and boom flying out to leeward, the other end of the yard is pulled down to the new bow with the tack line, the mainsheet is pulled in, and off you go.

Tack lines in all cases are "endless lines." The Oceanic lateen has both ends of the tack line tied to its yard butt, with the loop passing through two blocks located at the bows of the canoe. The Gibbons/Dierking rig has the two ends of the tack line attached to the two ends of the yard, and the loop also passes through two blocks at the bows of the canoe.

Steering a canoe rigged with the Oceanic lateen rig can be done with a steering oar in the usual way but can also be aided through sail trim and weight distribution. Sheeting in more than necessary will cause the canoe to turn away from the wind, and easing the sheet will cause it to turn toward the wind direction. This technique applies to close-hauled and beam-reaching courses. Broad-reaching will require the aid of a steering oar or paddle, and running dead downwind is not recommended at any time with a shunting rig because of the possibility of an accidental jibe and the resulting back-winding. Weight concentrated aft in the hull will turn the canoe away from the wind, while weight moved forward will turn the canoe toward the wind.

Sheet adjustments with the Gibbons/Dierking rig do not affect steering as much as in the Oceanic lateen rig. The shorter boom creates less turning

FIGURE 12-6. Oceanic lateen rig close-hauled on a port tack.

FIGURE 12-7. The canoe is steered onto a beam reach, and the mainsheet is released to allow the boom to swing out.

FIGURE 12-8. The tack line is used to pull the yard along the leeward side of the hull.

FIGURE 12-9. The tack line is secured in a cam cleat when the yard reaches the new bow.

FIGURE 12-10. The sail is sheeted in, and the canoe begins sailing on a starboard tack.

FIGURE 12-11. Gibbons/Dierking rig close-hauled on a port tack.

FIGURE 12-12. The canoe is steered onto a beam reach, and the mainsheet is released to allow the boom to swing out.

FIGURE 12-13. The forward tack line is released while the aft tack line is taken in, allowing the yard to pivot to a horizontal position. A light tension is kept on the tack line at both ends of the yard to avoid oscillation.

FIGURE 12-14. The tack of the sail is pulled down to the new bow, and the tack line is secured in a cam cleat.

FIGURE 12-15. The sail is sheeted in, and the canoe sails away on a starboard tack.

moment than the much longer boom used with the lateen.

Because shunting rigs are quite alien to most sailors, it can be a great help in visualizing the maneuver by making a small model with sticks and string. The effects of small alterations in geometry can readily be seen.

SWAMPING AND CAPSIZE

Flotation

During the thousands of years that outrigger canoes have been used for transportation and fishing, the most important safety device carried on board was between the ears of the crew. Nothing built in to the design or carried on board can replace prudent seamanship. It certainly helps if you grew up using small boats and occasionally got into harm's way. No book or lecture can come close to simply spending time on the water. Lessons learned on the water become a part of you and are never forgotten.

Traditional canoes being made of timber would not sink unless they were carrying a load of stone. They could certainly swamp, though, and Oceanic people became adept at getting the water back out again. A child or young person on board a sailing outrigger would be employed at bailing for much of the time.

I remember once watching a Tongan man paddling his outrigger canoe across a harbor on a choppy day. He had a full load of fruit and vegetables that put his freeboard down to nothing. The inevitable happened, and produce was floating everywhere. What amazed me was that he had the canoe bailed in a few seconds. It was a simple dugout with no fore or aft decks. He swam around to one end of the hull, and with a quick down-and-up motion, had all of the water going out the other end in one wave. Another few minutes for the produce retrieval and he was away again. For the rest of us who didn't grow up in the South Seas, some tangible safety devices are in order.

Flotation is the single most important way to stay alive, or to get your canoe on its way again. Unless you're an expert water person, wear your life jacket (PFD) and carry a knife. All of the designs described here have, at minimum, a sealed compartment at both ends of the hull defined by a watertight or collision bulkhead. An empty compartment will keep you afloat as long as it is sealed,

but if there was damage and it is leaking, you'll need a backup system. The lightest and cheapest solution is to fill your compartments with plastic soft-drink bottles or chunks of foam usually discarded from packing. Put the foam chunks in sealed plastic bags to keep the crumbs from getting loose.

The Ulua and the Wa'apa have a lot of interior volume that will be filled with water in the event of a capsize. If the waves are choppy, you may not be able to bail out the water faster than it's coming over the gunwales. Additional flotation would be a good idea if you frequent rough water or are often alone. Blocks of shaped foam can be fitted under the two seats. They can be nicely glassed or just strapped in with webbing belts. The seats can also be built with a sealed chamber beneath them that acts as flotation and dry storage space. There are also inflatable air bags available as standard equipment for sailing dinghies. Any additional flotation must be very securely fastened, as it will try to come out when it's submerged.

A hollow mast should have its ends sealed with plugs or foam. A mast filled with water makes recovery from a capsize more difficult.

Sailing canoes that race between the Hawaiian Islands use a *safety ama*. This is a second ama carried on the opposite side of the main ama. It is mounted differently in that it is closer to the main hull and is held well above the waterline. It only comes into play when a capsize is imminent and will, in most cases, prevent one. Iakos can be originally built longer to accommodate a safety ama, or short iako extensions can be lashed on with an overlap over the hull.

The safety ama does not require the sophisticated design of the main ama. It can, in fact, be a PVC pipe with its ends plugged, a simple foam-and-fiberglass log, or even the foam tubes used on swimming pool dividers, stiffened with a tube or dowel down its center. These can also be rigged as additional flotation in the interior of the hull in many ingenious ways.

The T2 has no need for extra flotation. In addition to the two sealed compartments in the end, it has a raised, sealed floor in the cockpit area that is above the waterline. Drain holes or *scuppers* are located at each end of the cockpit to drain out spray or the entire interior in the event of a capsize. A safety ama can also be rigged if you wish.

The Wa'apa has two sealed bow compartments that are adequate if it is being sailed as a 16-footer,

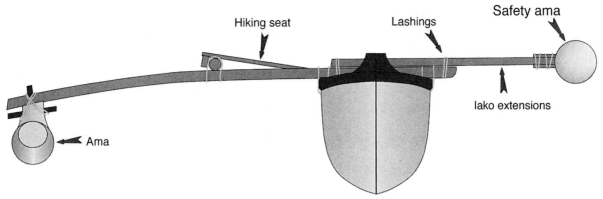

FIGURE 12-16. A safety ama rigged on an Ulua with short, overlapping beams lashed to the top of the main cross beams. A second hiking seat can be rigged on the safety ama side.

but that will allow a lot of water inside if it is rigged as a 24-footer. The center section can have foam blocks or other material under the seats. There is also the option of decking over the entire center section with hatches installed that, when open, would still allow a paddler to sit normally with his or her feet in the hull. A sealed bulkhead rather than the ring frame at the center of this section would make it even more secure. A safety ama or a double-outrigger setup will, of course, make it less likely to capsize in the first place.

Amas are made from either solid foam, or they can be made from hollow plywood or strip composite. It is wise to fill any hollow ama with foam chunks or plastic bottles, in case of a slow leak or major damage.

Recovering from a Capsize

The best way to prevent capsizing is to always keep a hand on or very near to the sheet controlling the sail. Don't forget to move onto the hiking seat

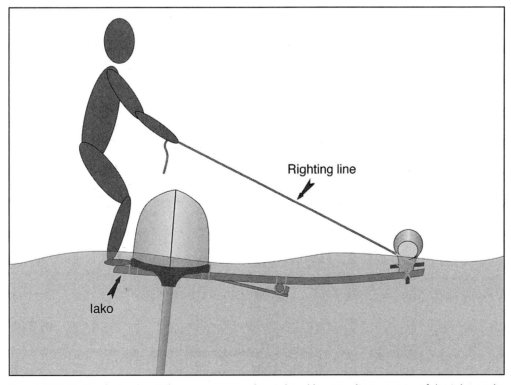

FIGURE 12-17. A capsized outrigger canoe can be righted by standing on one of the iako ends and pulling on a line attached to the ama.

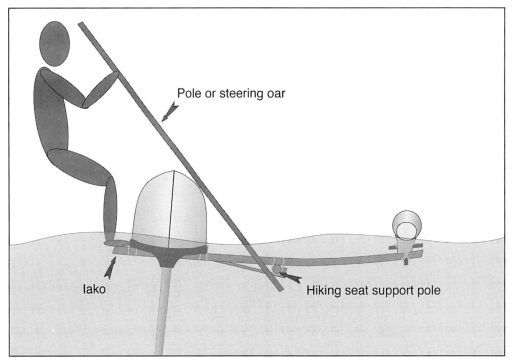

FIGURE 12-18. Using a righting pole or steering oar to right a capsized canoe.

when the ama is on the windward side. When jibing (turning the canoe with the stern passing through the eye of the wind), be sure to be in the hiking seat *before* you begin the jibe. In most cases, if you capsize in one of these canoes, it will stop with the ama up in the air. Most of the time you'll be thrown into the water to leeward and will have to swim around to the other side and pull the ama back down. Speed is of the essence, because the longer you take to get into position, the more likely it is that the wind will blow the canoe the rest of the way over. Release the mainsheet before you begin righting the canoe so that the sail can spill water and wind as it rises.

Traditional Oceanic canoes almost invariably used solid wood amas made from the lightest material available. The most common technique for righting a completely inverted canoe was to sink the ama, pushing it under the main hull. This was possible because of the limited buoyancy available from a solid log. Most amas attached to modern outriggers are hollow or foam-filled and are very difficult to sink unless you have several people to put their weight on them. A light, buoyant ama will have to be pulled over the top of the main hull.

A *righting line* can be kept rigged and stowed along underneath the iako and can be used to pull the ama up out of the water. A righting line is tied to the ama either at one of the attachment points or with a bridle to both of them, and is led back to the main hull. If you don't have one already rigged, always keep easily accessible pieces of line in the canoe that can also be used to fix many things.

A *righting pole* can also be used to gain more mechanical advantage in righting a capsized canoe. It can be stowed out on the iako alongside the pole that supports the hiking seat. A steering oar can also be used as a righting pole.

In the unlikely event that you have capsized a double outrigger, you can remove one of the amas and right the canoe as previously described. Lashings of rubber-strip or polyester line are normally used at the ama. If you carry a folding knife with a marline-spike in your pocket, you should be able to get even the nastiest knots undone.

Be sure that your mast has not come partly out of its step before you begin righting the canoe. This could cause severe damage to the mast and the collar.

Once the canoe is righted, you have to remove the water. A good-sized plastic bucket for each person on board is recommended. If you have more than one person on board, you may be able to get some of the water out of the hull by sinking the ama as much as possible and tipping the water out. Another tactic is to hang off of one end of the canoe and get a surge going to slop some of it out. It's not a bad idea to practice all of these things on a nice, warm day, and you'll be much better prepared if the real thing happens.

Be sure to have lanyards on the bailing buckets, paddles, and anything else carried in the hull.

Glossary

Aft—Toward the back end of a hull or opposite to the direction of travel.

Aka—A term sometimes used for the cross beams or iako.

Ama—The small hull or float attached to the ends of the outrigger beams used to stabilize a narrow hull.

Amidships—The midsection of a hull; halfway between the bow and stern.

Backstays—Lines leading from the top of the mast out to the two ends of the hull; backstays control the vertical angle of the mast.

Back-winding—In a shunting rig, the wind must always pass over the ama. If the canoe is allowed to turn with its ama away from the wind, the sail will flatten up against the spars and become unmanageable.

Ballast—Weight in the form of crew or inanimate objects used to counterbalance the force of the sail.

Batten—A semi-flexible length of fiberglass or wood used to stiffen parts of a sail.

Beam reach—Sailing with the wind coming from a direction at ninety degrees to the direction of travel.

Boom—The spar attached to the bottom edge or foot of a sail.

Bow—The forward end of a hull.

Brailing line—A line rigged through a block on the upper part of the mast; the brailing line is used to lift the boom. It can be used to reduce the effective sail area when you are sailing downwind.

Broad reach—Sailing with the wind at a forty-five-degree angle to the stern of the hull.

Broad-seaming—An overlapping seam in a sail where the amount of overlap is varied along its length to induce a three-dimensional shape in the sail.

Bulkhead—A solid panel at right angles to the keel that encloses compartments in the ends of the hull and adds structural strength.

CE—The center of effort of a sail. For calculation purposes, it is also the geometric center of the sail.

Chine—A hull joint where two panels meet. The ridge where the sides join the bottom in a flat-bottomed hull is the chine.

Clew—The outer aft corner of a sail, attached to the end of the boom.

CLR—The center of lateral resistance of the hull and any underwater appendages.

Collar—A loop of metal strap that holds the mast in place at deck level.

Dado—A rectangular groove cut into a piece of wood.

Dagger boards—Retractable fins that pass through the bottom of a hull to provide lateral resistance or steering.

Fairlead—A plastic or metal liner that fits into a hole through which a line can pass smoothly.

Foil—A wing-shaped, underwater appendage used for lateral resistance or steering. A sail is also a form of a foil.

Foot—The bottom edge of a sail.

Forestay—A line attached to the bow of a hull, leading up to a point on the mast, and used to hold up the mast or improve its bending characteristics.

Frame—A stiffening framework at right angles to the keel that helps the hull to maintain its shape.

Freeboard—The distance between the surface of the water and the gunwale of the hull.

Gibbons rig—A shunting rig originally used by Euell Gibbons in the 1950s. My version incorporates some windsurfing technology.

Gunwale—A narrow, wooden strip attached along the sheer. A two-piece gunwale consists of an *inwale* along the inside of the hull and an *outwale* along the outside.

Halyard—A line used to pull a sail or its yard up the mast.

Head—The top corner of a sail, or the top of the mast.

Hiking seat—A slatted or fabric seat for a crew member; it is rigged outboard of the hull to provide ballast to balance the force of the sail.

Iakos—Cross beams or outrigger booms used to hold the ama (outrigger float) at a set distance parallel to the hull.

In irons—Stalling or drifting backward when a tacking rig passes its bow through the eye of the wind.

Jib—A sail set forward of the mast.

Keel—The line that defines the center bottom line of the hull.

Keel rocker—The vertical curvature of the keel when viewed from the side. Increasing keel rocker makes the canoe turn quicker and tack easily but makes paddling in a straight line more difficult.

Lamination—A process where thin layers of wood are glued together to form larger and stronger parts. Curved members like cross beams are commonly laminated.

Lashings—Structural joints in traditional outrigger canoes are held together with small rope wrapped around the joint. Lashing has proved effective in reducing stress concentrations in multihulled craft and is still recommended in many applications.

Lateen—See Oceanic lateen.

Lazy jacks—Lines leading from the upper portion of the mast down to the boom. A pair of brailing lines can perform as lazy jacks and catch the sail as it is lowered.

Lead—The distance between the CE and the CLR.

Leeboard—A board held alongside the hull to prevent drift to leeward. A leeboard performs the same function as a dagger board but is mounted outside of the hull instead of through it.

Leech—The aft free edge of a sail. The leech is not usually attached to a spar.

Lee helm—The tendency for a sailing craft to turn away from the wind direction.

Leeward—Opposite to the direction from which the wind is blowing; i.e., downwind. If your hat blows off your head, it will fly to leeward.

Luff—The forward leading edge of a sail.

Mainsail—The sail that is attached along the aft side of the mast.

Mainsheet—The line connected to the boom that is used to pull the sail in or ease it out. The mainsheet controls the angle between the sail and the wind direction.

Manu—A Hawaiian term for the extended ends of the stem at the bow and stern. It is frequently carved into shapes resembling parts of a bird and is useful for cutting through wave tops.

Mast—The main spar of any sailing rig; used to hold up the sail and other spars.

Masthead—The top of the mast.

Mast shrouds—A line or lines holding the mast up in a lateral direction. Shunting proas have a shroud leading out to a bridle connecting the outer ends of the iakos.

Mold—A temporary shape cut from plywood or particle board that supports the hull planking before it is stiffened with fiberglass sheathing. Molds are removed from the hull later.

Oceanic lateen rig—A triangular sail rig consisting of an angled yard, a boom of equal or longer length, and a mast shorter than the other spars. It is used on shunting canoes where the yard is carried or pulled along from bow to bow.

Outboard bracket—A plywood bracket that clamps onto the aft iako. The outboard bracket is used to mount an outboard motor, a steering oar, or a rudder.

Outhaul—A line connecting the outer end of the boom and the clew corner of the sail.

Parrel—Wooden or plastic beads threaded onto a line and looped around a spar.

Pola—A Hawaiian term for the fore and aft members resting on the top of the iakos. These are used to support net, trampolines, or hiking seats and can be used to aid in carrying the canoe.

Port—The left-hand side of a canoe when facing the bow.

Port tack—Sailing with the wind coming over the left or port side of the canoe.

Proa—Originally, this Indonesian term just meant "boat," but the first shunting canoes observed by explorers were called "proas," or "praus," and the term is now commonly used to describe this type of sailing canoe.

Rake—The angle of a mast or other spar, when measured from vertical.

Reefing—Reducing the size of a sail by partially furling it or removing some of its area.

Reef points—Grommets located in a sail to allow partial furling.

Ring frame—A frame that attaches to the inner sides of the hull and under the deck, but is open in the middle.

Scarf joint—A long, tapered, overlapping joint used to produce long lengths of timber or plywood without a reduction in strength.

Scull—Using a long steering oar in a "fish tail" motion to propel a canoe.

Scupper—A drain hole on deck or in a cockpit.

Sharpie—A flat-bottomed hull similar that of a dory, but with less flare in the sides.

Sheer—The line that defines the upper edge of the hull viewed from the side.

Sheeting—Pulling or easing the mainsheet to adjust the angle of the sail.

Shunting—A maneuver during which a double-ended sailing canoe changes direction by reversing its ends. The bow becomes the stern and vice versa. A lateen sail will have its tack carried or pulled to the new bow. Some modern shunting rigs simply pivot their booms 180 degrees.

Spars—Timber, metal, or composite poles used to support the edges of a sail.

Spiller lines—See Brailing line.

Spinnaker—A large, lightweight sail used to sail on downwind and broad-reaching courses.

Splashboard—A shaped or angled board forward of an open cockpit; it is used to prevent water from entering the hull.

Sprit boom—A boom whose inner end is attached to the mast at a point higher than the tack of the sail.

Starboard—The right-hand side of a canoe when facing the bow.

Starboard tack—Sailing with the wind coming over the right or starboard side of the canoe.

Station—A longitudinal position shown in the hull plans and table of offsets. Stations are usually equally spaced and numbered sequentially.

Stay—A line used to hold up the mast.

Staysail—A small sail usually set between two larger sails.

Stem—The structural member at the bow of a hull that connects the two side panels.

Stern—The back end of a hull. The stern may be either pointed in a double-ended shunting canoe or have a transom, in the case of some tacking canoes.

Stringer—A longitudinal structural member used to stiffen hulls.

Strongback—A rigid, solid, and level framework upon which a hull can be built. It does not become a permanent part of the hull.

Tack—To change course by passing the bow through the eye of the wind. Also, the lower forward corner of a sail, at the intersection of the mast and boom.

Tacking rig—A sailing rig that works similarly to western rigs and turns through the eye of the wind to make progress to windward. Boats with tacking rigs have a permanent bow and stern.

Tack line—A rope used to pull the butt of the yard from bow to bow in a shunting proa.

Trimaran—A hull rigged with identical amas on both sides.

Wae—A Hawaiian term for spreaders or short beams located just below gunwale level to strengthen or stiffen the hull sides. These are usually located just below the iako and are sometimes lashed to it.

Weather helm—The tendency of a sailing craft to turn into the wind direction.

Windward—The side of a hull or rig that is exposed to the wind; or the direction from which the wind is blowing.

Wing mast—A mast that is normally larger in cross section and that is shaped like an aircraft wing.

Yard—The spar attached to the leading edge of an Oceanic lateen or Gibbons/Dierking rig.

Resources

TRADITIONAL OUTRIGGER CANOE CULTURE

Doran, Edwin, Jr. *Wangka: Austronesian Canoe Origins*. College Station, Texas: Texas A&M University Press, 1981.

Gillett, Robert, James Ianelli, Tevita Waqavaka-toqa, and Matai Qica. *Traditional Sailing Canoes in Lau*. Suva, Fiji: Institute of Pacific Studies, University of the South Pacific, 1993.

Gladwin, Thomas. *East is A Big Bird*. Boston: Harvard University Press, 1970.

Grimble, Rosemary. *Migrations, Myth and Magic from the Gilbert Islands*. London: Routledge and Kegan Paul Ltd., 1972.

Haddon, A.C., and J. Hornell. *Canoes of Oceania*. Honolulu, Hawaii: Bishop Museum Publications 27, 28, and 29. Reprinted as one volume, 1975.

Holmes, Tommy. *The Hawaiian Canoe*. Hanalei, Kauai, Hawaii: Editions Limited, 1981.

Horridge, Adrian. *Outrigger Canoes of Bali and Madura, Indonesia*. Honolulu, Hawaii: Bishop Museum Special Publication 77, 1987.

Lewis, David. *We, the Navigators*. Wellington, New Zealand: A.H. & A.W. Reed Ltd., 1972.

Siers, James. *Taratai, A Pacific Adventure*. Wellington, New Zealand: Millwood Press Ltd., 1977.

Siers, James. *Taratai II, A Continuing Pacific Adventure*. Wellington, New Zealand: Millwood Press Ltd., 1978.

BOATBUILDING

Bradshaw, Todd, *Canoe Rig, The Essence and the Art*. Brooklin, Maine: WoodenBoat Books, 2000.

Gougeon, Meade. *Gougeon Brothers on Boat Construction: Wood and West System Materials*, 5th ed. Bay City, Michigan: Gougeon Brothers, Inc., 2005.

Hazen, David. *The Stripper's Guide to Canoe Building*. Larkspur, California: Tamal Vista Publications, 1976.

Marino, Emiliano. *The Sailmaker's Apprentice*. Camden, Maine: International Marine, 2001.

Moores, Ted. *KayakCraft*. Brooklin, Maine: WoodenBoat Publications, 1999.

INTERNET RESOURCES

Full-sized paper patterns can be ordered from the author through the mail or online from the website.

Gary Dierking
1485 Long Bay Road
Coromandel 3506
New Zealand
Gary Dierking's website: http://gary.dierking.net
http://homepages.paradise.net.nz

Gougeon Brothers, Inc. (manufacturer of West System epoxy): http://www.westsystem.com

Proa links: http://www.wingo.com/proa/links.html

Yahoo proa group: http://groups.yahoo.com/group/proa_file

Proafile website: http://www.proafile.com/

Tim Anderson: http://www.mit.edu/people/robot/

Index

Numbers in **Bold** indicate pages with illustrations

C

cabins, 4
cable ties, 141
canoe houses, 75
capsize recovery, **157–59**
carpenters' glue, 62, 82, 103
center of effort (CE), 43, 53, 55, 147–**48**
center of lateral resistance (CLR), 121, 126, 127, 129, 147–**48**
checking, 59, 76
chines, 60, **96, 97, 98**
clamps, 59
close-hauled, **154, 155**
compressive loads, **46**, 134
connections. *See also* lashed connections
  direct and indirect methods, **105**–6, 110–**12**
  quick-connecting strut, **30**, 31, 111, **112**
  sticks, 110, **111**
crab-claw rigs, 90, 99, 127
cradle, 85, **116**

D

dagger boards, 124, **126, 127**
dagger rudders, **127**
dashboards, 88, **89**, 90, **94**
decks
  plywood construction, 98–99, **100, 101**
  strip-composite construction, **87–88, 89, 93**
delamination test, 60
double-outrigger canoes
  advantages, 31
  capsized, 158
  iakos, 31, 113, **115**
  tacking rig option, 31, **37**, 139
duct tape, 76
dust masks and respirators, 75

E

edge grain, 65
epoxy putties, 76
epoxy resin
  additives, 62, 69
  advantages, 61–62
  allergies to, 62, 75
  applying, 72
  choosing, 60
  clamping procedures, 62
  conditions for working with, 60, 72

filleting, 69, **70**
  mixing, 62
  safety gear, 62, 75
  scarf joints, 66, 67
  thinners, 62
  UV protection, 70, 74, 75–76

F

fairing, 70–**71**, 75, 85, **92**
fairing battens, 61, 81–**82**
false stem, 98
fasteners, 62–**63, 74**
feather board, **64**
fiberglass, joining plywood with, 67–**68**
fiberglass masts, **134**
fiberglass sheathing
  benefits of, 71
  maintenance and repair, 75–76
  plywood construction, 58–59, 71, 101
  procedures, 71–73
  strip-composite construction, 58, 62, 70, 71–72, 85, 86
  varnish-finished hulls, 70, 74, 75–76
filleting, 69, **70**
filleting tool, 69, **70**
filling, 69–70
finishes
  hull preparation, 69–**71**, 74
  painting and varnishing, 69–70, 74–75, 76
  UV protection, 70, 74, 75–76
flotation, 7, 156–**57**
foam and fiberglass amas, **103**–6, **112**
foam flotation, 156
foot pedals, 4, 8, 124, **125, 126**
forestay, 149, **150**

G

Ghylin, Clay, **91, 92, 93**
Gibbons, Euell, 17, 48
Gibbons/Dierking sailing rig
  booms, 50–**51**, 53, **54**
  characteristics, 50–**54**
  development of, 17
  masthead, **54**
  masts, **51, 53, 54**, 134
  rig setup, 149–52, **151**
  sailing with, 51, **52**, 53, 153, **155**–56
  sails, 53–54, **145–46**, 152
  spar specifications, 137–38